INSTANT POT DUO CRISP AIR FRYER COOKBOOK

By Katherine Rice

Copyright 2020.

All Rights Reserved.

All rights reserved. No part of this book may be reproduced or copied in any form or by any means, electronic or mechanical, including photocopying, recording or by any information storage and retrieval system, without written permission from the publisher, except for the inclusion of brief quotations in a review.

Warning-Disclaimer.

The aim of the information in this book is to be as accurate as possible. However this is not a medical book, so it is for informational purposes only and comes with no guarantees. The author and publisher shall have neither liability or responsibility to anyone with respect to any loss or damage caused, or alleged to be caused, directly or indirectly by the information provided in this book.

All product and company names used in this book are Trademarks™ or Registered® Trademarks of their respective holders. Their use in this book does not imply any affiliation with or endorsement by them. All trademarks and brand names used in this book are for clarifying purposes only.

INSTANT POT is a registered trademark of Double Insight Inc. This book is not sponsored or connected to Double Insight Inc in any way.

Contents

BREAKFAST 13
   1. Muffins with Cheese and Bacon [PC] 13
   2. Breakfast Brussels Sprouts [AF] 13
   3. Quinoa Porridge with Cranberries [PC] 13
   4. Breakfast Buckwheat Burgers [AF] 13
   5. Italian Stromboli Cups [PC] 13
   6. Classic Corn and Parsnip Burgers [AF] 14
   7. Puerto Rican Budin [PC] 14
   8. Country-Style Cornbread Tartles [AF] 14
   9. Keto Sausage Omelet [PC] 14
   10. Authentic German Meatballs [AF] 14
   11. Breakfast Ham and Mozzarella Cups [PC] 15
   12. Mozzarella, Tomato and Herb Frittata [AF] 15
   13. Mini Omelet Cups [PC] 15
   14. Vegetable Egg Cups [AF] 15
   15. Millet and Pistachio Porridge [PC] 15
   16. Parmesan Potato Croquettes [AF] 16
   17. Couscous Pudding with Orange and Almonds [PC] 16
   18. Breakfast Vegan Sausage [AF] 16
   19. Frittata with Cheese and Broccoli [PC] 16
   20. Authentic French Toast [AF] 16
   21. Chocolate and Apple Oatmeal [PC] 17
   22. Ricotta and Spinach Frittata [AF] 17
   23. Classic French Dip Sandwiches [PC+AF] 17
   24. Perfect Hard-Boiled Eggs [AF] 17
   25. Kamut Porridge with Coconut and Strawberries [PC] 17
   26. Crescent Dogs with Cheese [AF] 18
   27. Balkan-Style Rice Pudding (Sütlaç) [PC] 18
   28. Cauliflower and Feta Cheese Bombs [AF] 18
   29. Tangy Peach Sauce [PC] 18
   30. Authentic Potatoes Cakes [AF] 18
   31. Apricot and Lemon Jam [PC] 19
   32. Sicilian Arancini di Riso [AF] 19
   33. Breakfast Bulgur with Berries [PC] 19
   34. Creamed Egg Salad Sandwich [AF] 19
   35. Decadent Breakfast Brownie [PC] 19
   36. Quiche with Bacon Pie [AF] 20
   37. Vanilla Croissant Pudding with Dried Figs [PC] 20
   38. Classic Pigs in a Blanket [AF] 20
   39. Breakfast Mexican Rice Pudding [PC] 20
   40. Yorkshire Pudding Popovers [AF] 20
   41. Sweet Potato Frittata [PC] 21
   42. Buttery Brioche Grilled Cheese [AF] 21
   43. Pearl Barley and Cranberry Porridge [PC] 21
   44. Japanese-Style Tater Tots [AF] 21
   45. Perfect Steel Cut Oat Porridge [PC] 21
   46. Breakfast Egg Salad [AF] 22
   47. Sweet Farro Pudding [PC] 22
   48. Omelet with Mushrooms and Cheese [AF] 22
   49. Homemade Pear Sauce [PC] 22
   50. Double Cheese and Vegetable Croquettes [AF] 22
   51. Italian Bread Pudding [PC] 22
   52. Classic Griddle Cake [AF] 23
   53. Old-Fashioned Plum Jam [PC] 23
   54. Authentic Breakfast Rissoles [AF] 23
   55. German-Style Giant Pancake [PC] 23
   56. Breakfast Chickpea Bowl [AF] 24
   57. Breakfast Vanilla Risotto with Prunes [PC] 24
   58. Cottage Cheese and Egg Muffins [AF] 24
   59. Soy Pate with Sun-Dried Tomatoes [PC] 24
   60. Classic Cinnamon Butter Toast [AF] 24

VEGETABLES & SIDE DISHES 25
   61. Sticky Maple-Glazed Carrots [PC+AF] 25
   62. Cauliflower and Chickpea Salad [AF] 25
   63. Indian Masala Curry [PC] 25
   64. Old-Fashioned Crispy Eggplant [AF] 25
   65. Mediterranean-Style Eggplant Soup [PC] 26
   66. Classic Roasted Potatoes [AF] 26
   67. Easy Creamy Mashed Yams [PC] 26
   68. Crispy Yellow Beans [AF] 26
   69. Spicy Cream of Brussels Sprout Soup [PC] 26
   70. Roasted Bell Peppers [AF] 27
   71. Traditional Indian Raita [PC] 27
   72. Spicy Roasted Potatoes [AF] 27
   73. Baba Ganoush with a Twist [PC] 27
   74. Provençal Style Parsnips [AF] 27
   75. Harvest Vegetable Potage [PC] 28
   76. Classic Roasted Green Beans [AF] 28
   77. Herbed and Creamed Celery Soup [PC] 28
   78. Mushrooms with Garlic and Cilantro [AF] 28
   79. Easy Roasted Artichokes [PC+AF] 28
   80. Grandma's Beet Salad [AF] 29
   81. Classic Vegetarian Paprikash [PC] 29

82. Garlicky Brussels Sprouts [AF] 29
83. Pasta with Garden Vegetables [PC] 29
84. Rustic Paprika Cauliflower [AF] 29
85. Traditional Italian Ciambotta [PC] 30
86. Saucy Cremini Mushrooms [AF] 30
87. Brussels Sprout and Apple Bowl [PC] 30
88. Baked Parmesan Broccoli [PC+AF] 30
89. Thai-Style Cauliflower [PC] 31
90. Roasted Beets with Feta Cheese [AF] 31
91. The Best Peperonata Ever [PC] 31
92. Asian-Style Brussels Sprouts [AF] 31
93. Chinese-Style Braised Cabbage [PC] 31
94. Parmesan Eggplant Bites [AF] 32
95. Broccoli and Pepper Salad [PC] 32
96. Classic Roasted Vegetables [PC+AF] 32
97. Ginger Garlic Eggplant [PC] 32
98. Roasted Sweet Potatoes [AF] 32
99. Cajun Gumbo with Mushrooms [PC] 33
100. Green Bean Salad with Spinach [AF] 33
101. Easy Garden Vegetable Soup [PC] 33
102. Mushrooms with Cheddar Cheese [AF] 33
103. Carrot Salad with Garlic and Herbs [PC] 34
104. Traditional Indian Gujarati [AF] 34
105. Cheesy and Herby Squash [PC] 34
106. Bacon and Collard Greens Sautee [PC+AF] 34
107. Green Pea Medley [PC] 34
108. Eggs in Pepper Cups [AF] 35
109. Aromatic Roasted Fennel [AF] 35
110. Maple-Glazed Butternut Squash [PC] 35
111. Chinese Chili-Spiced Asparagus [AF] 35
112. Stuffed Tomatoes with Mushrooms and Goat Cheese
[PC+AF] 35
113. Parmesan Mushroom Patties [AF] 36
114. Chinese Ginger Carrot Soup [PC] 36
115. Sweet Potatoes with Salsa [AF] 36
116. Street-Style Corn on the Cob [PC] 36
117. Garlicky Potatoes with Oregano [AF] 36
118. Italian Eggplant Casserole [PC] 37
119. Mom's Vegetable Fritters [AF] 37
120. Creamed Corn Fried Cakes [AF] 37

PORK 38
121. Herbed Pork Shoulder [PC] 38
122. Paprika Pork Chops [AF] 38
123. Toulouse-Style Cassoulet [PC] 38
124. Dijon and Garlic Pork [AF] 38
125. Wine-Braised Pork Loin Roast [PC] 38
126. Easy BLT Sandwich [AF] 38
127. Juicy Mustard Pork [PC] 39
128. Orange-Glazed Smoked Ham [AF] 39
129. Old-Fashioned Pork Chops [PC] 39
130. Roasted Herbed Pork [AF] 39
131. Wine-Braised Pork Belly [PC] 39
132. Classic Dinner Rolls [AF] 40
133. Pork Chops with Red Wine [PC] 40
134. Easy Sausage Sandwich [AF] 40
135. Pork Loin Roast [PC] 40
136. Glazed Pork Belly [AF] 40
137. Southern Pork Chops [PC+AF] 40
138. Herbed Sausage with Brussels Sprouts [AF] 41
139. Hungarian Pork Stew (Pörkölt) [PC] 41
140. Easy Bacon Salad [AF] 41
141. Dijon Picnic Ham [PC] 41
142. Garlicky Pork Butt [AF] 41
143. Italian-Style Pork Soup [PC] 42
144. The Best Pork Roast Ever [AF] 42
145. Rustic Pork with Prunes [PC] 42
146. Pork Chops with Onions [AF] 42
147. Penne Pasta with Pork Sausage [PC] 42
148. Center Cut Rib Roast [AF] 42
149. Saucy Montreal-Style Pork [PC] 43
150. Mexican Tacos de Carnitas [AF] 43
151. Italian-Style Pork Sausage [PC] 43
152. Cuban Pork Sandwiches [AF] 43
153. Rustic Pork Stew [PC] 43
154. Dad's Bourbon Ribs [AF] 44
155. Italian-Style Cheeseburger Casserole [PC+AF] 44
156. Sweet Brats with Brussels Sprouts [AF] 44
157. Spicy Pork Bowls [PC+AF] 44
158. Easy Crispy Pork Cutlets [AF] 44
159. Grandma's Hot Ribs [PC] 44
160. Holiday Pork with Crackling [PC+AF] 45
161. Chunky Pork and Hash Brown Bake [PC] 45
162. Herbed Pork with Bell Peppers [AF] 45
163. Dad's Pork Salad [PC] 45
164. Country-Style Crispy Ribs [PC+AF] 45
165. Sticky Leg Steaks with Pineapple [PC] 46
166. Old-Fashioned Breakfast Patties [AF] 46
167. Mexican-Style Pork Carnitas [PC] 46
168. Sherry and Lime Glazed Ham [AF] 46

169. BBQ Spare Ribs [PC] 46
170. Crispy Bacon and Cauliflower Bites [AF] 46
171. Pork Butt with Vegetables [PC] 47
172. Pork Butt Roast with Sage and Applesauce [AF] 47
173. Rustic Pork Soup [PC] 47
174. Herbed Breakfast Sausage [AF] 47
175. Italian Meatballs with Marinara Sauce [PC] 47
176. Mediterranean-Style Pork Kebabs [AF] 48
177. Fall Off the Bone St Louis Style Ribs [PC] 48
178. Summer Pork Ribs [AF] 48
179. Pork with Green Beans [PC] 48
180. Asian-Style Back Ribs [PC+AF] 48

BEEF **49**
181. Roast Beef Sandwiches [PC] 49
182. Herbed Beef Eye Round Roast [AF] 49
183. Asian-Style Beef Bowl [PC] 49
184. Homemade Beef Burgers [AF] 49
185. French Au Jus [PC] 49
186. Skirt Steak Sliders [AF] 49
187. Wine-Braised Sirloin Steak [PC] 50
188. Easy Paprika Steak [AF] 50
189. Kielbasa Beef Soup [PC] 50
190. Beef Breakfast Cups [AF] 50
191. Herbed Top Sirloin Roast [PC] 50
192. Tangy and Herby London Broil [AF] 51
193. Bœuf à la Bourguignonne [PC] 51
194. Rump Roast with Red Wine [PC] 51
195. Beef and Bacon Mac and Cheese [PC+AF] 51
196. Summer Beef Brisket [AF] 51
197. Beef and Mushroom Casserole [PC] 52
198. T-Bone Steak Salad [AF] 52
199. Italian Osso Buco [PC] 52
200. Butter and Brandy Roast [AF] 52
201. Montreal-Style Beef [PC] 52
202. Filet Mignon with Herbs [AF] 53
203. Traditional Irish Beef Stew [PC] 53
204. Chinese-Style Beef [AF] 53
205. Smoked Beef Brisket [PC] 53
206. Classic Roast Beef [PC+AF] 53
207. Pearl Barley and Round Beef Soup [PC] 54
208. Decadent Coulotte Roast [AF] 54
209. Ribeye Steak Salad [PC] 54
210. Italian Sausage with Baby Potatoes [AF] 54
211. London Broil Medley [PC] 54
212. Broccoli and Beef Fritters [AF] 55
213. Saucy Beef Brisket [PC] 55
214. Ribeye Steak with Herbed Butter [AF] 55
215. Easy Beef Curry [PC] 55
216. Beef Scotch Tender Steak [AF] 55
217. Buttery Garlicky Steaks [PC+AF] 56
218. Ground Beef and Mushroom Cups [AF] 56
219. Beef Peppery Salad [PC] 56
220. Classic Beef Parmigiana [AF] 56
221. Beef Sausage with Yellow Potatoes [PC] 56
222. Aromatic Porterhouse Steak [AF] 57
223. Pakistani Karahi Keema [PC] 57
224. Rosemary Garlicky Steak [AF] 57
225. Asian-Style Round Steak [PC] 57
226. Roast Beef with Mediterranean Herbs [AF] 57
227. Saucy Top Sirloin [PC] 58
228. Grandma's Classic Meatloaf [AF] 58
229. Greek-Style Beef Bowl [PC] 58
230. Dijon and Paprika Steak [AF] 58
231. Spicy Cube Steak [PC] 58
232. Easy Mini Meatloaves [AF] 59
233. Mexican Meatball Soup (Albondigas Soup) [PC] 59
234. Mustard and Ketchup Glazed Beef [PC+AF] 59
235. Philly Cheesesteak Quiche [PC+AF] 59
236. Mustard Garlic Beef Shoulder [AF] 60
237. Autumn Braised Beef [PC] 60
238. Sticky Glazed Short Loin [AF] 60
239. Rib-Eye Steak with Mushrooms [PC] 60
240. Gyro Style Shredded Beef [AF] 60

POULTRY **61**
241. Chicken Noodle Soup [PC] 61
242. Easy Chicken Nuggets [AF] 61
243. Authentic Teriyaki Chicken [PC] 61
244. Homemade Chicken Burgers [AF] 61
245. Thai Spicy Duck Soup [PC] 61
246. Roasted Chicken Salad [AF] 62
247. BBQ Chicken Legs [PC] 62
248. Traditional Tacos Dorados [AF] 62
249. Chicken Breasts with Garlic and Wine [PC] 62
250. Classic Balsamic Chicken [AF] 62
251. Smothered Turkey Cutlets [PC] 63
252. Dijon Barbecued Turkey [AF] 63
253. Chicken Macaroni Soup [PC] 63
254. Stuffed Chicken Breasts [AF] 63

255. Classic Turkey Soup [PC] ... 63	300. English Muffin with Chicken [AF] ... 72
256. Mom's Famous Chicken Fingers [AF] ... 64	
257. Chunky Turkey Soup [PC] ... 64	**FISH & SEAFOOD ... 73**
258. Restaurant-Style Fried Chicken [AF] ... 64	301. Authentic Fish Biryani [PC] ... 73
259. Hungarian Chicken Stew (Gulyás) [PC] ... 64	302. Calamari in Sherry Sauce [AF] ... 73
260. Ground Turkey Sliders [AF] ... 64	303. Classic Codfish Curry [PC] ... 73
261. Thai Spicy Chicken Bowl [PC] ... 65	304. Mahi-Mahi with Butter and Herbs [AF] ... 73
262. Spicy Chicken Breasts [AF] ... 65	305. Halibut Fillets with Shallots [PC] ... 73
263. Shredded Chicken Sliders [PC] ... 65	306. Swordfish Steaks with Cilantro [AF] ... 74
264. Lemony Turkey Wings [AF] ... 65	307. Butter Paprika Salmon [PC] ... 74
265. Classic BBQ Turkey [PC] ... 65	308. Authentic Mediterranean Calamari [AF] ... 74
266. Duck a l'Orange [AF] ... 66	309. Grouper Fillets with Vegetables [PC] ... 74
267. Chicken Tenderloin with Feta Cheese [PC] ... 66	310. Mackerel Fillets with Classic Chimichurri [AF] ... 74
268. Fried Chicken Wings [AF] ... 66	311. Pancetta, Fish, and Cauliflower Stew [PC] ... 75
269. Murgh Kari (Indian Chicken Curry) [PC] ... 66	312. Fried Garlicky Shrimp [AF] ... 75
270. Authentic German Schweineschnitzel [AF] ... 66	313. Tuna Fillets with Tomatoes [PC] ... 75
271. Spicy Turkey Bolognese [PC] ... 67	314. Restaurant-Style Fish Fingers [AF] ... 75
272. Pomegranate-Glazed Duck [AF] ... 67	315. Classic Seafood Hot Pot [PC] ... 75
273. Traditional Chicken Chili [PC] ... 67	316. Dilled King Prawn Salad [AF] ... 76
274. Chicken Fillets with Peppers [AF] ... 67	317. Beer Crab Bowl [PC] ... 76
275. Colorful Chicken Salad [PC] ... 67	318. Halibut with Chives and Peppercorns [AF] ... 76
276. Spicy Ranch Chicken [AF] ... 68	319. Pasta and Tuna Casserole [PC+AF] ... 76
277. Decadent Duck with Prunes [PC] ... 68	320. Fried Paprika and Chive Prawns [AF] ... 76
278. Italian-Style Turkey Breasts [AF] ... 68	321. Fish and Vegetable Hot Pot [PC] ... 77
279. Chicken Cheese Pie [PC+AF] ... 68	322. Fish and Avocado Pita [AF] ... 77
280. Spicy Mustard Chicken Thighs [AF] ... 68	323. American-Style Cioppino [PC] ... 77
281. Apple Maple Turkey Tenderloin [PC] ... 69	324. Sea Bass with Butter and Wine [AF] ... 77
282. Greek Chicken Fillets [AF] ... 69	325. Seafood Salad with Olives and Cheese [PC] ... 78
283. Chicken Tikka Masala [PC] ... 69	326. Mediterranean Calamari Parmigiano [AF] ... 78
284. Saucy Turkey Wings [AF] ... 69	327. Creamy Codfish Pate [PC] ... 78
285. Turkey and Sweet Potato Stew [PC] ... 69	328. Mackerel Fish Cakes [AF] ... 78
286. Butter Paprika Chicken Cutlets [AF] ... 70	329. Asian-Style Mackerel [PC] ... 79
287. Duck Breast with Herbs and Wine [PC] ... 70	330. Fried Shrimp and Broccoli [AF] ... 79
288. Thai-Style Chicken Drumettes [AF] ... 70	331. Mussels Salad with Spinach [PC] ... 79
289. Smothered Chicken Fillets [PC] ... 70	332. Mexican Cod Fish Tacos [AF] ... 79
290. Easy Chicken Drumsticks [AF] ... 70	333. Creole Sea Bass with Tomato [PC] ... 79
291. Hungarian Paprika Chicken [PC] ... 71	334. Orange Roughy Fillets [AF] ... 80
292. Roasted Turkey Legs [PC] ... 71	335. Honey and Orange Tilapia [PC] ... 80
293. Easy Chinese Chicken [PC] ... 71	336. Sticky Trout Bites [AF] ... 80
294. Smoked Paprika and Butter Chicken Breasts [AF] ... 71	337. Traditional Italian Brodetto [PC] ... 80
295. Country-Style Duck with Walnuts [PC] ... 71	338. Hot and Spicy Squid [AF] ... 80
296. Chinese Duck with Hoisin Sauce [AF] ... 72	339. Asian Hong Shao Yu [PC] ... 80
297. Chicken Fillets with Wine [PC] ... 72	340. Tangy Minty Swordfish [AF] ... 81
298. Garlic and Parm Chicken Wings [AF] ... 72	341. Herb Garlic Mussels [PC] ... 81
299. Sticky Chicken Wings [PC] ... 72	342. Thai-Style Sea Bass [AF] ... 81

343. Chilean Caldillo de Mariscos [PC] 81
344. Fried Calamari Rings [AF] 82
345. Catfish and Mushroom Medley [PC] 82
346. Salmon Fillets with Lemon and Herbs [AF] 82
347. Tilapia with Cremini Mushroom Sauce [PC] 82
348. Spicy Fish Patties [AF] 83
349. Salmon and Broccoli Quiche [PC+AF] 83
350. American-Style Fried Shrimp [AF] 83
351. Herbed Fish Boil [PC] 83
352. Sea Scallops with Rosemary and Wine [AF] 83
353. Spicy Tilapia Hot Pot [PC] 84
354. Tuna Steak Salad with Spinach [AF] 84
355. Saucy Tilapia Fillets with Wine [PC] 84
356. Italian Sausage-Stuffed Squid [AF] 84
357. Fish and Bacon Chowder [PC] 85
358. Sea Scallop and Baby Greens Bowl [AF] . 85
359. Cod with Coconut Yogurt Sauce [PC] 85
360. Salmon Salad with Aleppo Pepper [AF] .. 85

RICE & GRAINS 86

361. Shrimp, Couscous, and Feta Salad [PC] .. 86
362. Risotto with Cauliflower and Mozzarella [AF] 86
363. Brown Rice Porridge [PC] 86
364. Porridge with Applesauce and Walnut [AF] 86
365. Authentic Asian Congee [PC] 86
366. Brioche Bread Pudding with Almonds [AF] 87
367. Wheat Berry and Anasazi Bean Salad [PC] 87
368. Spiced Banana Oatmeal [AF] 87
369. Indian Daliya Khichdi [PC] 87
370. Multigrain Pilaf with Herbs [AF] 87
371. Jasmine Rice and Pecan Bowl [PC] 88
372. Herb Corn Fritters [AF] 88
373. Spanish Oat Groat Stew [PC] 88
374. Bread Pudding with Prunes [AF] 88
375. Brioche Bread Pudding [PC] 88
376. Vanilla and Cinnamon French Toast [AF] 89
377. Spelt Berry and Spinach Bowl [PC] 89
378. Breakfast Muffins with Apples [AF] 89
379. Millet and Pumpkin Bowl [PC] 89
380. Asian Wontons with Chicken [PC+AF] ... 89
381. Wild Rice Salad with Greens [PC] 90
382. South Indian Pakoda [AF] 90
383. Bulgur Pilaf with Mushrooms [PC] 90
384. The Best Granola Ever [AF] 90
385. Barley Porridge with Cinnamon [PC] 90
386. British Buttermilk Scones [AF] 91
387. Millet Congee with a Twist [PC] 91
388. Vanilla Oatmeal with Almonds [AF] 91
389. Wild Rice Porridge [PC] 91
390. Spicy Macaroni and Cheese [AF] 91
391. Couscous with Cauliflower and Feta Cheese [PC] ... 92
392. Indian Curry with Scallions [PC+AF] 92
393. Classic Wild Rice Soup [PC] 92
394. Orange and Apricot Porridge [AF] 92
395. Provencal Farro Soup [PC] 92
396. Old-Fashioned Mocha Muffins [AF] 93
397. Spicy Spelt Berry Salad [PC] 93
398. Pakora Fritters with Cheese [AF] 93
399. Sweet Risotto with Almonds and Pears [PC+AF] 93
400. Fried Chinese Rice [PC+AF] 93
401. Chicken Legs with Bulgur [PC] 94
402. Italian Rice Casserole [PC+AF] 94
403. Asian-Style Quinoa Pilaf [PC] 94
404. Crescent Dinner Rolls with Blueberries [AF] 94
405. Mac and Cheese with Herbs [PC+AF] 94
406. Creamy Risotto with Parmesan Cheese [PC+AF] ... 95
407. Indian Kambu Koozh [PC] 95
408. Easy Mediterranean Harcha [AF] 95
409. Autumn Squash and Oat Porridge [PC] .. 95
410. Herbed Millet Croquettes [AF] 95
411. Indian Sweet Pongal [PC] 96
412. Mini Cornbread Muffins [AF] 96
413. Creamed Quinoa Salad [PC] 96
414. Oregano Polenta Bites [AF] 96
415. Kamut and Sausage Medley [PC+AF] 96
416. Bread Pudding with Dried Berries [AF] . 97
417. Green Rice Porridge [PC] 97
418. Traditional Italian Arancini [AF] 97
419. Dijon and Honey Sorghum Salad [PC] ... 97
420. Savory Breakfast Cups [AF] 97

VEGAN 98

421. Wild Rice with Spinach and Wine [PC] . 98
422. Perfect Crispy Falafel [AF] 98
423. Vegetable Millet Porridge [PC] 98
424. Eggplant with Red Lentils [AF] 98
425. Cremini Mushroom and Barley Stew [PC] 98
426. Fried Cucumber Bites [AF] 99
427. Greek Sweet Potato Stew [PC] 99
428. Aromatic Roasted Peppers [AF] 99

429. One-Pot Vegan Minestrone [PC] 99
430. Moroccan-Spiced Carrot [AF] 99
431. Sorghum, Spinach, and Avocado Bowl [PC] 100
432. Easy Garlic Cabbage [AF] 100
433. Rich and Easy Vegan Biryani [PC] 100
434. The Best Chickpea Fritters Ever [AF] 100
435. Herb Vegetable Soup [PC] 100
436. Parsnip Fries with Mayonnaise [AF] 101
437. Thai-Style Butternut Squash Curry [PC] 101
438. Beets with Tofu Cheese [AF] 101
439. Barley Pilaf with Herbs [PC] 101
440. Polenta Bites with Peppers [AF] 101
441. Green Pea and Farro Stew [PC] 102
442. Japanese Broccoli Tempura [AF] 102
443. Easy Yellow Lentil Curry [PC] 102
444. Vegan Smoked Sausage [PC+AF] 102
445. Country-Style Vegetable Soup [PC] 102
446. Italian-Style Zucchini [AF] 103
447. Spicy Kale Pilaf [PC] 103
448. Stuffed Peppers with Tofu and Corn [AF] 103
449. Classic Vegan Stroganoff [PC] 103
450. Baby Potatoes with Mediterranean Herbs [AF] 103
451. Easy French Lentil Salad [PC] 104
452. Asian Spicy Tofu [AF] 104
453. Two Bean Peppery Salad [PC] 104
454. Homemade Lebanese Falafel [AF] 104
455. Vegan Irish Stew with Guinness [PC] 104
456. Fingerling Potatoes with Tofu and Herbs [AF] 104
457. Classic Tabbouleh Salad [PC] 105
458. Chinese Broccoli Florets [AF] 105
459. Creamed Mushroom and Shallot Soup [PC] 105
460. Sticky Red Beets [AF] 105
461. Squash and Spinach Medley [PC] 105
462. Paprika Green Beans [AF] 106
463. Za'atar and White Wine Cauliflower [PC] 106
464. Asian Fried Tempeh [AF] 106
465. Old-Fashioned Cabbage Soup [PC] 106
466. Crispy Baby Bellas [AF] 106
467. Mexican Kidney Bean Chili [PC] 106
468. Vegan Moroccan Kefta [AF] 107
469. Chickpea and Avocado Salad [PC] 107
470. Tangy Roasted Cabbage [AF] 107
471. Creamed Corn and Split Pea Chowder [PC] 107
472. Spicy Potato Wedges [AF] 108
473. Vegetable and Lentil Mélange [PC] 108

474. Breakfast Red Bean Sausage [AF] 108
475. Vanilla Oatmeal with Almonds [PC] 108
476. Fried Bok Choy [AF] 108
477. Quinoa with Butternut Squash and Leeks [PC] 109
478. Potato Wedges with Italian Herbs [AF] 109
479. Chili with White Wine and Spinach [PC] 109
480. Dijon Fried Tofu Cubes 109

SNACKS & APPETIZERS 110

481. Restaurant-Style Buffalo Chicken Wings [PC+AF] 110
482. Restaurant-Style Onion Rings [AF] 110
483. Sticky Little Smokies [PC] 110
484. Crispy Chicken Wings [AF] 110
485. Spiced Butternut Squash [PC] 110
486. Honey and Wine Baby Carrots [AF] 111
487. Corn on the Cob with Herb Butter [PC] 111
488. Homemade Apple Chips [AF] 111
489. Hot 'n' Spicy Spareribs [PC] 111
490. Spicy Chicken Drumettes [AF] 111
491. Sweet and Spicy Chicken Drumettes [PC] 111
492. Mediterranean-Style Eggplant Chips [AF] 112
493. Crab Legs with Herbs [PC] 112
494. Parmesan Green Bean Chips [AF] 112
495. Moroccan Spiced Sweet Potatoes [PC] 112
496. Cheese Zucchini Fries [AF] 112
497. Italian-Style Pepperoni Dip [PC+AF] 113
498. Tomato Chips with Herbs [AF] 113
499. BBQ Spicy Broccoli Bites [PC] 113
500. Chinese Potato Chips [AF] 113
501. Street-Style Corn on the Cob [PC] 113
502. Spicy Mixed Nuts [AF] 114
503. Hot Paprika Potato Bites with Bacon [PC] 114
504. Homemade Yam Chips [AF] 114
505. Beet, Arugula, and Orange Salad [PC] 114
506. Golden Beet Fries [AF] 114
507. Buttery Mashed Cauliflower [PC] 114
508. Gochugaru Chicken Drumettes [AF] 115
509. Autumn Acorn Squash [PC] 115
510. Herbed Carrot Bites [AF] 115
511. Asparagus Bites with Parmesan Cheese [PC] 115
512. Homemade Tortilla Chips [AF] 115
513. Sticky Baby Carrots [PC] 116
514. Parmesan Zucchini Chips [AF] 116
515. Dijon Sticky Cocktail Meatballs [PC] 116
516. Asian-Style Ribs [AF] 116

517. Artichokes with Herbs and Cheese [PC] 116
518. Cheddar Cauliflower Balls [AF] 117
519. Sweet Vanilla Popcorn [PC] 117
520. Cheese and Garlic Broccoli Florets [AF] 117
521. Grape Jelly Party Kielbasa [PC] 117
522. Green Tomato Crisps [AF] 117
523. Vegetarian Cauliflower Wings [PC] 118
524. Double Cheese Jalapeno Poppers [AF] 118
525. Potato Wedges with Tomato Sauce [PC] 118
526. Crispy Cauliflower Bites [AF] 118
527. Vanilla Ginger Yam Bites [PC] 118
528. Grandma's Pumpkin Chips [AF] 119
529. Easy Mashed Pumpkin [PC] 119
530. Mediterranean Sweet Potato Bites [AF] 119
531. Herbed Brussels Sprouts [PC] 119
532. Dijon and Pancetta Shrimp [AF] 119
533. Seafood and Bacon Dip [PC+AF] 120
534. Greek Potato Bites [AF] 120
535. Ricotta and Chicken Dipping Sauce [PC] 120
536. Cheese and Bacon-Stuffed Poblanos [AF] 120
537. Creamed Stuffed Eggs [PC] 121
538. Beer Battered Sweet Onion Rings [AF] 121
539. Pizza Dipping Sauce [PC] 121
540. Mom's Famous Kale Chips [AF] 121

DESSERTS **122**
541. Crumble Cake with Blueberries [PC] 122
542. Nutty Chocolate Cake [AF] 122
543. Classic Mini Cheesecakes [PC] 122
544. Chocolate and Coconut Brownies [AF] 122
545. Pear Crisp with a Twist [PC] 123
546. Old-Fashioned Brownie Muffins [AF] 123
547. Greek Blueberry Cheesecake [PC] 123
548. Grandma's Caramelized Plums [AF] 123
549. White Chocolate Chip Fudge [PC] 124
550. Fried Plantain with Raisins [AF] 124
551. Pumpkin Pie with Pecans [PC] 124
552. Souffle Apple Pancakes [AF] 124
553. Fudgy Mocha Cake [PC] 124
554. French Toast Bake [AF] 125
555. Chocolate Banana Cake [PC] 125
556. French-Style Cronuts [AF] 125
557. Peach Cake with Pecans [PC] 125

558. Almond Chocolate Cake [AF] 126
559. Greek Dried Fruit Compote (Hosafi) [PC] 126
560. Classic Cranberry Scones [AF] 126
561. Classic Apple Crumble [PC] 126
562. Cinnamon Baked Donuts [AF] 126
563. Cinnamon Rolls with Apples and Walnuts [PC] 127
564. Cinnamon Baked Peaches [AF] 127
565. Stuffed Pears with Pistachios and Sultanas [PC] 127
566. Pumpkin Pie with Walnuts [AF] 127
567. Greek Risogalo (Rice Pudding) [PC] 127
568. Moist Raisin and Chocolate Cupcakes [AF] 128
569. Indian Chai Hot Chocolate [PC] 128
570. Vegan Chocolate Chip Cake [AF] 128
571. Chocolate Chip Bread Pudding [PC] 128
572. Baked Apples with Sultanas and Pecans [PC+AF] 128
573. Kid-Friendly Mini Cheesecakes [PC] 129
574. Plum Mini Tarts [AF] 129
575. Honey Vanilla Pudding [PC] 129
576. Vanilla Chocolate Cupcakes [AF] 129
577. Berry Cobbler Pie [PC] 130
578. Grilled Fruit Skewers [AF] 130
579. Middle Eastern Pudding (Sahlab) [PC] 130
580. Coconut and Blueberry Fritters [AF] 130
581. Chocolate and Peanut Butter Fudge [PC] 130
582. Classic Cinnamon Rolls [AF] 131
583. The Best Dulce de Leche Ever [PC] 131
584. Chocolate Mug Cake [AF] 131
585. Caramel Chocolate Cake [PC] 131
586. Apricots with Mascarpone Cheese and Coconut [AF] 132
587. Gooey Pinch Me Cake [PC] 132
588. Banana Rum Galettes [AF] 132
589. Ginger Crumb Cake with Berries [PC] 132
590. Traditional Unnakai Malabar [AF] 132
591. Apple Walnut Crisp Cake [PC] 133
592. Fluffy Apple Crumble Cake [AF] 133
593. Raspberry Peanut Butter Cake [PC] 133
594. Old-Fashioned Almond Cupcakes [AF] 133
595. Baked Apples with Honey and Raisins [PC] 134
596. Better-Than-Box-Mix Brownies [AF] 134
597. Apple Pie and Ginger Curd [PC] 134
598. Dutch Baby Pancake [PC+AF] 134
599. Lebanese Moghli Pudding [PC] 135
600. Classic Apple and Cranberry Cookies [PC+AF] 135

INTRODUCTION

Like most of us, I want to make delicious and nutritious meals most efficiently. I also want to cook my favorite restaurant foods such as fish and chips as well as the professionals. A few months ago, I stumbled upon the Instant Pot Duo Crisp on a food website and it seemed like a good idea. From this point of view, I can say that the Instant Pot Duo Crisp gave me much-needed change in my cooking routine. In all modesty, I think this is one of the best things to ever enter my kitchen! If you think that cooking great-tasting meals requires special skills and extra effort, think twice! All that's required is a change of your tools! With my new multi-cooker, I can make nutritious and freshly-prepared home-cooked meals in no time. I can save my money, my time, and my nerves. Win-win!

Favorite homemade meals with just the push of a button! Is this possible? Soups, stews, and chilies are done within 15-20 minutes; steamed or roasted veggies in 3-5 minutes! Chip cuts of meat turn out moist, tender, and succulent. Pressure-cooked or air-fried vegetables maintain their flavor instead of tasting like the soup base or fat. The Instant Pot Duo Crisp uses the power of sealed steam and high temperature to cook your food faster than ever before. Indeed, the Duo Crisp + Air Fryer is the secret to incredibly fast and outrageously delicious meals. It is also a breeze to clean and fun-filled! It is very simple to use, it has a great user-friendly control panel with buttons that are very basic. People who have used this revolutionary cooker have confirmed that the Instant Pot Duo Crisp works just as promised and advertised.

Healthy eating doesn't have to be boring or time-consuming – The Duo Crisp + Air Fryer produces versatile and immensely creative recipes. My eating plan focuses on the high consumption of local, unprocessed foods, emphasizing fresh foods and aromatic spices. Fast food, prepackaged foods and unhealthy fats are off limits here. In developing this recipe collection, I studied culinary classics and modern creations, adapting them for use in the Instant Pot Duo Crisp. Let's begin with an overview of the Instant Pot Duo Crisp.

What is so Special About an Instant Pot Duo Crisp?

If you do not own an Instant Pot or an Air Fryer before, it is time to check out a new revolutionary kitchen appliance named Instant Pot Duo Crisp + Air Fryer. This multipurpose kitchen appliance has a special airtight cooking pot that cooks foods faster using high pressures and high temperatures. In addition, you can fry your food without oil by replacing a pressure cooking lid with an air fryer (crisping) lid. Simply put, the Instant Pot Duo Crisp is an electric pressure cooker and air fryer in one! It can perform various cooking functions such as pressure cooking, steaming, sauteing, baking, air frying, and even dehydrating! In general, multi-cookers are known for their efficiency, ease of use, and eco-friendliness.

The Duo Crisp + Air Fryer has two lids – a pressure cooker lid and air fryer (crisping) lid. It means that you can pressure cook or air fry your food in only one pot. It also means that you can pressure cook your food, and then, easily switch lids and crisp the food to perfection. That sounds pretty good, doesn't it?

Do you want to make a seriously decadent Macaroni and Cheese, so nice, ooey gooey and creamy? You can cook your pasta in the pressure cooker, and, then, switch the lids, add the mixture of crushed Ritz crackers and melted butter to the top, and Voila! You will have this perfect crunchy top. You can do this right in the pot, without transferring your macaroni and cheese to a baking pan and preheating an oven. Once you select your desired cook mode, a default time for that mode will show on the digital display. However, you can choose your desired time and temperature by pressing the Time Adjustment button. Moreover, you can select the Delay Start Timer and cook your food at a later time (for a minimum of 10 minutes to a maximum of 24 hours).

Smart Programs
The Duo Crisp + Air Fryer uses pressurized steam to cook your dish evenly and richly – you will be amazed by how well it cooks your food!

Pressure Cook – it is a "multi-purpose" pressure cooking program. When cooking beans or grains, make sure to follow the grain-to-water ratios.

Sauté – you can sauté, brown, stir fry and sear your ingredients before pressure cooking or thicken the sauces and simmer the cooking liquid. It is similar to using a skillet, frying pan, or griddle. Sautéing is one of the best flavor-boosting techniques, it allows inexpensive and humble dishes to release some of their hidden flavors. Add a splash of dry wine or broth to start the magic! Use a wooden or silicone scraper to loosen bits that may be stuck to the bottom of the pot.

Slow Cook – you can use your multi-cooker as a conventional slow cooker. If you're craving some good old-fashioned meals, this smart program is your first choice. This is the perfect program for budget-friendly cuts of meat, rustic stews, and fall-off-the-bone meats, just like grandma used to make!

Steam – this program is designed for delicate foods such as vegetables, fish, and seafood. Be careful and use 1 cup of water and a steamer basket with this function.

Sous Vide – this program is for cooking vacuum-sealed food to mouthwatering perfection, maintaining a very accurate temperature for a long period of time. After sous vide cooking, sear the meat on the Sauté function to ensure the best possible flavor.

Smart Programs: Air Frying
This is perfect for making fried foods with little to no oil. If you want a golden, crispy top, simply replace the lids and choose the "Air Fry" or "Broil" smart program. With these smart cooking programs, making your favorite fried food items becomes a breeze!

Air fry – enjoy your favorites without soaking them in unhealthy oil.

Roast – as the name indicates, you can roast your favorite meat and vegetables to perfection. You can cook your food in the air fryer basket, oven-safe cookware, or directly in the inner pot. The program works as a tiny oven

Bake – this program applies rapid air circulation to cook your food to perfection, just like a small convection oven. You can bake amazing desserts, puffy cupcakes, and bread pudding.

Broil – it blows hot air inside the cooking chamber, providing your dish with a crispy golden finish, without using an oven.

Dehydrate – this program uses low heat for a long period of time to safely dry out your foods. You can prepare vegetable chips, dried fruits, raw desserts, and many more food items.

Top 5 Benefits of the Instant Pot Duo Crisp

There are numerous benefits of the Instant Pot Duo Crisp. It allows you to cook a wide range of dishes, from appetizers and soups to desserts and sauces. Here are some of the key benefits of the Instant Pot Duo Crisp.

Health benefits. Feeding your body nutrient-dense foods may help improve your immune system and overall health; it may boost your metabolism and help you to lose weight. Pressure cooking and air frying are more likely to preserve nutrients compared to other cooking methods. These recipes focus on consuming natural food and home-cooked meals. It means that a healthy diet doesn't have to be complicated.

Convenience of one-pot cooking. Forget about overcooked, mushy vegetables, burned pies, and unhealthy dip-fried foods. Adapting classic recipes to the Instant Pot Duo Crisp is fun and easy, too. This recipe collection proves that! Cooking on a stovetop generates a lot of heat and steam in the kitchen; on the other hand, heat and steam cannot escape from your electric pressure cooker. If you tend to cook frozen foods, you do not need to defrost it before cooking; you should add an extra 10 minutes of cooking time. This possibility would be highly beneficial for large households during busy weeknights. Wonderfully convenient!

Space and cost-saving solution. Good and healthy eating doesn't have to be expensive. Turn inexpensive cuts of meat, leftovers, bones, and root vegetables into delicious family meals! With your Instant Pot Duo Crips, you do not have to buy extra pans, rice cookers, slow cookers, and similar appliances. Moreover, all oven-safe cookware and air frying accessories are safe for use in the inner pot.

Time-saving solution. The sealed steam raises the temperature in your pressure cooker, reducing cooking time and retaining more nutrients in your food. Whether you are a novice cook or a culinary expert, the Instant Pot Duo Crisp will save your time, allowing you to enjoy quality time with your family. That's what I call "instant"!

Energy efficiency. Instant Pot Duo Crips uses less energy (about 70%) than many other kitchen appliances. Go ahead and go green!

Guide to Using This Recipe Collection

This cookbook provides a compilation of the best pressure cooker and air fryer recipes I have ever tried. These recipes illustrate the power of pressure cooking and air frying in one kitchen appliance. You won't miss the fun! Every recipe includes the number of serving, estimated cook time, list of ingredients, and nutritional analysis. In addition, with the step-by-step process of cooking any of the foods, you would not miss anything out. Last but not least, you will find the method used in the recipe listed along with each title, for your easy reference. I used these labels to explain the cooking method called for in each recipe.

[PC] is an abbreviation for Pressure Cooking, which means that pressure cooking is the method used in the recipe;

[AF] is an abbreviation for Air Frying while the label

[PC+AF] means that both methods, Pressure Cooking and Air Frying, are used in the recipe.

This cookbook promotes both a modern and old-fashioned approach to cooking, focusing on inventive cooking methods and various food combinations. Therefore, instead of throwing vegetables and meat into your pot, you can enjoy cooking with this versatile kitchen device. Happy cooking!

BREAKFAST

1. Muffins with Cheese and Bacon [PC]

(Ready in about 15 minutes | Servings 6)

Ingredients

7 eggs
2 tablespoons olive oil
1 teaspoon cayenne pepper
Sea salt and ground black pepper, to taste
2 ounces bacon, chopped
1/4 cup Colby cheese, shredded
2 tablespoons scallions, chopped
1 tomato, chopped
1 cup spinach, chopped

Directions

Place 1 cup of water and metal trivet in the inner pot of your Instant Pot Duo Crisp.

Thoroughly combine all the ingredients until everything is well incorporated. Pour the mixture into silicone molds.

Lower the silicone molds onto the prepared trivet. Secure the pressure-cooking lid.

Pressure cook for 10 minutes at High pressure. Once cooking is complete, use a quick pressure release; carefully remove the lid.

Bon appétit!

Per serving: Calories: 189; Fat: 15.1g; Carbs: 2.6g; Protein: 9.5g; Sugars: 1.3g; Fiber: 0.6g

2. Breakfast Brussels Sprouts [AF]

(Ready in about 15 minutes | Servings 4)

Ingredients

1 pound Brussels sprouts, trimmed
1 tablespoon peanut oil
Sea salt and freshly ground black pepper, to season
2 ounces ham, diced

Directions

Toss the Brussels sprouts with the remaining ingredients; then, arrange the Brussels sprouts in the Air Fryer basket.

Secure the air-frying lid.

Cook the Brussels sprouts at 380 degrees F for 13 minutes, shaking the basket halfway through the cooking time.

Serve warm and enjoy!

Per serving: Calories: 93; Fat: 4.3g; Carbs: 10.2g; Protein: 6.2g; Sugars: 2.4g; Fiber: 4.3g

3. Quinoa Porridge with Cranberries [PC]

(Ready in about 10 minutes | Servings 4)

Ingredients

1 cup quinoa, rinsed
4 tablespoons brown sugar
1/2 cup dried cranberries
2 tablespoons flax seeds, ground
2 tablespoons coconut oil
1/2 teaspoon ground cinnamon
1 cup almond milk
1 cup water

Directions

Place all the ingredients in the inner pot and secure the pressure-cooking lid.

Pressure cook for 5 minutes at High pressure. Once cooking is complete, use a quick pressure release; carefully remove the lid.

Fluff your quinoa with a fork and serve at room temperature.

Bon appétit!

4. Breakfast Buckwheat Burgers [AF]

(Ready in about 20 minutes | Servings 4)

Per serving: Calories: 198; Fat: 8.7g; Carbs: 24.2g; Protein: 8g; Sugars: 2.2g; Fiber: 5.3g

Ingredients

1 cup buckwheat, soaked overnight and rinsed
1 cup canned kidney beans, drained and well rinsed
1/4 cup walnuts, chopped
1 tablespoon olive oil
1 small onion, chopped
1 teaspoon smoked paprika
Sea salt and ground black pepper, to taste
1/2 cup bread crumbs

Directions

Mix all the ingredients until everything is well combined. Form the mixture into four patties and arrange them in a lightly greased Air Fryer basket.

Secure the air-frying lid.

Cook the burgers at 380 degrees F for about 15 minutes or until cooked through. Tun them over halfway through the cooking time.

Bon appétit!

Per serving: Calories: 327; Fat: 13.6g; Carbs: 44g; Protein: 8.7g; Sugars: 14.7g; Fiber: 3.5g

5. Italian Stromboli Cups [PC]

(Ready in about 15 minutes | Servings 6)

Ingredients

7 eggs, whisked
1 cup kale leaves, torn into pieces
1 bell pepper, seeded and chopped
1/2 cup grape tomatoes, chopped
1 teaspoon paprika
Kosher salt and ground black pepper, to taste
1 teaspoon Italian seasoning mix
2 tablespoons butter
1 cup goat cheese, crumbled

Directions

Place 1 cup of water and metal trivet in the inner pot of your Instant Pot Duo Crisp.

Thoroughly combine all the ingredients in a mixing bowl. Spoon the mixture into lightly oiled silicone molds.

Lower the silicone molds onto the prepared trivet. Secure the pressure-cooking lid.

Pressure cook for 10 minutes at High pressure. Once cooking is complete, use a quick pressure release; carefully remove the lid.

Bon appétit!

Per serving: Calories: 205; Fat: 15.3g; Carbs: 3.3g; Protein: 12.4g; Sugars: 1.5g; Fiber: 0.7g

6. Classic Corn and Parsnip Burgers [AF]

(Ready in about 20 minutes | Servings 3)

Ingredients

3/4 pound peeled parsnips, shredded
1/4 cup all-purpose flour
1/4 cup corn flour
1 egg, lightly beaten
1 teaspoon cayenne pepper
Sea salt and ground black pepper, to taste

Directions

Mix all the ingredients until everything is well combined. Form the mixture into three patties.

Secure the air-frying lid.

Cook the burgers at 380 degrees F for about 15 minutes or until cooked through.

Bon appétit!

Per serving: Calories: 179; Fat: 2.2g; Carbs: 35.9g; Protein: 4.9g; Sugars: 5.6g; Fiber: 6.5g

7. Puerto Rican Budin [PC]

(Ready in about 55 minutes | Servings 7)

Ingredients

12 Hawaiian sweet rolls, torn into pieces
6 large eggs, beaten
1/3 cup maple syrup
1 cup coconut cream
1 teaspoon cinnamon powder
1/2 teaspoon ground cloves
1 teaspoon vanilla essence

Directions

Place 1 cup of water and a metal trivet in the inner pot of your Instant Pot Duo Crisp. Arrange the pieces of sweet rolls in a lightly oiled casserole dish.

Mix the remaining ingredients and pour the mixture over the pieces of sweet bread. Let it stand for 20 minutes, pressing down with a wide spatula until bread is covered.

Secure the pressure-cooking lid.

Pressure cook for 25 minutes at High pressure. Once cooking is complete, use a natural pressure release for 10 minutes; carefully remove the lid.

Bon appétit!

Per serving: Calories: 522; Fat: 28.1g; Carbs: 57.1g; Protein: 11.4g; Sugars: 36.6g; Fiber: 3g

8. Country-Style Cornbread Tartles [AF]

(Ready in about 20 minutes | Servings 4)

Ingredients

1/2 cup corn flour
1/2 cup plain flour
1 teaspoon baking soda
1/2 teaspoon salt
A pinch of grated nutmeg
2 eggs, whisked
2 tablespoons lard, melted
1 cup buttermilk

Directions

Spritz mini muffin cups with a nonstick cooking oil. In a mixing bowl, thoroughly combine all the ingredients.

Pour the mixture into the prepared mini muffin cups and lower them into the Air Fryer basket.

Secure the air-frying lid.

Cook your tartlets at 350 degrees F for approximately 15 minutes, or until a toothpick comes out dry and clean.

Bon appétit!

Per serving: Calories: 223; Fat: 9.7g; Carbs: 26.5g; Protein: 7.4g; Sugars: 3.2g; Fiber: 1.6g

9. Keto Sausage Omelet [PC]

(Ready in about 20 minutes | Servings 4)

Ingredients

6 eggs
1/4 cup heavy cream
1 onion, chopped
1 garlic clove, minced
4 ounces smoked sausage
1/2 teaspoon red pepper flakes
Sea salt and ground black pepper, to taste

Directions

Prepare your Instant Pot Duo Crisp by adding 1 cup of water and metal trivet to the bottom.

Whisk the eggs with heavy cream in a measuring cup. Add in the other ingredients; whisk to combine.

Scrape the egg mixture into a heatproof dish. Lower the dish onto the metal trivet. Secure the pressure-cooking lid.

Pressure cook for 14 minutes at High pressure. Once cooking is complete, use a natural pressure release for 5 minutes; carefully remove the lid

Enjoy!

Per serving: Calories: 228; Fat: 17.2g; Carbs: 5.2g; Protein: 12.4g; Sugars: 2.3g; Fiber: 0.7g

10. Authentic German Meatballs [AF]

(Ready in about 20 minutes | Servings 4)

Ingredients

1/3 pound ground beef
1/2 pound ground turkey
1 egg, slightly beaten
1/4 cup tortilla chips, crushed
1/2 cup cheddar cheese, grated
1 small onion, chopped
1 teaspoon garlic, minced
Sea salt and fresh ground black pepper, to taste
1 teaspoon dried parsley flakes
1 teaspoon dried oregano
1 teaspoon dried basil

Directions

Mix all the ingredients until everything is well combined. Form the mixture into balls.

Secure the air-frying lid.

Cook the meatballs at 380 degrees F for about 15 minutes or until cooked through, shaking the basket halfway through the cooking time. Bon appétit!

Per serving: Calories: 256; Fat: 14.6g; Carbs: 8.7g; Protein: 22.3g; Sugars: 1g; Fiber: 0.8g

BREAKFAST

11. Breakfast Ham and Mozzarella Cups [PC]

(Ready in about 20 minutes | Servings 4)

Ingredients

8 eggs
1/4 cup cream cheese
Sea salt and freshly ground black pepper, to taste
1/2 teaspoon hot paprika
2 ounces ham, chopped
1/2 cup mozzarella cheese, shredded

Directions

In a mixing dish, whisk together the eggs and cream cheese. Stir in the remaining ingredients; whisk until everything is well incorporated.

Pour the egg mixture into a heat-resistant dish.

Add 1 cup of water and a metal rack to the inner pot. Lower the dish onto the rack. Secure the pressure-cooking lid.

Pressure cook for 18 minutes at High pressure. Once cooking is complete, use a quick pressure release; carefully remove the lid.

Bon appétit!

Per serving: Calories: 208; Fat: 13.1g; Carbs: 1.9g; Protein: 19g; Sugars: 1.1g; Fiber: 0.6g

12. Mozzarella, Tomato and Herb Frittata [AF]

(Ready in about 20 minutes | Servings 3)

Ingredients

4 tablespoons sour cream
5 eggs
1/4 cup mozzarella cheese, crumbled
2 tablespoons olive oil
1 medium tomato, chopped
1/4 cup fresh parsley, chopped
1/4 cup fresh chives, chopped
1/2 teaspoon dried oregano
Sea salt and ground black pepper, to taste

Directions

Brush the sides and bottom of a baking pan with a nonstick cooking oil.

In a mixing bowl, thoroughly combine all the ingredients. Pour the mixture into the prepared baking pan.

Then, lower the pan into the Air Fryer basket. Secure the air-frying lid.

Cook your frittata at 350 degrees F for about 15 minutes, or until a toothpick comes out dry and clean.

Bon appétit!

Per serving: Calories: 236; Fat: 17.9g; Carbs: 5.5g; Protein: 13g; Sugars: 2.3g; Fiber: 1.2g

13. Mini Omelet Cups [PC]

(Ready in about 20 minutes | Servings 4)

Ingredients

8 eggs
1/4 cup heavy cream
1 shallot, chopped
2 bell peppers, chopped
1 jalapeno pepper, chopped
1/2 cup Monterey-Jack cheese, shredded
Sea salt and cayenne pepper, to taste

Directions

Prepare your Instant Pot Duo Crisp by adding 1 cup of water and a metal trivet to the bottom.

Whisk the eggs with heavy cream in a measuring cup. Add in the other ingredients; whisk to combine.

Scrape the egg mixture into a mini-muffin tin. Lower the muffin tin onto the metal trivet. Secure the pressure-cooking lid.

Pressure cook for 12 minutes at High pressure. Once cooking is complete, use a natural pressure release for 5 minutes; carefully remove the lid

Enjoy!

Per serving: Calories: 225; Fat: 15.2g; Carbs: 4.7g; Protein: 15.4g; Sugars: 2.6g; Fiber: 0.7g

14. Vegetable Egg Cups [AF]

(Ready in about 20 minutes | Servings 4)

Ingredients

4 eggs
4 tablespoons cream cheese
1 tablespoon butter, melted
Sea salt and ground black pepper, to taste
1/2 teaspoon cayenne pepper
1 cup baby spinach, chopped
1 small tomato, chopped
2 garlic cloves, minced

Directions

Brush silicone molds with a nonstick cooking oil.

In a mixing bowl, thoroughly combine all the ingredients. Pour the mixture into the prepared silicone molds

Then, lower the molds into the Air Fryer basket. Secure the air-frying lid.

Air fry the egg cups at 350 degrees F for approximately 15 minutes, or until a toothpick comes out dry and clean.

Bon appétit!

Per serving: Calories: 146; Fat: 11.9g; Carbs: 3.6g; Protein: 7.3g; Sugars: 1.9g; Fiber: 1g

15. Millet and Pistachio Porridge [PC]

(Ready in about 15 minutes | Servings 4)

Ingredients

1 cup millet, rinsed
1 cup water
3/4 cup coconut milk
2 ounces pistachios, toasted
4 tablespoons maple syrup

Directions

Place all the ingredients in the inner pot of your Instant Pot Duo Crisp. Stir to combine and secure the pressure-cooking lid.

Pressure cook for 12 minutes at High pressure. Once cooking is complete, use a quick pressure release; carefully remove the lid.

Bon appétit!

Per serving: Calories: 349; Fat: 10.2g; Carbs: 55.3g; Protein: 15.5g; Sugars: 2.9g; Fiber: 5.4g

BREAKFAST

16. Parmesan Potato Croquettes [AF]

(Ready in about 15 minutes | Servings 4)

Ingredients

1/2 cup all-purpose flour
3/4 pound potatoes, peeled and grated
2 eggs, whisked
2 tablespoons butter
2 ounces Parmesan cheese, grated
2 ounces breadcrumbs
2 tablespoons olive oil
1 teaspoon paprika
Kosher salt and freshly ground black pepper, to taste

Directions

Mix all the ingredients in a bowl. Shape the mixture into bite-sized balls and place them in a lightly oiled Air Fryer cooking basket.

Secure the air-frying lid.

Air fry the croquettes at 400 degrees F for about 14 minutes, shaking the basket halfway through the cooking time.

Bon appétit!

Per serving: Calories: 363; Fat: 19g; Carbs: 36.2g; Protein: 11.5g; Sugars: 1.6g; Fiber: 2.9g

17. Couscous Pudding with Orange and Almonds [PC]

(Ready in about 5 minutes | Servings 4)

Ingredients

1 cup couscous
2 cups water
4 tablespoons brown sugar
1/2 teaspoon ground cinnamon
1/2 teaspoon ground cardamom
2 teaspoons rose water
1 orange, peeled and chopped
1/2 cup almonds, slivered

Directions

Place all the ingredients in the inner pot of your Instant Pot Duo Crisp. Gently stir to combine and secure the pressure-cooking lid.

Pressure cook for 3 minutes at High pressure. Once cooking is complete, use a quick pressure release; carefully remove the lid.

Bon appétit!

Per serving: Calories: 298; Fat: 7.1g; Carbs: 51g; Protein: 8.7g; Sugars: 13.3g; Fiber: 5g

18. Breakfast Vegan Sausage [AF]

(Ready in about 20 minutes | Servings 4)

Ingredients

1 cup cooked quinoa
10 ounces canned red kidney beans, rinsed and dried
1/2 cup walnuts, ground
1 red onion, chopped
2 cloves garlic, minced
1 teaspoon smoked paprika
Sea salt and ground black pepper, to taste

Directions

Mix all the ingredients in your blender or food processor. Form the mixture into logs and arrange them in a lightly greased Air Fryer basket.

Secure the air-frying lid.

Cook the sausages at 380 degrees F for about 15 minutes or until cooked through. Tun them over halfway through the cooking time.

Bon appétit!

Per serving: Calories: 228; Fat: 8.2g; Carbs: 30.7g; Protein: 9.6g; Sugars: 5.1g; Fiber: 6.7g

19. Frittata with Cheese and Broccoli [PC]

(Ready in about 30 minutes | Servings 5)

Ingredients

2 tablespoons butter
1/2 cup scallions, chopped
2 cloves garlic, minced
1 pound button mushrooms, chopped
9 large eggs, whisked
1/2 cup double cream
1 cup cheddar cheese, shredded
Kosher salt and ground black pepper, to taste
2 cups small broccoli florets

Directions

Press the "Sauté" button and melt the butter; cook the scallions, garlic, and mushrooms for about 3 minutes or until tender and aromatic.

Now, add in the remaining ingredients; spoon the mixture into a casserole dish.

Lower the casserole dish onto the trivet and secure the pressure-cooking lid. Pressure cook for 10 minutes at High pressure.

Once cooking is complete, use a natural release for 15 minutes; carefully remove the lid.

Serve warm and enjoy!

Per serving: Calories: 349; Fat: 25.9g; Carbs: 9g; Protein: 21.7g; Sugars: 4.4g; Fiber: 2.3g

20. Authentic French Toast [AF]

(Ready in about 10 minutes | Servings 2)

Ingredients

2 tablespoons butter, melted
2 eggs, whisked
4 tablespoons coconut milk
1/2 teaspoon ground cinnamon
1/2 teaspoon vanilla extract
4 tablespoons brown sugar
4 slices stale French bread

Directions

In a mixing bowl, thoroughly combine the butter, eggs, coconut milk, cinnamon, vanilla, and brown sugar.

Then dip each piece of bread into the egg mixture; place the bread slices in a lightly greased baking pan.

Secure the air-frying lid.

Air Fryer the bread slices at 330 degrees F for about 4 minutes; turn them over and cook for a further 3 to 4 minutes. Enjoy!

Per serving: Calories: 192; Fat: 9.1g; Carbs: 21.5g; Protein: 5.5g; Sugars: 10.1g; Fiber: 0.8g

21. Chocolate and Apple Oatmeal [PC]

(Ready in about 10 minutes | Servings 4)

Ingredients

1 ½ cups rolled oats
3 cups water
1 apple, peeled, cored and chopped
1/2 cup bittersweet chocolate chunks
1/2 teaspoon ground cloves
1/3 teaspoon ground cinnamon
1/4 teaspoon grated nutmeg

Directions

Simply place all ingredients in the inner pot of your Instant Pot Duo Crisp. Secure the pressure-cooking lid.

Pressure cook for 4 minutes at High pressure. Once cooking is complete, use a quick pressure release; carefully remove the lid. Bon appétit!

Per serving: Calories: 342; Fat: 10.5g; Carbs: 52.2g; Protein: 11.2g; Sugars: 8.3g; Fiber: 9g

22. Ricotta and Spinach Frittata [AF]

(Ready in about 20 minutes | Servings 3)

Ingredients

6 eggs
6 tablespoons half-and-half
1/4 teaspoon salt
1/4 teaspoon ground black pepper
3 ounces Ricotta cheese crumbled
2 cups baby spinach
1 tablespoon fresh cilantro, chopped
2 tablespoons olive oil

Directions

Brush the sides and bottom of a baking pan with a nonstick cooking oil.

In a mixing bowl, thoroughly combine all the ingredients. Pour the mixture into the prepared baking pan and lower the pan into the Air Fryer basket.

Secure the air-frying lid.

Cook your frittata at 350 degrees F for approximately 15 minutes, or until a toothpick comes out dry and clean.

Bon appétit!

Per serving: Calories: 277; Fat: 21.5g; Carbs: 5g; Protein: 15.6g; Sugars: 1.9g; Fiber: 0.5g

23. Classic French Dip Sandwiches [PC+AF]

(Ready in about 50 minutes | Servings 6)

Ingredients

2 tablespoons olive oil
2 pounds eye of round roast, thinly sliced into strips
1 red chili, thinly sliced
Sea salt and ground black pepper, to taste
1/4 cup tomato paste
2 cups beef bone broth
1 onion, chopped
2 garlic cloves, chopped
6 rolls
6 slices provolone cheese

Directions

Heat the olive oil on the "Sauté" mode and sear the eye of round roast for about 5 minutes or until no longer pink.

Add in the other ingredients; secure the pressure-cooking lid.

Pressure cook for 35 minutes at High pressure. Once cooking is complete, use a quick pressure release; carefully remove the lid.

Shred the beef and arrange your sandwiches with rolls and provolone cheese. Secure the air-frying lid and press the "Broil" function.

Broil your sandwiches for 5 to 6 minutes or until the cheese melts. Bon appétit!

Per serving: Calories: 477; Fat: 22.2g; Carbs: 26.2g; Protein: 43.2g; Sugars: 5.3g; Fiber: 1.8g

24. Perfect Hard-Boiled Eggs [AF]

(Ready in about 20 minutes | Servings 2)

Ingredients

4 eggs
Sea salt, to taste

Directions

Place the eggs in the Air Fryer cooking basket. Secure the air-frying lid.

Air fry your eggs at 270 degrees F for about 15 minutes.

Peel the eggs and season them with the salt. Bon appétit!

Per serving: Calories: 144; Fat: 9.6g; Carbs: 0.7g; Protein: 12.3g; Sugars: 0.2g; Fiber: 0g

25. Kamut Porridge with Coconut and Strawberries [PC]

(Ready in about 15 minutes | Servings 4)

Ingredients

1 cup kamut berries
1 cup water
1 cup coconut milk
A pinch of kosher salt
A pinch of grated nutmeg
1/2 teaspoon ground cinnamon
2 tablespoons coconut oil
4 tablespoons agave syrup
4 tablespoons strawberries, halved
2 tablespoons coconut chips

Directions

Add the kamut berries, water, coconut milk, salt, nutmeg, cinnamon, coconut oil, and agave syrup to the inner pot. Secure the pressure-cooking lid.

Pressure cook for 11 minutes at High pressure. Once cooking is complete, use a quick pressure release; then, carefully remove the lid.

Ladle the kamut pudding into serving bowls; garnish with strawberries and coconut chips. Bon appétit!

Per serving: Calories: 346; Fat: 12.3g; Carbs: 54.6g; Protein: 9.1g; Sugars: 24.5g; Fiber: 6.2g

26. Crescent Dogs with Cheese [AF]

(Ready in about 15 minutes | Servings 4)

Ingredients

6 ounces refrigerated crescent dinner rolls
1/2 pound smoked sausage, chopped
4 ounces Swiss cheese, shredded
1/2 teaspoon dried oregano
2 tablespoons tomato paste

Directions

Separate the dough into rectangles. In a bowl, combine the remaining ingredients.

Spread each rectangle with the sausage mixture; roll them up tightly. Arrange the rolls in the Air Fryer cooking basket.

Secure the air-frying lid.

Air fry the crescent rolls at 300 degrees F for about 5 minutes; turn them over and bake for a further 5 minutes.

Bon appétit!

Per serving: Calories: 412; Fat: 26.1g; Carbs: 24g; Protein: 18.3g; Sugars: 2g; Fiber: 2g

27. Balkan-Style Rice Pudding (Sütlaç) [PC]

(Ready in about 5 minutes | Servings 4)

Ingredients

1 cup white rice
1 cup milk
1 cup water
1/2 teaspoon vanilla extract
8 tablespoons brown sugar
1/2 teaspoon ground cinnamon
1/4 teaspoon ground cardamom

Directions

Place all the ingredients in the inner pot of your Instant Pot Duo Crisp. Secure the pressure-cooking lid.

Pressure cook for 4 minutes at High pressure. Once cooking is complete, use a quick pressure release; carefully remove the lid.

Bon appétit!

Per serving: Calories: 288; Fat: 2.3g; Carbs: 60.1g; Protein: 8.7g; Sugars: 22.3g; Fiber: 1.5g

28. Cauliflower and Feta Cheese Bombs [AF]

(Ready in about 20 minutes | Servings 4)

Ingredients

2 cups cauliflower florets
4 tablespoons butter
1 teaspoon dried parsley flakes
1 teaspoon dried rosemary
2 garlic cloves, minced
Sea salt and ground black pepper, to taste
1/2 cup feta cheese

Directions

Arrange the cauliflower florets in a lightly greased Air Fryer basket.

Secure the air-frying lid.

Cook the cauliflower florets at 400 degrees F for about 15 minutes, shaking the basket halfway through the cooking time.

Chop the roasted cauliflower and combine it with the remaining ingredients. Shape the mixture into balls.

Bon appétit!

Per serving: Calories: 180; Fat: 15.2g; Carbs: 5g; Protein: 4.6g; Sugars: 2.3g; Fiber: 1.3g

29. Tangy Peach Sauce [PC]

(Ready in about 10 minutes | Servings 9)

Ingredients

2 pounds peaches, pitted
2 tablespoons fresh lemon juice
4 ounces agave syrup
1 cinnamon stick
1 vanilla bean

Directions

Simply add all the ingredients to the inner pot and secure the pressure-cooking lid.

Pressure cook for 6 minutes at High pressure. Once cooking is complete, use a quick pressure release; carefully remove the lid.

Blend the cooked peaches using an immersion blender or food processor.

Enjoy!

Per serving: Calories: 56; Fat: 0.1g; Carbs: 13.8g; Protein: 0.4g; Sugars: 3.2g; Fiber: 0.5g

30. Authentic Potatoes Cakes [AF]

(Ready in about 20 minutes | Servings 4)

Ingredients

3/4 cup all-purpose flour
1 cup boiled potatoes, mashed
2 eggs, whisked
1 tablespoon fresh parsley, chopped
1 tablespoon fresh cilantro, chopped
2 tablespoons fresh scallions, chopped
Sea salt and ground black pepper, to taste
1/2 cup fresh breadcrumbs
2 tablespoons olive oil

Directions

Mix all the ingredients in a bowl. Shape the mixture into bite-sized balls and place them in a lightly oiled Air Fryer cooking basket.

Secure the air-frying lid.

Cook the potato cakes at 400 degrees F for about 14 minutes, shaking the basket halfway through the cooking time.

Bon appétit!

Per serving: Calories: 232; Fat: 9.3g; Carbs: 30.3g; Protein: 6.6g; Sugars: 1.4g; Fiber: 1.8g

31. Apricot and Lemon Jam [PC]

(Ready in about 30 minutes | Servings 8)

Ingredients

1 pound dried apricots, chopped
2 lemons, squeezed
1 ½ cups caster sugar
1 teaspoon whole cloves
1 cinnamon stick

Directions

Place all the ingredients in the inner pot and secure the pressure-cooking lid.

Pressure cook for 10 minutes at High pressure. Once cooking is complete, use a natural pressure release for 15 minutes; carefully remove the lid.

Puree the ingredients in your blender or food processor.

Bon appétit!

Per serving: Calories: 213; Fat: 0.4g; Carbs: 55.2g; Protein: 1.9g; Sugars: 48.3g; Fiber: 4.2g

32. Sicilian Arancini di Riso [AF]

(Ready in about 20 minutes | Servings 4)

Ingredients

1 ½ cups cooked Arborio rice
1/2 cup Parmesan cheese, grated
1 cup panko crumbs
2 large eggs, whisked
1 teaspoon dried parsley flakes
Kosher salt and freshly ground black pepper, to taste
2 tablespoons butter

Directions

Mix all the ingredients until everything is well combined. Form the mixture into balls.

Secure the air-frying lid.

Air fry the balls at 380 degrees F for about 15 minutes or until cooked through, shaking the basket halfway through the cooking time. Bon appétit!

Per serving: Calories: 248; Fat: 12.5g; Carbs: 23.9g; Protein: 9.4g; Sugars: 0.8g; Fiber: 2g

33. Breakfast Bulgur with Berries [PC]

(Ready in about 25 minutes | Servings 4)

Ingredients

1 cup medium-grind bulgur
2 cups water
1 cup milk
A pinch of sea salt
A pinch of grated nutmeg
4 tablespoons brown sugar
1 cup mixed berries

Directions

Add all the ingredients to the inner pot of your Instant Pot Duo Crisp. Secure the pressure-cooking lid.

Pressure cook for 20 minutes at High pressure. Once cooking is complete, use a quick pressure release; carefully remove the lid.

Spoon the bulgur porridge into serving bowls and enjoy!

Per serving: Calories: 313; Fat: 5.6g; Carbs: 60.2g; Protein: 7.7g; Sugars: 23g; Fiber: 5.4g

34. Creamed Egg Salad Sandwich [AF]

(Ready in about 25 minutes | Servings 3)

Ingredients

6 eggs
2 tablespoons scallions, chopped
2 garlic cloves, minced
1/4 cup sour cream
1/4 cup mayonnaise
1 teaspoon yellow mustard
Sea salt and ground black pepper, to taste
1 garlic clove, minced
6 slices whole-grain bread

Directions

Place the eggs in the Air Fryer cooking basket. Secure the air-frying lid.

Air fry your eggs at 270 degrees F for about 15 minutes.

Peel and chop the eggs; place them in a salad bowl and add in the remaining ingredients. Gently toss to combine.

Secure the air-frying lid.

Air fry the bread slices at 330 degrees F for about 4 minutes; turn them over and cook for a further 3 to 4 minutes.

Lastly, assemble your sandwiches with the egg salad and toasted bread.

Bon appétit!

Per serving: Calories: 503; Fat: 27.2g; Carbs: 40.2g; Protein: 23.4g; Sugars: 6.6g; Fiber: 6.5g

35. Decadent Breakfast Brownie [PC]

(Ready in about 30 minutes | Servings 8)

Ingredients

1 stick butter, melted
1 cup caster sugar
2 large eggs
1/2 teaspoon ground cinnamon
1/2 teaspoon ground cardamom
1 teaspoon vanilla extract
1/2 cup cake flour
1/4 cup almond flour
1/2 cup cocoa powder

Directions

Add 1 cup of water and a metal trivet to the inner pot. Spritz a baking pan with a nonstick cooking spray.

Then, thoroughly combine all the ingredients in a mixing bowl. Scrape the batter into the prepared pan.

Lower the baking pan onto the trivet. Secure the pressure-cooking lid.

Pressure cook for 20 minutes at High pressure. Once cooking is complete, use a natural pressure release for 5 minutes; carefully remove the lid.

Transfer the cake to a cooling rack. Bon appétit!

Per serving: Calories: 268; Fat: 13.4g; Carbs: 35.2g; Protein: 3.9g; Sugars: 25.4g; Fiber: 1.9g

BREAKFAST

36. Quiche with Bacon Pie [AF]

(Ready in about 20 minutes | Servings 4)

Ingredients

6 eggs, whisked
6 tablespoons all-purpose flour
1/2 teaspoon baking soda
6 tablespoons full-fat milk
4 ounces Canadian bacon, diced
1 tablespoon olive oil
2 cups baby spinach
1 tomato, chopped
1 Serrano peppers, chopped
Kosher salt and freshly ground black pepper, to taste

Directions

Spritz the sides and bottom of a baking pan with a nonstick cooking oil. In a mixing bowl, thoroughly combine all the ingredients.

Pour the mixture into the prepared baking pan and lower the pan into the Air Fryer basket.

Secure the air-frying lid.

Cook the pie at 350 degrees F for approximately 15 minutes, or until a toothpick comes out dry and clean.

Bon appétit!

Per serving: Calories: 220; Fat: 11.3g; Carbs: 12.5g; Protein: 16.4g; Sugars: 2.6g; Fiber: 1.5g

37. Vanilla Croissant Pudding with Dried Figs [PC]

(Ready in about 20 minutes | Servings 4)

Ingredients

1/2 cup brown sugar
1/2 cup full-fat milk
1/2 cup double cream
4 tablespoons rum
1 teaspoon vanilla essence
1/4 teaspoon ground cinnamon
2 large eggs, beaten
4 medium-sized stale croissants, torn into pieces
4 dried figs, chopped

Directions

In a mixing bowl, thoroughly combine the sugar, milk, cream, rum, vanilla, cinnamon, and eggs.

Fold in croissants and let them soak for about 20 minutes. Spoon the mixture into the inner pot and fold in the chopped figs; secure the pressure-cooking lid.

Pressure cook for 15 minutes at High pressure. Once cooking is complete, use a quick pressure release; carefully remove the lid.

Bon appétit!

Per serving: Calories: 491; Fat: 20.7g; Carbs: 61.4g; Protein: 8.2g; Sugars: 39.9g; Fiber: 2.3g

38. Classic Pigs in a Blanket [AF]

(Ready in about 10 minutes | Servings 4)

Ingredients

4 ounces refrigerated crescent rolls
1 tablespoon Dijon mustard
8 cocktail sausages

Directions

Separate the dough into triangles. Cut them lengthwise into triangles. Spread each triangle with mustard.

Place a cocktail sausage on the shortest side of each triangle and roll it up.

Place the rolls in the Air Fryer cooking basket. Secure the air-frying lid.

Bake the rolls at 320 degrees F for about 8 minutes, turning them over halfway through the cooking time.

Bon appétit!

Per serving: Calories: 342; Fat: 25g; Carbs: 14.9g; Protein: 13.3g; Sugars: 1.6g; Fiber: 0.8g

39. Breakfast Mexican Rice Pudding [PC]

(Ready in about 20 minutes | Servings 4)

Ingredients

1 cup long-grain white rice
1 cup water
1 cup almond milk
1/4 cup agave syrup
1 teaspoon whole cloves
1 vanilla bean
1 cinnamon stick

Directions

Combine all the ingredients in the inner pot and secure the pressure-cooking lid.

Pressure cook for 5 minutes at High pressure. Once cooking is complete, use a natural pressure release for 10 minutes; carefully remove the lid.

Enjoy!

Per serving: Calories: 267; Fat: 2.4g; Carbs: 56.2g; Protein: 5.4g; Sugars: 19.1g; Fiber: 0.6g

40. Yorkshire Pudding Popovers [AF]

(Ready in about 20 minutes | Servings 4)

Ingredients

6 large-sized eggs
1/2 cup all-purpose flour
1/2 teaspoon baking powder
4 tablespoons butter, melted
1/2 cup milk
1/2 teaspoon granulated sugar
1/4 teaspoon kosher salt
1 teaspoon dried rosemary

Directions

Brush mini muffin cups with a nonstick cooking oil. In a mixing bowl, thoroughly combine all the ingredients.

Pour the mixture into the prepared mini muffin cups and lower them into the Air Fryer basket.

Secure the air-frying lid.

Cook your popovers at 350 degrees F for approximately 15 minutes, or until a toothpick comes out dry and clean.

Bon appétit!

Per serving: Calories: 299; Fat: 20.6g; Carbs: 14.3g; Protein: 13.3g; Sugars: 2.2g; Fiber: 0.5g

41. Sweet Potato Frittata [PC]

(Ready in about 20 minutes | Servings 4)

Ingredients

8 large eggs, whisked
2 tablespoons butter
8 tablespoons milk
1 pound sweet potatoes, peeled and sliced
1 onion, thinly sliced
8 ounces deli ham, chopped
1 teaspoon hot pepper sauce
Sea salt and ground black pepper, to taste
1 cup Colby cheese, shredded

Directions

Prepare your Instant Pot Duo Crisp by adding 1 cup of water and a metal trivet to the bottom.

Whisk the eggs, butter, and milk in a mixing bowl. Add in the other ingredients; whisk to combine.

Scrape the egg mixture into lightly greased ramekins. Lower the ramekins onto the metal trivet.

Secure the pressure-cooking lid. Pressure cook for 14 minutes at High pressure. Once cooking is complete, use a natural pressure release for 5 minutes; carefully remove the lid

Enjoy!

Per serving: Calories: 497; Fat: 28.7g; Carbs: 25.7g; Protein: 33.7g; Sugars: 4.2g; Fiber: 3g

42. Buttery Brioche Grilled Cheese [AF]

(Ready in about 10 minutes | Servings 3)

Ingredients

2 ounces goat cheese, crumbled
1 ounce butter, melted
1 ounce yogurt
2 eggs
1/4 teaspoon sea salt
3 stale Brioche bread slices

Directions

In a mixing bowl, thoroughly combine the cheese, butter, yogurt, eggs, and sea salt.

Then dip each piece of bread into the egg mixture; place the bread slices in a lightly greased baking pan.

Secure the air-frying lid.

Air fry the bread slices at 330 degrees F for about 4 minutes; turn them over and cook for a further 3 to 4 minutes. Enjoy!

Per serving: Calories: 255; Fat: 17.6g; Carbs: 10.9g; Protein: 12.3g; Sugars: 2g; Fiber: 0.5g

43. Pearl Barley and Cranberry Porridge [PC]

(Ready in about 25 minutes | Servings 4)

Ingredients

1 cup pearl barley, coarsely ground
1 ½ cups water
1 cup coconut milk
2 tablespoons coconut oil
4 tablespoons dates, pitted and coarsely chopped
4 tablespoons dried cranberries

Directions

Add all the ingredients to the inner pot. Secure the pressure-cooking lid.

Pressure cook for 22 minutes at High pressure. Once cooking is complete, use a quick pressure release; carefully remove the lid.

Bon appétit!

Per serving: Calories: 408; Fat: 21.1g; Carbs: 51g; Protein: 6.6g; Sugars: 9.7g; Fiber: 21.5g

44. Japanese-Style Tater Tots [AF]

(Ready in about 20 minutes | Servings 4)

Ingredients

1 cup boiled potato, mashed
1 cup cheddar, grated
1 tablespoon miso paste
1 cup all-purpose flour
1/2 teaspoon coriander seeds
Sea salt and ground black pepper, to taste
1 egg, beaten
1 cup breadcrumbs
2 tablespoons Kewpie Japanese mayonnaise

Directions

Mix all the ingredients, except for the breadcrumbs, in a bowl. Press the mixture into a parchment-lined baking sheet and allow it to freeze until firm.

Cut the mixture into sticks and roll them into the breadcrumbs; place the sticks in a lightly oiled Air Fryer cooking basket.

Secure the air-frying lid.

Air fry the sticks at 400 degrees F for about 14 minutes, shaking the basket halfway through the cooking time.

Bon appétit!

Per serving: Calories: 364; Fat: 15.5g; Carbs: 40.5g; Protein: 16g; Sugars: 2g; Fiber: 2.5g

45. Perfect Steel Cut Oat Porridge [PC]

(Ready in about 10 minutes | Servings 4)

Ingredients

1 cup steel-cut oats
2 cups water
1 cup almond milk
2 tablespoons coconut oil
A pinch of sea salt
A pinch of grated nutmeg
1/2 teaspoon ground cinnamon
1/2 cup dates, pitted
1/2 cup walnuts, roughly chopped

Directions

Add all the ingredients to the inner pot and secure the pressure-cooking lid.

Pressure cook for 5 minutes at High pressure. Once cooking is complete, use a quick pressure release and carefully remove the lid.

Serve in individual bowls. Bon appétit!

Per serving: Calories: 366; Fat: 18.1g; Carbs: 44.1g; Protein: 10.4g; Sugars: 14.8g; Fiber: 6.4g

46. Breakfast Egg Salad [AF]

(Ready in about 20 minutes | Servings 4)

Ingredients

6 eggs
4 tablespoons Greek-style yogurt
4 tablespoons mayonnaise
3 tablespoons scallions, chopped
1 tablespoon Dijon mustard
Sea salt and ground black pepper, to taste

Directions

Place the eggs in the Air Fryer cooking basket. Secure the air-frying lid.

Air fry your eggs at 270 degrees F for about 15 minutes.

Peel and chop the eggs; place them in a salad bowl and add in the remaining ingredients. Gently toss to combine.

Place the salad in your refrigerator until ready to serve. Bon appétit!

Per serving: Calories: 206; Fat: 16.7g; Carbs: 2.7g; Protein: 10.1g; Sugars: 1.6g; Fiber: 0.5g

47. Sweet Farro Pudding [PC]

(Ready in about 15 minutes | Servings 4)

Ingredients

1 cup farro
2 cups water
4 tablespoons honey
1/2 teaspoon ground cardamom
1/2 teaspoon ground cinnamon

Directions

Simply place all the ingredients in the inner pot of your Instant Pot Duo Crisp. Stir to combine and secure the pressure-cooking lid.

Pressure cook for 12 minutes at High pressure. Once cooking is complete, use a quick pressure release and carefully remove the lid.

Spoon your pudding into serving bowls and enjoy!

Per serving: Calories: 186; Fat: 0.5g; Carbs: 43.6g; Protein: 4.3g; Sugars: 17.3g; Fiber: 4.4g

48. Omelet with Mushrooms and Cheese [AF]

(Ready in about 20 minutes | Servings 3)

Ingredients

6 eggs
1/4 cup sour cream
1/2 cup Swiss cheese, shredded
Kosher salt and ground black pepper, to taste
1 teaspoon hot paprika
2 tablespoons olive oil
2 cloves garlic, crushed
6 ounces brown mushrooms, sliced
2 tablespoons fresh parsley, roughly chopped

Directions

In a mixing bowl, thoroughly combine all the ingredients.

Pour the mixture into a lightly greased baking pan; lower the pan into the Air Fryer basket.

Secure the air-frying lid.

Cook your omelet at 350 degrees F for approximately 15 minutes, or until a toothpick comes out dry and clean. Bon appétit!

Per serving: Calories: 340; Fat: 25.2g; Carbs: 8.5g; Protein: 19.6g; Sugars: 2.6g; Fiber: 1.5g

49. Homemade Pear Sauce [PC]

(Ready in about 10 minutes | Servings 8)

Ingredients

1 ½ pounds pears, cored, peeled and diced
1 cup water
2 tablespoons fresh orange juice
1/2 teaspoon ground cinnamon
1/2 teaspoon ground ginger
1 teaspoon vanilla essence

Directions

Add all the ingredients to the inner pot and secure the pressure-cooking lid.

Pressure cook for 6 minutes at High pressure. Once cooking is complete, use a quick pressure release; carefully remove the lid.

Transfer the cooked pears to your blender or food processor; blend to desired consistency and spoon into sterilized jars.

Enjoy!

Per serving: Calories: 66; Fat: 0.1g; Carbs: 13.6g; Protein: 0.4g; Sugars: 8.7g; Fiber: 2.4g

50. Double Cheese and Vegetable Croquettes [AF]

(Ready in about 15 minutes | Servings 4)

Ingredients

2 eggs, whisked
1/2 cup chickpea flour
2 ounces feta cheese, crumbled
2 ounces Swiss cheese, shredded
1 bell pepper, chopped
1 small zucchini, chopped
1 clove garlic, minced
1/2 teaspoon smoked paprika
Kosher salt and freshly ground black pepper, to taste
2 tablespoons butter, melted

Directions

Mix all the ingredients in a bowl. Shape the mixture into bite-sized balls and place them in a lightly oiled Air Fryer cooking basket.

Secure the air-frying lid.

Cook your croquettes at 400 degrees F for about 14 minutes, shaking the basket halfway through the cooking time.

Bon appétit!

Per serving: Calories: 227; Fat: 15.5g; Carbs: 9.5g; Protein: 12.6g; Sugars: 2.6g; Fiber: 1.5g

51. Italian Bread Pudding [PC]

(Ready in about 40 minutes | Servings 7)

Ingredients

2 tablespoons butter, melted
1 ¾ cups coconut milk
1/4 cup brandy
2 eggs, beaten
1 cup brown sugar
1 teaspoon vanilla essence
1/4 cup prunes, pitted and chopped
1 Italian bread, torn into pieces

BREAKFAST

Directions

In a mixing bowl, thoroughly combine the butter, coconut milk, brandy, eggs, brown sugar, and vanilla.

Fold in the bread pieces and let it soak for about 20 minutes. Spoon the mixture into the inner pot.

Fold in the prunes and secure the pressure-cooking lid.

Pressure cook for 15 minutes at High pressure. Once cooking is complete, use a quick pressure release; carefully remove the lid.

Bon appétit!

Per serving: Calories: 476; Fat: 21.7g; Carbs: 66.4g; Protein: 6.7g; Sugars: 34.1g; Fiber: 3g

52. Classic Griddle Cake [AF]

(Ready in about 15 minutes | Servings 4)

Ingredients

3/4 cup all-purpose flour
1/2 teaspoon baking powder
2 tablespoons brown sugar
1/2 cup yogurt
2 eggs, whisked
1/2 teaspoon ground cinnamon
1/2 teaspoon vanilla extract

Directions

In a mixing bowl, thoroughly combine all the ingredients.

Drop a spoonful of batter onto the greased Air Fryer pan. Secure the air-frying lid.

Cook in the preheated Air Fryer at 360 degrees F for 10 minutes, flipping them halfway through the cooking time.

Repeat with the remaining batter and serve warm. Enjoy!

Per serving: Calories: 163; Fat: 3.3g; Carbs: 23.2.9g; Protein: 6.5g; Sugars: 5.6g; Fiber: 0.9g

53. Old-Fashioned Plum Jam [PC]

(Ready in about 20 minutes | Servings 9)

Ingredients

2 pounds plums, pitted
2 cups brown sugar
1 cinnamon stick
1 vanilla bean
1 teaspoon whole cloves

Directions

Toss the plums and sugar into the inner pot of your Instant Pot Duo Crisp. Press the "Sauté" button and let it cook for 2 to 3 minutes or until just tender.

Now, add in the spices and gently stir to combine. Secure the pressure-cooking lid.

Pressure cook for 2 minutes at High pressure. Once cooking is complete, use a natural pressure release for 15 minutes; carefully remove the lid.

Bon appétit!

Per serving: Calories: 133; Fat: 0.4g; Carbs: 33.3g; Protein: 0.5g; Sugars: 31.6g; Fiber: 1.4g

54. Authentic Breakfast Rissoles [AF]

(Ready in about 20 minutes | Servings 4)

Ingredients

1 slice bread, crusts removed and soaked
1 shallot, chopped
2 cloves garlic, minced
1/2 pound ground beef
1/2 pound pork sausage, crumbled
1 egg, beaten
Sea salt and ground black pepper, to taste

Directions

Mix all the ingredients until everything is well combined. Form the mixture into balls.

Secure the air-frying lid.

Cook the meatballs at 380 degrees F for about 15 minutes or until cooked through, shaking the basket halfway through the cooking time.

Bon appétit!

Per serving: Calories: 342; Fat: 26.2g; Carbs: 5g; Protein: 21.3g; Sugars: 1.1g; Fiber: 0.5g

55. German-Style Giant Pancake [PC]

(Ready in about 30 minutes | Servings 5)

Ingredients

1 ½ cups plain flour
1 teaspoon baking powder
1/2 teaspoon baking soda
1 tablespoon granulated sugar
1/2 teaspoon ground cinnamon
2 eggs, whisked
1 ½ cups milk

Directions

Add 1 cup water and a metal rack to the inner pot. Line the bottom of a springform pan with parchment paper; brush the bottom and sides of the pan with a nonstick spray.

Mix all the ingredients until well combined. Now, spoon the batter into the prepared pan. Lower the pan onto the rack. Secure the pressure-cooking lid.

Pressure cook for 25 minutes at High pressure. Once cooking is complete, use a quick pressure release; carefully remove the lid.

Enjoy!

Per serving: Calories: 231; Fat: 4.4g; Carbs: 34.1g; Protein: 8.4g; Sugars: 5.4g; Fiber: 1.2g

BREAKFAST

56. Breakfast Chickpea Bowl [AF]

(Ready in about 30 minutes | Servings 3)

Ingredients

8 ounces chickpeas, drained and rinsed
2 tablespoons olive oil
Sea salt and ground black pepper, to taste
1 teaspoon paprika
2 bell peppers, seeded and halved
1 small onion, thinly sliced
2 cups baby spinach
2 lemon wedges

Directions

Toss the chickpeas with the olive oil, salt, black pepper, and paprika in the Air Fryer cooking basket.

Secure the air-frying lid.

Air fry the chickpeas at 390 degrees F for about 13 minutes, tossing the basket a couple of times; reserve.

Then, air fry the peppers at 400 degrees F for about 15 minutes, shaking the basket halfway through the cooking time.

Arrange the bowl with the roasted chickpeas, peppers, and the other ingredients. Bon appétit!

Per serving: Calories: 240; Fat: 11.2g; Carbs: 29.9g; Protein: 8.6g; Sugars: 7.1g; Fiber: 7.4g

57. Breakfast Vanilla Risotto with Prunes [PC]

(Ready in about 10 minutes | Servings 4)

Ingredients

1 cup jasmine rice
1 cup water
1/2 cup milk
1/2 teaspoon vanilla paste
1/4 cup brown sugar
8 prunes, chopped

Directions

Place all the ingredients in the inner pot and secure the pressure-cooking lid.

Pressure cook for 4 minutes at High pressure. Once cooking is complete, use a quick pressure release; carefully remove the lid.

Bon appétit!

Per serving: Calories: 300; Fat: 1.4g; Carbs: 67.3g; Protein: 5g; Sugars: 7.6g; Fiber: 1.3g

58. Cottage Cheese and Egg Muffins [AF]

(Ready in about 20 minutes | Servings 4)

Ingredients

6 eggs
6 tablespoons Cottage cheese, crumbled
2 tablespoons scallions, chopped
1 teaspoon garlic, minced
3 ounces bacon, chopped
1 teaspoon paprika
Sea salt and ground black pepper, to taste

Directions

Start by preheating your Air Fryer to 350 degrees F. Then, spritz silicone molds with a nonstick cooking oil.

In a mixing bowl, thoroughly combine all the ingredients.

Pour the mixture into the prepared silicone molds and lower them into the Air Fryer basket.

Secure the air-frying lid.

Cook the egg muffins in the preheated Air Fryer for approximately 15 minutes, or until a toothpick comes out dry and clean.

Bon appétit!

Per serving: Calories: 205; Fat: 14.5g; Carbs: 3.3g; Protein: 14.6g; Sugars: 1.6g; Fiber: 0.6g

59. Soy Pate with Sun-Dried Tomatoes [PC]

(Ready in about 50 minutes | Servings 8)

Ingredients

1 cup soybeans
2 cups water
1/2 teaspoon smoked paprika
2 tablespoons sun-dried tomatoes in olive oil
1 tablespoon tahini
1/2 small shallot
1 garlic clove, peeled
Sea salt and freshly ground black pepper, to taste

Directions

Add the soybeans and water to the inner pot and secure the pressure-cooking lid.

Pressure cook for 45 minutes at High pressure. Once cooking is complete, use a natural pressure release; carefully remove the lid.

Drain the soybeans and let them cool.

In your blender or food processor, blend all the ingredients until creamy and uniform. Bon appétit!

Per serving: Calories: 146; Fat: 9g; Carbs: 7.6g; Protein: 8.8g; Sugars: 1.7g; Fiber: 2.5g

60. Classic Cinnamon Butter Toast [AF]

(Ready in about 10 minutes | Servings 2)

Ingredients

2 bread slices
1 teaspoon ground cinnamon
2 tablespoons butter, softened

Directions

Toss the bread slices with the cinnamon and butter.

Secure the air-frying lid.

Air fry the bread slices at 330 degrees F for about 4 minutes; turn them over and cook for a further 3 to 4 minutes.

Bon appétit!

Per serving: Calories: 169; Fat: 12.2g; Carbs: 11g; Protein: 1.9g; Sugars: 1.6g; Fiber: 1.2g

BREAKFAST

VEGETABLES & SIDE DISHES

61. Sticky Maple-Glazed Carrots [PC+AF]

(Ready in about 10 minutes | Servings 4)

Ingredients

- 1 ½ pounds baby carrots
- 1/4 cup coconut oil
- 1/4 cup maple syrup
- 1/2 cup water
- Kosher salt and ground white pepper, to taste
- 1/2 teaspoon ground allspice

Directions

Place 1 cup of water and a steamer basket in the inner pot of your Instant Pot Duo Crisp. Place the carrots in the steamer basket.

Secure the pressure-cooking lid. Choose the "Steam" mode and cook for 3 minutes at High pressure. Once cooking is complete, use a quick pressure release; carefully remove the lid.

Toss the carrots with the remaining ingredients. Secure the air-frying lid and choose the "Broil" mode and cook for 2 minutes or until caramelized.

Bon appétit!

Per serving: Calories: 233; Fat: 13.9g; Carbs: 28.4g; Protein: 1.3g; Sugars: 20.3g; Fiber: 5.2g

62. Cauliflower and Chickpea Salad [AF]

(Ready in about 15 minutes + chilling time | Servings 4)

Ingredients

- 1 pound cauliflower florets
- 1 cup chickpeas, canned or boiled
- 1/4 cup mayonnaise
- 1 teaspoon Dijon mustard
- 1 teaspoon ancho chili powder
- Sea salt and ground black pepper, to taste
- 2 tablespoons fresh chives, chopped
- 2 tablespoons apple cider vinegar

Directions

Arrange the cauliflower florets in a lightly greased Air Fryer basket.

Air fry the cauliflower florets at 400 degrees F for 12 minutes, shaking the basket halfway through the cooking time.

Thoroughly combine the cauliflower florets with the remaining ingredients. Serve well-chilled and enjoy!

Per serving: Calories: 192; Fat: 11.8g; Carbs: 17.2g; Protein: 6.1g; Sugars: 4.3g; Fiber: 5.7g

63. Indian Masala Curry [PC]

(Ready in about 25 minutes | Servings 4)

Ingredients

- 2 tablespoons olive oil
- 2 cardamom pods
- 2 whole cloves
- 1 teaspoon fresh ginger, peeled and minced
- 1 onion, sliced
- 1 red chili pepper, seeded and chopped
- 1/2 teaspoon curry powder
- Kosher salt and freshly ground black pepper, to taste
- 2 cups vegetable broth
- 1 teaspoon garam masala
- 1 cup full-fat coconut milk

Directions

Press the "Sauté" button and heat the olive oil; then, sauté the cardamom pods, cloves, and ginger for about 1 minute or until fragrant.

Stir in the onion, chili pepper, curry, salt, black pepper, vegetable broth, and garam masala.

Secure the pressure-cooking lid. Choose the "Pressure Cook" mode; cook for 20 minutes at High pressure. Once cooking is complete, use a quick pressure release; carefully remove the lid.

Mix the ingredients with the coconut milk using your immersion blender until creamy and uniform.

Bon appétit!

Per serving: Calories: 224; Fat: 21.2g; Carbs: 5.4g; Protein: 4.1g; Sugars: 2.8g; Fiber: 1.7g

64. Old-Fashioned Crispy Eggplant [AF]

(Ready in about 15 minutes | Servings 3)

Ingredients

- Sea salt and freshly ground black pepper, to taste
- 1/2 cup all-purpose flour
- 2 eggs
- 3/4 pound eggplant, sliced
- 1/2 cup bread crumbs

Directions

In a shallow bowl, mix the salt, black pepper, and flour. Whisk the eggs in a second bowl, and place the breadcrumbs in a third bowl.

Dip the eggplant slices in the flour mixture, then in the whisked eggs; finally, roll the eggplant slices over the breadcrumbs until they are well coated on all sides.

Arrange the eggplant in the Air Fryer basket. Secure the air-frying lid.

Cook the eggplant at 400 degrees F for about 13 minutes, shaking the basket halfway through the cooking time.

Bon appétit!

Per serving: Calories: 187; Fat: 1.4g; Carbs: 36.5g; Protein: 8g; Sugars: 5.3g; Fiber: 4.8g

65. Mediterranean-Style Eggplant Soup [PC]

(Ready in about 25 minutes | Servings 4)

Ingredients

- 2 tablespoons olive oil
- 1 small shallot, chopped
- 2 garlic cloves, minced
- 1 ½ pounds eggplant, peeled and diced
- 1 jalapeno pepper, chopped
- 4 cups vegetable broth
- 1 tablespoon Mediterranean spice mix
- Kosher salt and ground black pepper, to taste
- 1/2 cup sour cream

Directions

Press the "Sauté" button to preheat your Instant Pot Duo Crisp; heat the olive oil until sizzling.

Once hot, sauté the shallot and garlic for about 2 minutes until they've softened. Add in the remaining ingredients, except for the sour cream.

Secure the pressure-cooking lid. Pressure cook for 20 minutes at High pressure. Once cooking is complete, use a quick pressure release; carefully remove the lid.

Fold in the sour cream and blend the soup until it is creamy and smooth. Taste and adjust seasonings, if desired.

Bon appétit!

Per serving: Calories: 193; Fat: 11.6g; Carbs: 15.5g; Protein: 7.7g; Sugars: 7.3g; Fiber: 5.4g

66. Classic Roasted Potatoes [AF]

(Ready in about 20 minutes | Servings 3)

Ingredients

- 3/4 pound Yukon Gold potatoes, peeled and cut into 1-inch chunks
- 1 tablespoon olive oil
- Sea salt and ground black pepper, to taste
- 1/2 turmeric powder
- 1/2 teaspoon garlic powder
- 1/2 teaspoon paprika

Directions

Toss the potatoes with the remaining ingredients until well coated on all sides.

Arrange the potatoes in the Air Fryer basket. Secure the air-frying lid.

Choose the "Roast" mode and cook the potatoes at 400 degrees F for about 13 minutes, shaking the basket halfway through the cooking time.

Bon appétit!

Per serving: Calories: 127; Fat: 4.7g; Carbs: 19.6g; Protein: 2.5g; Sugars: 1g; Fiber: 2.5g

67. Easy Creamy Mashed Yams [PC]

(Ready in about 10 minutes | Servings 5)

Ingredients

- 2 pounds yams, peeled and diced
- 1 tablespoon butter
- Sea salt and red pepper, to taste
- 1 cup half-and-half cream

Directions

Place the yams, butter, salt, and red pepper in the inner pot. Add in 1 cup of water.

Secure the pressure-cooking lid. Pressure cook for 6 minutes at High pressure. Once cooking is complete, use a quick pressure release; carefully remove the lid.

Lastly, puree the ingredients with half-and-half cream until it is creamy and smooth.

Bon appétit!

Per serving: Calories: 266; Fat: 3.3g; Carbs: 55.3g; Protein: 4.4g; Sugars: 3.8g; Fiber: 7.6g

68. Crispy Yellow Beans [AF]

(Ready in about 9 minutes | Servings 3)

Ingredients

- 1/2 pound yellow beans, trimmed
- 2 small tomatoes, sliced
- 1 tablespoon sesame oil
- Sea salt and ground black pepper, to taste

Directions

Toss the green beans and tomatoes with the olive oil, salt, and black pepper; toss until they are well coated.

Arrange the vegetables in the Air Fryer basket. Secure the air-frying lid.

Cook the green beans at 390 degrees F for 8 minutes; make sure to stir your vegetables halfway through the cooking time.

Taste, adjust the seasonings, and serve immediately. Bon appétit!

Per serving: Calories: 75; Fat: 4.8g; Carbs: 7g; Protein: 2g; Sugars: 4g; Fiber: 2.8g

69. Spicy Cream of Brussels Sprout Soup [PC]

(Ready in about 12 minutes | Servings 4)

Ingredients

- 2 tablespoons butter
- 1/2 cup leeks, chopped
- 2 garlic cloves, minced
- 1 chili pepper, chopped
- 1 pound Brussels sprouts
- Sea salt and ground black pepper, to taste
- 4 cups vegetable broth

Directions

Press the "Sauté" button and melt the butter until hot.

Once hot, cook the leeks, garlic, and chili pepper until just fragrant. Add in the remaining ingredients.

Secure the pressure-cooking lid. Pressure cook for 10 minutes at High pressure. Once cooking is complete, use a quick pressure release; carefully remove the lid.

Using your blender or food processor, blend the soup until it is completely smooth. Ladle into individual bowls and serve warm. Bon appétit!

Per serving: Calories: 157; Fat: 7.7g; Carbs: 15.3g; Protein: 9.4g; Sugars: 4.3g; Fiber: 4.7g

VEGETABLES & SIDE DISHES

70. Roasted Bell Peppers [AF]

(Ready in about 15 minutes | Servings 3)

Ingredients

1 pound bell peppers, seeded and halved
1 chili pepper, seeded
2 tablespoons olive oil
Kosher salt and ground black pepper, to taste
1 teaspoon granulated garlic

Directions

Toss the peppers with the remaining ingredients; place them in the Air Fryer basket. Secure the air-frying lid.

Cook the peppers at 400 degrees F for about 15 minutes, shaking the basket halfway through the cooking time.

Taste, adjust the seasonings and serve at room temperature. Bon appétit!

Per serving: Calories: 128; Fat: 9.2g; Carbs: 11.2g; Protein: 2g; Sugars: 0.6g; Fiber: 1.6g

71. Traditional Indian Raita [PC]

(Ready in about 20 minutes | Servings 4)

Ingredients

1 pound small beets, greens removed
1/4 teaspoon cumin seeds, ground
1 cup yogurt
1 garlic clove, minced
Kosher salt and ground black pepper, to taste
1 teaspoon red chili powder

Directions

Place 1 cup of water and a steamer basket in the inner pot. Place the beets in the steamer basket.

Secure the pressure-cooking lid. Choose the "Steam" mode and cook for 15 minutes at High pressure. Once cooking is complete, use a quick pressure release; carefully remove the lid.

Peel the beets and chop them into bite-sized pieces. Add in the remaining ingredients and toss to combine well. Bon appétit!

Per serving: Calories: 94; Fat: 2.3g; Carbs: 15.1g; Protein: 4.3g; Sugars: 11g; Fiber: 3.6g

72. Spicy Roasted Potatoes [AF]

(Ready in about 20 minutes | Servings 4)

Ingredients

1 pound potatoes, diced into bite-sized chunks
1 tablespoon olive oil
Sea salt and ground black pepper, to taste
1 teaspoon chili powder

Directions

Toss the potatoes with the remaining ingredients until well coated on all sides.

Arrange the potatoes in the Air Fryer basket and secure the air-frying lid. Choose the "Roast" function.

Cook the potatoes at 400 degrees F for about 13 minutes, shaking the basket halfway through the cooking time. Bon appétit!

Per serving: Calories: 117; Fat: 3.5g; Carbs: 19.5g; Protein: 2.3g; Sugars: 1g; Fiber: 2.5g

73. Baba Ganoush with a Twist [PC]

(Ready in about 10 minutes | Servings 5)

Ingredients

2 tablespoon olive oil
1 onion, chopped
2 cloves garlic, minced
1 pound eggplant, peeled and diced
2 tablespoons fresh parsley, chopped
2 tablespoons fresh cilantro, chopped
1 tablespoon fresh rosemary, chopped
Sea salt and ground black pepper, to taste
4 tablespoons heavy whipping cream

Directions

Choose the "Sauté" function and heat the olive oil until sizzling; then, sauté the onion and garlic for about 3 minutes or until tender and aromatic.

Add in the remaining ingredients and stir to combine. Secure the pressure-cooking lid.

Pressure cook for 6 minutes at High pressure. Once cooking is complete, use a quick pressure release; carefully remove the lid.

Puree the sauce using a blender or food processor. Bon appétit!

Per serving: Calories: 128; Fat: 10g; Carbs: 9.2g; Protein: 1.7g; Sugars: 4.9g; Fiber: 3.4g

74. Provençal Style Parsnips [AF]

(Ready in about 15 minutes | Servings 4)

Ingredients

1 pound parsnips, trimmed
1 tablespoon olive oil
1 teaspoon Herbs de province
1 teaspoon cayenne pepper
Sea salt and ground black pepper, to taste

Directions

Toss the parsnip with olive oil and spices until they are well coated on all sides; then, arrange the parsnip in the Air Fryer basket.

Secure the air-frying lid.

Cook the parsnip at 380 degrees F for 10 minutes, shaking the basket halfway through the cooking time.

Bon appétit!

Per serving: Calories: 117; Fat: 3.7g; Carbs: 20.5g; Protein: 1.3g; Sugars: 5.3g; Fiber: 5.6g

75. Harvest Vegetable Potage [PC]
(Ready in about 15 minutes | Servings 4)

Ingredients
- 1 tablespoon butter
- 1 cup yellow onion, sliced
- 1 celery stalk, sliced
- 2 garlic cloves, minced
- 1 cup broccoli florets
- 1 cup cauliflower florets
- 1 cup frozen petite green peas
- 4 cups chicken broth
- 1 tablespoon fresh lemon juice
- Kosher salt and ground black pepper, to taste

Directions
Choose the "Sauté" mode and melt the butter; once hot, cook the onion, celery, and garlic for about 3 minutes or until they've softened.

Stir the remaining ingredients, except for the lemon juice, into the inner pot.

Secure the pressure-cooking lid. Pressure cook for 10 minutes at High pressure. Once cooking is complete, use a quick pressure release; carefully remove the lid.

Puree the ingredients in your blender or food processor. Ladle your potage into soup bowls and serve with a few drizzles of lemon juice. Enjoy!

Per serving: Calories: 138; Fat: 7g; Carbs: 10.8g; Protein: 9g; Sugars: 4.4g; Fiber: 3.1g

76. Classic Roasted Green Beans [AF]
(Ready in about 9 minutes | Servings 4)

Ingredients
- 1 pound fresh green beans, cleaned and trimmed
- 1/2 teaspoon garlic powder
- 1/2 teaspoon cumin powder
- 1/2 teaspoon onion powder
- 1/2 teaspoon dried dill weed
- 1 teaspoon olive oil
- Sea salt and red pepper flakes, to taste

Directions
Toss the green beans with the remaining ingredients until they are well coated.

Arrange the green beans in the Air Fryer basket. Choose the "Roast" function and secure the air-frying lid.

Cook the green beans at 375 degrees F for 7 minutes; make sure to check the green beans halfway through the cooking time.

Taste, adjust the seasonings, and serve warm. Bon appétit!

Per serving: Calories: 45; Fat: 1.3g; Carbs: 7g; Protein: 2.1g; Sugars: 3.6g; Fiber: 3.1g

77. Herbed and Creamed Celery Soup [PC]
(Ready in about 15 minutes | Servings 4)

Ingredients
- 2 tablespoons olive oil
- 4 garlic cloves, minced
- 1 medium onion, chopped
- 1 ½ pounds celery, trimmed and chopped
- 4 cups vegetable stock
- 1 tablespoon fresh mint, chopped
- 1 tablespoon fresh cilantro, chopped
- Sea salt and ground black pepper, to taste

Directions
Press the "Sauté" button and heat the olive oil; then, sauté the garlic and onion until just tender and fragrant.

Stir the remaining ingredients into the inner pot.

Secure the pressure-cooking lid. Pressure cook for 10 minutes at High pressure. Once cooking is complete, use a quick pressure release; carefully remove the lid.

Lastly, blend the soup until it is completely smooth. Bon appétit!

Per serving: Calories: 144; Fat: 9g; Carbs: 9.4g; Protein: 7.2g; Sugars: 4g; Fiber: 3.4g

78. Mushrooms with Garlic and Cilantro [AF]
(Ready in about 12 minutes | Servings 3)

Ingredients
- 3/4 pound button mushrooms, cleaned and cut into halves
- 2 tablespoons olive oil
- 1 garlic clove, pressed
- Sea salt and ground black pepper, to taste
- 1 tablespoon fresh lemon juice
- 1 tablespoon fresh cilantro, chopped

Directions
Toss your mushrooms with the olive oil, garlic, salt, and black pepper.

Arrange them on a lightly oiled Air Fryer basket and secure the air-frying lid.

Air fry the mushrooms at 375 degrees F for about 10 minutes, shaking the basket halfway through the cooking time.

Drizzle fresh lemon juice over the mushroom and serve with fresh cilantro. Enjoy!

Per serving: Calories: 114; Fat: 9.4g; Carbs: 5.9g; Protein: 3.9g; Sugars: 3.1g; Fiber: 1.4g

79. Easy Roasted Artichokes [PC+AF]
(Ready in about 15 minutes | Servings 4)

Ingredients
- 1 ½ pounds artichokes, trimmed
- 1 teaspoon garlic, crushed
- 2 tablespoons olive oil
- 2 tablespoons fresh lemon juice
- Sea salt and ground black, to taste

VEGETABLES & SIDE DISHES

Directions

Add 1 cup of water and a steamer basket to the inner pot. Toss your artichokes with the remaining ingredients.

Lower the artichokes into the steamer basket.

Secure the pressure-cooking lid. Pressure cook for 9 minutes at High pressure. Once cooking is complete, use a quick pressure release; carefully remove the lid.

Secure the air-frying lid and cook for 3 minutes or until just crisp.

Serve the roasted artichokes with a dipping sauce of your choice. Bon appétit!

Per serving: Calories: 143; Fat: 7g; Carbs: 18.6g; Protein: 5.8g; Sugars: 1.7g; Fiber: 9.2g

80. Grandma's Beet Salad [AF]

(Ready in about 45 minutes | Servings 4)

Ingredients

1 pound beets, whole
1/2 teaspoon cumin seeds
Sea salt and red pepper flakes, to taste
2 tablespoons apple cider vinegar
4 tablespoons olive oil
1 teaspoon garlic, pressed

Directions

Arrange your beats in the Air Fryer basket. Secure the air-frying lid.

Cook the beats at 400 F for 40 minutes, shaking the basket halfway through the cooking time. Let them cool completely.

Peel the beets and cut them into thin slices; transfer to a salad bowl. Add in the remaining ingredients and stir to combine.

Bon appétit!

Per serving: Calories: 172; Fat: 13.2g; Carbs: 11.2g; Protein: 1.9g; Sugars: 3.2g; Fiber: 7.7g

81. Classic Vegetarian Paprikash [PC]

(Ready in about 25 minutes | Servings 4)

Ingredients

2 tablespoons olive oil
1 large onion, chopped
3 cloves garlic, chopped
2 bell peppers, chopped
1 celery stick, diced
1 chili pepper, chopped
Kosher salt and ground black pepper, to taste
1 teaspoon Hungarian paprika
3 cups vegetable broth

Directions

Press the "Sauté" button and heat the olive oil; now, sauté the onion and garlic for about 2 minutes or until fragrant.

Add in the remaining ingredients.

Secure the pressure-cooking lid. Pressure cook for 20 minutes at High pressure. Once cooking is complete, use a quick pressure release; carefully remove the lid.

Bon appétit!

Per serving: Calories: 123; Fat: 8.1g; Carbs: 8.3g; Protein: 5g; Sugars: 3.3g; Fiber: 1.6g

82. Garlicky Brussels Sprouts [AF]

(Ready in about 15 minutes | Servings 3)

Ingredients

3/4 pound Brussels sprouts
2 tablespoons butter, melted
2 garlic cloves, crushed
Kosher salt and ground black pepper, to taste

Directions

Toss the Brussels sprouts with the remaining ingredients until well coated.

Arrange the Brussels sprouts in the Air Fryer basket. Secure the air-frying lid.

Cook the Brussels sprouts at 380 degrees F for 14 minutes, shaking the basket halfway through the cooking time. Bon appétit!

Per serving: Calories: 121; Fat: 8g; Carbs: 10.2g; Protein: 4g; Sugars: 2.6g; Fiber: 4.5g

83. Pasta with Garden Vegetables [PC]

(Ready in about 15 minutes | Servings 4)

Ingredients

2 tablespoons olive oil
1 medium onion, chopped
2 garlic cloves, sliced
1 zucchini, diced
1 bell pepper, seeded and diced
2 cups vegetable broth
9 ounces spaghetti
2 tomatoes, pureed
1/2 teaspoon dried basil
1/2 teaspoon dried oregano
1/2 teaspoon dried oregano
1 teaspoon kosher salt

Directions

Press the "Sauté" button and heat the olive oil.

Then, sauté the onion and garlic for about 2 minutes until just tender. Add in the zucchini and bell pepper and continue sautéing for 2 minutes more.

Add the remaining ingredients to the inner pot.

Secure the pressure-cooking lid. Pressure cook for 10 minutes at High pressure. Once cooking is complete, use a quick pressure release; carefully remove the lid. Bon appétit!

Per serving: Calories: 349; Fat: 8.6g; Carbs: 54.5g; Protein: 12.1g; Sugars: 5g; Fiber: 3.6g

84. Rustic Paprika Cauliflower [AF]

(Ready in about 15 minutes | Servings 3)

Ingredients

3/4 pound cauliflower florets
1 large onion, cut into wedges
2 cloves garlic, pressed
1 tablespoon olive oil
Sea salt and ground black pepper, to taste
1 teaspoon paprika

Directions

Toss the cauliflower florets and onion with the garlic, olive oil, and spices. Toss until they are well coated on all sides.

Arrange the vegetables in the Air Fryer basket. Secure the air-frying lid.

Cook the vegetables at 400 degrees F for about 13 minutes, shaking the basket halfway through the cooking time. Bon appétit!

Per serving: Calories: 92; Fat: 4.8g; Carbs: 10.9g; Protein: 2.9g; Sugars: 4.3g; Fiber: 3g

VEGETABLES & SIDE DISHES

85. Traditional Italian Ciambotta [PC]

(Ready in about 15 minutes | Servings 4)

Ingredients
- 2 tablespoons olive oil
- 1 small onion, chopped
- 1 teaspoon garlic, chopped
- 1 stalk celery, chopped
- 1 pound potatoes, peeled and cubed
- 2 cups brown mushrooms, sliced
- 2 cups vegetable broth
- 1 teaspoon Italian seasoning mix
- 2 tomatoes, chopped
- Sea salt and ground black pepper, to taste
- 1 tablespoon corn starch

Directions
Press the "Sauté" button and heat the olive oil; now, sauté the onion and garlic for about 2 minutes or until fragrant.

Stir in the celery and potatoes and continue sautéing for about 4 minutes or until tender. Add in the remaining ingredients.

Secure the pressure-cooking lid. Pressure cook for 10 minutes at High pressure. Once cooking is complete, use a natural pressure release; carefully remove the lid.

Bon appétit!

Per serving: Calories: 213; Fat: 7.9g; Carbs: 29.6g; Protein: 7.1g; Sugars: 4.8g; Fiber: 4.4g

86. Saucy Cremini Mushrooms [AF]

(Ready in about 9 minutes | Servings 4)

Ingredients
- 1 pound cremini mushrooms, sliced
- 2 tablespoons olive oil
- 1/2 teaspoon shallot powder
- 1/2 teaspoon garlic powder
- 1 tablespoon coconut aminos
- 1 tablespoon white wine
- Sea salt and ground black pepper, to taste
- 1 tablespoon fresh parsley, chopped

Directions
Toss the mushrooms with the remaining ingredients. Toss until they are well coated on all sides.

Arrange the mushrooms in the Air Fryer basket. Secure the air-frying lid.

Cook your mushrooms at 400 degrees F for about 7 minutes, shaking the basket halfway through the cooking time.

Garnish with fresh herbs, if desired. Bon appétit!

Per serving: Calories: 95; Fat: 7g; Carbs: 6g; Protein: 2.9g; Sugars: 3.6g; Fiber: 1.8g

87. Brussels Sprout and Apple Bowl [PC]

(Ready in about 10 minutes | Servings 4)

Ingredients
- 1 pound Brussels sprouts, halved
- 1 apple, peeled, cored, and diced
- 1 tablespoon fresh lemon juice
- 1 tablespoon apple cider vinegar
- 1/4 cup pomegranate arils
- 1/4 cup extra-virgin olive oil
- 2 tablespoons honey
- 1 teaspoon Dijon mustard
- Sea salt and ground black pepper, to taste

Directions
Place 1 cup of water and a steamer basket in the inner pot. Place the Brussels sprouts in the steamer basket.

Secure the pressure-cooking lid. Choose the "Steam" mode and cook for 3 minutes at High pressure. Once cooking is complete, use a quick pressure release; carefully remove the lid.

Toss the Brussels sprouts with the remaining ingredients.

Bon appétit!

Per serving: Calories: 245; Fat: 14.4g; Carbs: 29.3g; Protein: 4.5g; Sugars: 18.5g; Fiber: 6.4g

88. Baked Parmesan Broccoli [PC+AF]

(Ready in about 8 minutes | Servings 3)

Ingredients
- 3/4 pound broccoli florets
- 1 tablespoon olive oil
- 1/2 teaspoon dried dill weed
- Coarse sea salt and freshly ground black pepper, to taste
- 2 ounces parmesan cheese, freshly grated

Directions
Add 1 cup of water and a steamer basket to the inner pot. Lower the broccoli florets into the steamer basket and place the steamer basket in the inner pot.

Secure the pressure-cooking lid. Choose the "Steam" mode and cook for 2 minutes at High pressure. Once cooking is complete, use a quick pressure release; carefully remove the lid.

Toss the steamed broccoli with the remaining ingredients. Secure the air-frying lid.

Air fry the broccoli florets at 395 degrees F for 3 minutes, shaking the basket halfway through the cooking time.

Bon appétit!

Per serving: Calories: 159; Fat: 10.2g; Carbs: 10.2g; Protein: 8.3g; Sugars: 1.9g; Fiber: 3g

VEGETABLES & SIDE DISHES

89. Thai-Style Cauliflower [PC]

(Ready in about 10 minutes | Servings 4)

Ingredients

2 tablespoons butter, at room temperature
1 small onion, chopped
2 cloves garlic, minced
1 pound cauliflower florets
1 cup butternut squash, peeled and diced
1 teaspoon curry powder
Sea salt and ground black pepper, to taste
2 cups chicken broth
1 cup coconut milk

Directions

Press the "Sauté" and melt the butter; once hot, sauté the onion and garlic until tender and aromatic or about 2 minutes.

Add in the cauliflower, squash, spices, and broth.

Secure the pressure-cooking lid. Pressure cook for 5 minutes at High pressure. Once cooking is complete, use a quick pressure release; carefully remove the lid.

Pour in the milk; cover with the air-frying lid and cook for 5 minutes or until cooked through.

Enjoy!

Per serving: Calories: 169; Fat: 8.7g; Carbs: 16.3g; Protein: 7.5g; Sugars: 7.1g; Fiber: 3.7g

90. Roasted Beets with Feta Cheese [AF]

(Ready in about 45 minutes | Servings 4)

Ingredients

1 pound beets, whole
Sea salt and red pepper flakes, to taste
2 tablespoons apple cider vinegar
4 tablespoons olive oil
1 teaspoon garlic powder
4 ounces feta cheese, crumbled

Directions

Arrange your beets in the Air Fryer basket. Secure the air-frying lid.

Air fry the beats for 40 minutes at 400 F, shaking the basket halfway through the cooking time. Let your beets cool completely.

Peel the beets and cut them into thin slices; transfer to a salad bowl. Add in the remaining ingredients and stir to combine.

Bon appétit!

Per serving: Calories: 252; Fat: 19.3g; Carbs: 13.2g; Protein: 6.1g; Sugars: 9.6g; Fiber: 3.7g

91. The Best Peperonata Ever [PC]

(Ready in about 15 minutes | Servings 4)

Ingredients

2 tablespoons olive oil
1 onion, sliced
3 cloves garlic, chopped
1 pound bell peppers, seeded and sliced
2 tomatoes, chopped
1 cup vegetable broth
1 teaspoon cayenne pepper
Sea salt and ground black pepper, to taste

Directions

Press the "Sauté" button and heat the olive oil; cook the onion and garlic for about 2 minutes or until they've softened.

Stir in the peppers, tomatoes, broth, cayenne pepper, salt, and black pepper.

Secure the pressure-cooking lid. Pressure cook for 10 minutes at High pressure. Once cooking is complete, use a quick pressure release; carefully remove the lid. Bon appétit!

Per serving: Calories: 136; Fat: 7.5g; Carbs: 15.6g; Protein: 4.5g; Sugars: 8.1g; Fiber: 2.9g

92. Asian-Style Brussels Sprouts [AF]

(Ready in about 15 minutes | Servings 2)

Ingredients

1/2 pound Brussels sprouts, trimmed
2 tablespoons sesame oil
Sea salt and ground black pepper, to taste
1 teaspoon Five-spice powder
1 teaspoon soy sauce
1 teaspoon rice vinegar

Directions

Toss the Brussels sprouts with the oil until well coated on all sides; then, arrange the Brussels sprouts in the Air Fryer basket.

Secure the air-frying lid. Air fry the Brussels sprouts at 380 degrees F for 10 minutes, shaking the basket halfway through the cooking time.

Toss them with the remaining ingredients and continue to cook for 3 to 4 minutes more. Serve warm and enjoy!

Per serving: Calories: 187; Fat: 14.2g; Carbs: 13.2g; Protein: 4.4g; Sugars: 3.8g; Fiber: 4.9g

93. Chinese-Style Braised Cabbage [PC]

(Ready in about 10 minutes | Servings 4)

Ingredients

2 tablespoons ghee, room temperature
1 onion, chopped
2 pounds cabbage, cut into wedges
1 cup dashi stock
4 garlic cloves, minced
Sea salt and ground black pepper, to taste
1 teaspoon Five-spice powder
2 bay leaves

Directions

Press the "Sauté" button and melt the ghee. Then, cook the onion until tender and fragrant.

Now, stir in the garlic and continue to sauté for 30 seconds more, stirring frequently.

Add the remaining ingredients to the inner pot and stir to combine.

Secure the pressure-cooking lid. Pressure cook for 8 minutes at High pressure. Once cooking is complete, use a quick pressure release; carefully remove the lid.

Serve in individual bowls and enjoy!

Per serving: Calories: 144; Fat: 6.4g; Carbs: 20.3g; Protein: 5g; Sugars: 9.5g; Fiber: 5.5g

94. Parmesan Eggplant Bites [AF]

(Ready in about 15 minutes | Servings 4)

Ingredients

2 eggs, whisked
1/2 cup almond flour
1/2 cup Parmesan cheese, grated
1 teaspoon Italian seasoning mix
3/4 pound eggplant, peeled and sliced

Directions

In a mixing bowl, thoroughly combine the eggs, almond flour, cheese, and Italian seasoning mix.

Dip the eggplant slices in the egg/flour mixture until they are well coated on all sides.

Arrange the eggplant in the Air Fryer basket. Secure the air-frying lid.

Air fry the eggplant at 400 degrees F for about 13 minutes, shaking the basket halfway through the cooking time.

Bon appétit!

Per serving: Calories: 210; Fat: 14.2g; Carbs: 10.2g; Protein: 11.4g; Sugars: 3.9g; Fiber: 4.1g

95. Broccoli and Pepper Salad [PC]

(Ready in about 5 minutes + chilling time| Servings 4)

Ingredients

1 pound broccoli florets
Sea salt and ground black pepper, to taste
2 tablespoons olive oil
1 tablespoon white vinegar
1 bell pepper, seeded and sliced
2 garlic cloves, minced
2 tablespoons pumpkin seeds, lightly roasted

Directions

Add 1 cup of water and a steamer basket to the inner pot. Lower the broccoli florets into the steamer basket and place the steamer basket in the inner pot.

Secure the pressure-cooking lid. Choose the "Steam" mode and cook for 2 minutes at High pressure. Once cooking is complete, use a quick pressure release; carefully remove the lid.

Toss the steamed broccoli with the remaining ingredients and serve at room temperature. Bon appétit!

Per serving: Calories: 133; Fat: 9g; Carbs: 10.6g; Protein: 4.8g; Sugars: 3.1g; Fiber: 3.6g

96. Classic Roasted Vegetables [PC+AF]

(Ready in about 20 minutes | Servings 4)

Ingredients

1 carrot, trimmed and sliced
1 parsnip, trimmed and sliced
1 celery stalk, trimmed and sliced
1 onion, peeled and diced
2 tablespoons olive oil
Sea salt and ground black pepper, to taste
1 teaspoon red pepper flakes, crushed

Directions

Toss all the ingredients in the Air Fryer basket. Secure the air-frying lid.

Cook your vegetables at 380 degrees F for about 15 minutes, shaking the basket halfway through the cooking time.

Bon appétit!

Per serving: Calories: 119; Fat: 7g; Carbs: 15g; Protein: 1.2g; Sugars: 6.6g; Fiber: 2.8g

97. Ginger Garlic Eggplant [PC]

(Ready in about 10 minutes | Servings 4)

Ingredients

1 tablespoon olive oil
1 shallot, chopped
2 cloves garlic, minced
1 (1-inch) piece fresh ginger, minced
1 pound eggplant
1/2 teaspoon cumin powder
1/2 teaspoon mustard powder
Kosher salt and ground black pepper, to taste
1 cup vegetable broth

Directions

Preheat your Instant Pot Do Crisp on the "Sauté" function; heat the oil and sauté the shallot and garlic for about 2 minutes or until tender and aromatic.

Add in the remaining ingredients.

Secure the pressure-cooking lid. Pressure cook for 4 minutes at High pressure. Once cooking is complete, use a quick pressure release; carefully remove the lid.

Bon appétit!

Per serving: Calories: 69; Fat: 3.6g; Carbs: 8.5g; Protein: 5.6g; Sugars: 4.8g; Fiber: 3.7g

98. Roasted Sweet Potatoes [AF]

(Ready in about 40 minutes | Servings 4)

Ingredients

1 pound sweet potatoes, scrubbed and halved
3 tablespoons olive oil
1 teaspoon paprika
Sea salt and ground black pepper, to taste

Directions

Toss the sweet potatoes with the olive oil, paprika, salt, and black pepper. Secure the air-frying lid.

Choose the "Roast" function. Air fry the sweet potatoes at 380 degrees F for 35 minutes, shaking the basket halfway through the cooking time.

Taste and adjust the seasonings. Bon appétit!

Per serving: Calories: 187; Fat: 10.2g; Carbs: 22.9g; Protein: 1.7g; Sugars: 4.7g; Fiber: 3.5g

VEGETABLES & SIDE DISHES

99. Cajun Gumbo with Mushrooms [PC]

(Ready in about 25 minutes | Servings 4)

Ingredients

- 2 tablespoons ghee
- 1 medium-sized white onion, chopped
- 1 teaspoon garlic, minced
- 1 ½ cups baby bella mushrooms, diced
- 1 bell pepper, seeded and chopped
- 1 ½ pounds okra, trimmed
- Kosher salt and ground black pepper, to taste
- 1 tablespoon hot pepper sauce
- 1 teaspoon Cajun seasoning blend
- 2 tomatoes, chopped

Directions

Press the "Sauté" button and melt the ghee; then, sauté the onion for about 2 minutes or until just tender.

Add in the garlic and continue sautéing an additional 30 seconds or so.

Stir in the remaining ingredients.

Secure the pressure-cooking lid. Pressure cook for 20 minutes at High pressure. Once cooking is complete, use a quick pressure release; carefully remove the lid.

Bon appétit!

Per serving: Calories: 145; Fat: 6g; Carbs: 20.5g; Protein: 5.6g; Sugars: 6.6g; Fiber: 7.3g

100. Green Bean Salad with Spinach [AF]

(Ready in about 10 minutes | Servings 3)

Ingredients

- 3/4 pound fresh green beans, washed and trimmed
- 2 tablespoons olive oil
- 1/2 cup green onions, thinly sliced
- 2 cups baby spinach
- 1 tablespoon fresh basil, chopped
- 1 green pepper, sliced
- 2 tablespoons fresh lemon juice
- Sea salt and ground black pepper, to taste

Directions

Toss the green beans with 1 tablespoon of the olive oil. Arrange the green beans in the Air Fryer basket. Secure the air-frying lid.

Cook the green beans at 375 degrees F for 7 minutes; make sure to check the green beans halfway through the cooking time.

Add the green beans to a salad bowl; add in the remaining ingredients and stir to combine well. Enjoy!

Per serving: Calories: 132; Fat: 9.4g; Carbs: 11.4g; Protein: 3.7g; Sugars: 5.1g; Fiber: 4g

101. Easy Garden Vegetable Soup [PC]

(Ready in about 25 minutes | Servings 4)

Ingredients

- 2 tablespoons olive oil
- 1 large onion, peeled and chopped
- 2 cloves garlic, minced
- 2 tomatoes, chopped
- 1 carrot, chopped
- 4 cups vegetable broth
- Sea salt and ground black pepper, to taste
- 6 ounces frozen corn

Directions

Press the "Sauté" button and heat the olive oil; then, sauté the onion and garlic for about 2 minutes or until fragrant.

Stir in the tomatoes, carrot, broth, salt, and black pepper.

Secure the pressure-cooking lid. Pressure cook for 15 minutes at High pressure. Once cooking is complete, use a natural pressure release; carefully remove the lid.

Fold in the corn, cover, and let it sit in the residual heat for about 5 minutes or until heated through.

Bon appétit!

Per serving: Calories: 193; Fat: 9g; Carbs: 20.6g; Protein: 6.1g; Sugars: 7.8g; Fiber: 3.3g

102. Mushrooms with Cheddar Cheese [AF]

(Ready in about 9 minutes | Servings 3)

Ingredients

- 3/4 pound button mushrooms, halved
- 1 tablespoon oil
- Sea salt and ground black pepper, to taste
- 1/2 teaspoon garlic powder
- 3 ounces cheddar cheese, cubed

Directions

Toss the mushrooms with the olive oil, salt, black pepper, and garlic powder. Toss until they are well coated on all sides.

Divide the cheese cubes between the prepared mushrooms. Arrange the mushrooms in the Air Fryer basket. Secure the air-frying lid.

Air fry your mushrooms at 400 degrees F for about 7 minutes, shaking the basket halfway through the cooking time.

Bon appétit!

Per serving: Calories: 124; Fat: 7.6g; Carbs: 8g; Protein: 7.7g; Sugars: 5g; Fiber: 1.4g

VEGETABLES & SIDE DISHES

103. Carrot Salad with Garlic and Herbs [PC]

(Ready in about 10 minutes + chilling time | Servings 4)

Ingredients

1 pound carrots, sliced
1 cup water
2 tablespoons extra-virgin olive oil
Sea salt and red pepper flakes, to taste
1 teaspoon garlic, crushed
1/4 teaspoon cumin seeds
1 tablespoon fresh parsley, chopped
1 tablespoon fresh chives, chopped

Directions

Place 1 cup of water and a steamer basket in the inner pot. Place the carrots in the steamer basket.

Secure the pressure-cooking lid. Choose the "Steam" mode and cook for 3 minutes at High pressure. Once cooking is complete, use a quick pressure release; carefully remove the lid.

Toss the carrots with the remaining ingredients.

Bon appétit!

Per serving: Calories: 108; Fat: 7g; Carbs: 11.3g; Protein: 1.5g; Sugars: 5.3g; Fiber: 3.4g

104. Traditional Indian Gujarati [AF]

(Ready in about 10 minutes | Servings 3)

Ingredients

3/4 pound fresh green beans, trimmed
1 garlic clove, minced
2 tablespoons olive oil
1 tablespoon soy sauce
1 teaspoon black mustard seeds
1 dried red chili pepper, crushed
Sea salt and ground black pepper, to taste

Directions

Toss the green beans with the remaining ingredients; then, arrange them in the Air Fryer basket.

Secure the air-frying lid.

Air fry the green beans at 380 degrees F for 8 minutes, tossing the basket halfway through the cooking time.

Enjoy!

Per serving: Calories: 136; Fat: 10.4g; Carbs: 9.8g; Protein: 2.7g; Sugars: 4.8g; Fiber: 3.3g

105. Cheesy and Herby Squash [PC]

(Ready in about 10 minutes | Servings 4)

Ingredients

2 teaspoons butter, at room temperature
1 tablespoon fresh sage, chopped
1 tablespoon fresh rosemary, chopped
Sea salt and ground black pepper, to taste
1 pound acorn squash, peeled and diced
1/2 cup Provolone cheese, shredded

Directions

Add all ingredients, except for the cheese, to the inner pot of your Instant Pot Duo Crisp.

Secure the pressure-cooking lid. Pressure cook for 4 minutes at High pressure. Once cooking is complete, use a quick pressure release; carefully remove the lid.

Top the squash with the cheese. Secure the air-frying lid and cook for 2 minutes or until the cheese melts.

Bon appétit!

Per serving: Calories: 122; Fat: 6.5g; Carbs: 12.5g; Protein: 5.2g; Sugars: 0.1g; Fiber: 2g

106. Bacon and Collard Greens Sautee [PC+AF]

(Ready in about 10 minutes | Servings 4)

Ingredients

2 ounces smoked bacon, diced
1 onion, thinly sliced
2 cloves garlic, thinly sliced
1 ½ pounds collard greens
2 cups vegetable broth
Sea salt and ground black pepper, to taste

Directions

Press the "Sauté" button to preheat your Instant Pot Duo Crisp. Sauté the bacon for about 2 minutes or until crisp.

Add in the remaining ingredients; stir to combine. Secure the air-frying lid and cook for 3 minutes or until cooked through.

Bon appétit!

Per serving: Calories: 139; Fat: 7.3g; Carbs: 11.4g; Protein: 9.8g; Sugars: 1.7g; Fiber: 7g

107. Green Pea Medley [PC]

(Ready in about 10 minutes | Servings 4)

Ingredients

2 tablespoons olive oil
2 cloves garlic, minced
1 cup scallions, sliced
1 jalapeno pepper, chopped
1 pound frozen green peas
1 tomato, pureed
Sea salt and ground black pepper, to taste
1 bay laurel
2 tablespoons fresh cilantro, chopped

Directions

Press the "Sauté" button and heat the olive oil; one hot, sauté the garlic, scallions, and pepper for about 1 minute or until aromatic.

Stir the remaining ingredients into the inner pot; stir to combine well.

Secure the pressure-cooking lid. Pressure cook for 5 minutes at High pressure. Once cooking is complete, use a quick pressure release; carefully remove the lid.

Bon appétit!

Per serving: Calories: 169; Fat: 7.3g; Carbs: 19g; Protein: 6.7g; Sugars: 7g; Fiber: 6.3g

VEGETABLES & SIDE DISHES

108. Eggs in Pepper Cups [AF]

(Ready in about 15 minutes | Servings 3)

Ingredients

3 bell peppers, seeded and halved
1 tablespoon olive oil
3 eggs
3 tablespoons green onion, chopped
Sea salt and ground black pepper

Directions

Toss the peppers with the oil; place them in the Air Fryer basket.

Crack an egg into each bell pepper half. Sprinkle your peppers with the salt and black pepper. Secure the air-frying lid.

Air fry the peppers at 400 degrees F for about 10 minutes. Top the peppers with green onions. Continue to cook for 4 minutes more.

Bon appétit!

Per serving: Calories: 143; Fat: 9g; Carbs: 7.8g; Protein: 6.4g; Sugars: 5.4g; Fiber: 2.6g

109. Aromatic Roasted Fennel [AF]

(Ready in about 20 minutes | Servings 4)

Ingredients

1 pound fennel bulbs, trimmed and sliced
2 tablespoons olive oil
1 teaspoon fresh garlic, minced
1 teaspoon dried parsley flakes
Kosher salt and ground black pepper, to taste

Directions

Toss all the ingredients in a mixing bowl.

Add the fennel slice to the Air Fryer basket. Secure the air-frying lid.

Cook the fennel at 370 degrees F for about 15 minutes or until cooked through; check your fennel halfway through the cooking time. Bon appétit!

Per serving: Calories: 97; Fat: 6.9g; Carbs: 8.4g; Protein: 1.4g; Sugars: 4.4g; Fiber: 3.5g

110. Maple-Glazed Butternut Squash [PC]

(Ready in about 10 minutes | Servings 4)

Ingredients

1 pound butternut squash, peeled, seeded, and diced
1 cup vegetable broth
2 tablespoons butter
2 tablespoons maple syrup
Sea salt and crushed red pepper, to taste

Directions

Add all the ingredients to the inner pot and stir to combine.

Secure the pressure-cooking lid. Pressure cook for 3 minutes at High pressure. Once cooking is complete, use a quick pressure release; carefully remove the lid.

Bon appétit!

Per serving: Calories: 137; Fat: 6.2g; Carbs: 19.8g; Protein: 2.9g; Sugars: 6.9g; Fiber: 1.9g

111. Chinese Chili-Spiced Asparagus [AF]

(Ready in about 10 minutes | Servings 4)

Ingredients

1 pound asparagus
4 teaspoons Chinese chili oil
1/2 teaspoon garlic powder
1 tablespoon soy sauce
1/2 teaspoon red pepper flakes, crushed

Directions

Toss the asparagus with the remaining ingredients. Arrange the asparagus spears in the Air Fryer cooking basket. Secure the air-frying lid.

Cook the asparagus at 400 degrees F for about 6 minutes, tossing them halfway through the cooking time.

Bon appétit!

Per serving: Calories: 75; Fat: 6g; Carbs: 5.6g; Protein: 2.8g; Sugars: 2.8g; Fiber: 2.5g

112. Stuffed Tomatoes with Mushrooms and Goat Cheese [PC+AF]

(Ready in about 15 minutes | Servings 4)

Ingredients

2 tablespoons olive oil
2 garlic cloves, minced
1 cup brown mushrooms, chopped
Sea salt and ground black pepper, to taste
1/2 teaspoon dried basil
4 tomatoes, tops, seeds, and pulp removed
2 ounces goat cheese, shredded

Directions

Press the "Sauté" button and heat the olive oil; now, sauté garlic and mushrooms for about 2 minutes or until the mushrooms release the liquid.

Stir in the salt, black pepper, and basil; stir to combine. Fill the tomatoes with the prepared mixture and arrange them in the inner pot of your Instant Pot; add in 1/2 cup of water.

Secure the pressure-cooking lid. Pressure cook for 4 minutes at High pressure. Once cooking is complete, use a quick pressure release; carefully remove the lid.

Top them with the cheese and secure the air-frying lid. Air fry for 3 to 4 minutes or until the cheese melts.

Bon appétit!

Per serving: Calories: 166; Fat: 12.2g; Carbs: 9g; Protein: 7g; Sugars: 1.2g; Fiber: 1.8g

VEGETABLES & SIDE DISHES

113. Parmesan Mushroom Patties [AF]

(Ready in about 20 minutes | Servings 3)

Ingredients

- 3/4 pound brown mushrooms, chopped
- 1 large eggs, whisked
- 1/2 cup breadcrumbs
- 1/2 cup parmesan cheese, grated
- 1 small onion, minced
- 1 garlic clove, minced
- Sea salt and ground black pepper, to taste
- 1 tablespoon olive oil

Directions

Mix all the ingredients until everything is well combined. Form the mixture into three patties.

Secure the air-frying lid.

Cook the patties at 380 degrees F for about 15 minutes or until cooked through.

Bon appétit!

Per serving: Calories: 184; Fat: 11.1g; Carbs: 14g; Protein: 9.4g; Sugars: 4g; Fiber: 1.5g

114. Chinese Ginger Carrot Soup [PC]

(Ready in about 20 minutes | Servings 4)

Ingredients

- 2 teaspoons ghee, at room temperature
- 1 sweet onion, diced
- 2 cloves garlic, minced
- 1 teaspoon fresh ginger, minced
- 1 teaspoon fennel seeds
- 1 teaspoon red curry paste
- 1 pound carrots, chopped
- 2 cups vegetable stock
- 1 cup coconut yogurt
- Kosher salt and red pepper, to taste

Directions

Press the "Sauté" button and melt the ghee; now, sauté the onion and garlic for about 2 minutes or until it has softened.

Stir in the ginger, fennel seeds, curry paste, carrots, and vegetable stock.

Secure the pressure-cooking lid. Pressure cook for 15 minutes at High pressure. Once cooking is complete, use a quick pressure release; carefully remove the lid.

Afterwards, blend the soup with the coconut yogurt until creamy and uniform. Season the soup with the salt and red pepper to taste.

Bon appétit!

Per serving: Calories: 150; Fat: 5.2g; Carbs: 20.4g; Protein: 6.6g; Sugars: 12.2g; Fiber: 4.2g

115. Sweet Potatoes with Salsa [AF]

(Ready in about 40 minutes | Servings 4)

Ingredients

- 1 pound sweet potatoes, scrubbed, prick with a fork
- 1 tablespoon olive oil
- Coarse sea salt and ground black pepper, to taste
- 1/2 teaspoon cayenne pepper
- 4 tablespoons salsa

Directions

Sprinkle the sweet potatoes with olive oil, salt, black pepper, and cayenne pepper.

Add the sweet potatoes to the Air Fryer basket. Secure the air-frying lid.

Cook the sweet potatoes at 380 degrees F for 35 minutes, checking them halfway through the cooking time.

Split the tops open with a knife. Top each potato with salsa and serve. Bon appétit!

Per serving: Calories: 128; Fat: 3.5g; Carbs: 22.1g; Protein: 3g; Sugars: 2.1.8g; Fiber: 3g

116. Street-Style Corn on the Cob [PC]

(Ready in about 10 minutes | Servings 4)

Ingredients

- 4 ears corn on the cob
- 4 teaspoons butter
- 1 teaspoon red chili powder
- Sea salt, to taste

Directions

Add 1 cup of water and a metal trivet to the inner pot. Place the corn on the trivet.

Secure the pressure-cooking lid. Pressure cook for 2 minutes at High pressure. Once cooking is complete, use a quick pressure release; carefully remove the lid.

Mix the butter, red chili powder, and sea salt. Spread the butter mixture over the corn on the cob.

Secure the air-frying lid and cook for 3 minutes or until golden brown. Bon appétit!

Per serving: Calories: 158; Fat: 4.9g; Carbs: 29g; Protein: 4.3g; Sugars: 1g; Fiber: 3.7g

117. Garlicky Potatoes with Oregano [AF]

(Ready in about 20 minutes | Servings 3)

Ingredients

- 3/4 pound potatoes, quartered
- 1 tablespoon butter, melted
- 1 teaspoon garlic, pressed
- 1 teaspoon dried oregano
- Sea salt and ground black pepper, to taste

Directions

Toss the potatoes with the remaining ingredients until well coated on all sides.

Arrange the potatoes in the Air Fryer basket. Secure the air-frying lid.

Cook the potatoes at 400 degrees F for about 18 minutes, shaking the basket halfway through the cooking time.

Serve warm and enjoy!

Per serving: Calories: 123; Fat: 4g; Carbs: 20.1g; Protein: 2.3g; Sugars: 0.9g; Fiber: 2.5g

118. Italian Eggplant Casserole [PC]

(Ready in about 20 minutes | Servings 4)

Ingredients

2 tablespoons olive oil
1 medium onion, chopped
2 garlic cloves, minced
1 pound eggplant, peeled and cut into chunks
2 medium tomatoes, pureed
1 tablespoon Italian seasoning
Sea salt and ground black pepper, to taste
2 cups vegetable broth
7 ounces fusilli pasta
1 cup cheddar cheese, shredded

Directions

Press the "Sauté" button to preheat your Instant Pot Duo Crisp; heat the olive oil.

Then, sauté the onion and garlic for about 2 minutes until just tender. Add in the eggplant and continue to cook for 2 minutes more.

Meanwhile, cook the pasta according to the package directions. Toss the pasta with the sautéed vegetables, tomatoes, and spices. Pour in the vegetable broth.

Secure the pressure-cooking lid. Pressure cook for 10 minutes at High pressure. Once cooking is complete, use a quick pressure release; carefully remove the lid.

Top with cheddar cheese, cover with the air-frying lid and cook for 5 minutes or until the cheese is melted and bubbly.

Bon appétit!

Per serving: Calories: 435; Fat: 18.4g; Carbs: 54.4g; Protein: 15.2g; Sugars: 7.8g; Fiber: 10.6g

119. Mom's Vegetable Fritters [AF]

(Ready in about 20 minutes | Servings 3)

Ingredients

1 carrot, shredded
1 parsnip, shredded
1 onion, chopped
1 garlic clove, minced
1/2 cup all-purpose flour
1 teaspoon cayenne pepper
Sea salt and ground black pepper, to taste
2 eggs, whisked

Directions

Mix all the ingredients until everything is well combined. Form the mixture into three fritters.

Secure the air-frying lid. Cook the fritters at 380 degrees F for about 15 minutes or until cooked through.

Bon appétit!

Per serving: Calories: 184; Fat: 3.3g; Carbs: 31.1g; Protein: 8.1g; Sugars: 5.6g; Fiber: 4.3g

120. Creamed Corn Fried Cakes [AF]

(Ready in about 20 minutes | Servings 4)

Ingredients

1 cup all-purpose flour
1/2 teaspoon baking powder
1 cup sweet corn kernels, canned and drained
2 eggs
1/4 cup buttermilk
1/2 teaspoon sea salt
1/4 teaspoon freshly ground black pepper, or more to taste
1 garlic clove, minced
1 tablespoon butter, melted
2 ounces Swiss cheese, shredded

Directions

Start by preheating your Air Fryer to 380 degrees F.

Mix all the ingredients until everything is well combined. Form the mixture into patties.

Secure the air-frying lid. Cook the fritters at 380 degrees F for about 15 minutes or until cooked through.

Turn them over halfway through the cooking time. Bon appétit!

Per serving: Calories: 296; Fat: 12.7g; Carbs: 32.5g; Protein: 13g; Sugars: 2.3g; Fiber: 1.8g

VEGETABLES & SIDE DISHES

PORK

121. Herbed Pork Shoulder [PC]

(Ready in about 30 minutes | Servings 4)

Ingredients

- 1 ½ pounds pork shoulder
- 3 garlic cloves, minced
- 1 teaspoon dried sage
- 1 teaspoon dried rosemary
- 1 teaspoon dried thyme
- 1 cup chicken bone broth

Directions

Place all the ingredients in the inner pot and secure the pressure-cooking lid.

Pressure cook for 25 minutes at High pressure. Once cooking is complete, use a quick pressure release; carefully remove the lid.

Bon appétit!

Per serving: Calories: 416; Fat: 25.2g; Carbs: 1.4g; Protein: 42.5g; Sugars: 0.7g; Fiber: 0.4g

122. Paprika Pork Chops [AF]

(Ready in about 20 minutes | Servings 4)

Ingredients

- 1 pound pork loin chops
- 1 tablespoon olive oil
- Sea salt and ground black pepper, to taste
- 1 tablespoon smoked paprika

Directions

Place all the ingredients in a lightly greased Air Fryer basket. Secure the air-frying lid.

Air fry the chops at 400 degrees F for 15 minutes, turning them over halfway through the cooking time.

Bon appétit!

Per serving: Calories: 332; Fat: 13.3g; Carbs: 1.9g; Protein: 23.4g; Sugars: 0.8g; Fiber: 0.8g

123. Toulouse-Style Cassoulet [PC]

(Ready in about 30 minutes | Servings 6)

Ingredients

- 1 pound pork belly, slice into strips
- 1 cup tomato sauce
- 1 onion, chopped
- 2 garlic cloves, minced
- Sea salt and ground black pepper, to season
- 1 teaspoon cayenne pepper
- 1 cup canned white beans, drained

Directions

Place the pork belly, tomato sauce, onion, garlic, salt, black pepper, and cayenne pepper in the inner pot; secure the pressure-cooking lid.

Pressure cook for 20 minutes at High pressure. Once cooking is complete, use a natural pressure release; carefully remove the lid.

Add in the canned white beans. Secure the air-frying lid and cook at 380 degrees F for 5 minutes or until everything is thoroughly cooked. Bon appétit!

Per serving: Calories: 501; Fat: 40.4g; Carbs: 21.2g; Protein: 11.8g; Sugars: 6.1g; Fiber: 5.3g

124. Dijon and Garlic Pork [AF]

(Ready in about 20 minutes | Servings 4)

Ingredients

- 1 ½ pounds top loin roasts, sliced into four pieces
- 2 tablespoons olive oil
- 1 teaspoon hot paprika
- Sea salt and ground black pepper
- 1 tablespoon Dijon mustard
- 1 teaspoon garlic, pressed

Directions

Place all the ingredients in a lightly greased Air Fryer basket. Secure the air-frying lid.

Cook the pork at 400 degrees F for 15 minutes, turning it over halfway through the cooking time. Bon appétit!

Per serving: Calories: 352; Fat: 21.1g; Carbs: 1.9g; Protein: 36.4g; Sugars: 0.6g; Fiber: 0.6g

125. Wine-Braised Pork Loin Roast [PC]

(Ready in about 45 minutes | Servings 4)

Ingredients

- 1 tablespoon butter
- 1 ½ pounds pork loin roast
- Kosher salt and ground black pepper, to season
- 1 tablespoon poultry seasoning mix
- 1 cup chicken stock
- 1/2 cup white wine

Directions

Press the "Sauté" button and melt the butter; once hot, sear the pork loin roast for about 4 minutes.

Stir in the remaining ingredients and secure the pressure-cooking lid.

Pressure cook for 40 minutes at High pressure. Once cooking is complete, use a quick pressure release; carefully remove the lid.

Serve warm and enjoy!

Per serving: Calories: 327; Fat: 17.3g; Carbs: 2.1g; Protein: 38.1g; Sugars: 1g; Fiber: 0.3g

126. Easy BLT Sandwich [AF]

(Ready in about 15 minutes | Servings 3)

Ingredients

- 6 ounces bacon, thick-cut
- 2 tablespoons brown sugar
- 2 teaspoons chipotle chili powder
- 1 teaspoon cayenne pepper
- 1 tablespoon Dijon mustard
- 1 heads lettuce, torn into leaves
- 2 medium tomatoes, sliced
- 6 (1/2-inch) slices white bread

Directions

Toss the bacon with the sugar, chipotle chili powder, cayenne pepper, and mustard.

Place the bacon in the Air Fryer basket. Secure the air-frying lid.

Air fry the bacon at 400 degrees F for approximately 10 minutes, tossing the basket halfway through the cooking time.

Assemble your sandwiches with the bacon, lettuce, and tomato.

Bon appétit!

Per serving: Calories: 401; Fat: 23.3g; Carbs: 32.3g; Protein: 14.1g; Sugars: 9.5g; Fiber: 6.3g

127. Juicy Mustard Pork [PC]

(Ready in about 30 minutes | Servings 4)

Ingredients

1 tablespoon butter
1 pound sirloin pork, diced
1 teaspoon stone-ground mustard
1 cup vegetable broth

Directions

Place all the ingredients in the inner pot and secure the pressure-cooking lid.

Pressure cook for 25 minutes at High pressure. Once cooking is complete, use a quick pressure release; carefully remove the lid.

Bon appétit!

Per serving: Calories: 270; Fat: 17.4g; Carbs: 0.4g; Protein: 21.5g; Sugars: 0.1g; Fiber: 0.1g

128. Orange-Glazed Smoked Ham [AF]

(Ready in about 1 hour | Servings 4)

Ingredients

1 ½ pounds smoked and cooked ham
1/4 cup honey
1 small-sized orange, freshly squeezed
1 tablespoon balsamic vinegar
1 tablespoon stone-ground mustard
1/2 teaspoon red pepper flakes, crushed
Freshly ground black pepper, to taste

Directions

Start by preheating your Air Fryer to 400 degrees F for about 13 minutes.

In a mixing bowl, whisk all the remaining ingredients to make the glaze.

Wrap the ham in a piece of aluminum foil and lower it into the Air Fryer basket. Reduce the temperature to 375 degrees F and cook the ham for about 30 minutes.

Remove the top foil, turn the temperature to 400 degrees F, and continue to cook an additional 15 minutes, coating the ham with the glaze every 5 minutes.

Bon appétit!

Per serving: Calories: 368; Fat: 15.3g; Carbs: 27.8g; Protein: 28.9g; Sugars: 20.3g; Fiber: 3g

129. Old-Fashioned Pork Chops [PC]

(Ready in about 4 hours 5 minutes | Servings 5)

Ingredients

2 pounds pork blade chops, bone-in
2 tablespoons sea salt
2 tablespoons granulated sugar
1 cup chicken bone broth
2 bay leaves
2 garlic cloves, crushed
1 pound broccoli florets

Directions

Place the pork, salt, sugar, broth, bay leaves, and garlic in the inner pot of your Instant Pot Duo Crisp. Fill the inner pot with warm water up to 1/2 line.

Secure the pressure-cooking lid. Choose the "Sous Vide" program. Cook the pork at 140 degrees F for 4 hours.

Add in the broccoli, choose the "Pressure Cook" function and continue to cook for 3 minutes or until tender.

Serve warm. Bon appétit!

Per serving: Calories: 316; Fat: 11.1g; Carbs: 9.8g; Protein: 42.1g; Sugars: 4.7g; Fiber: 2.4g

130. Roasted Herbed Pork [AF]

(Ready in about 55 minutes | Servings 4)

Ingredients

1 ½ pounds pork butt
1 teaspoon olive oil
1 teaspoon dried rosemary
1 teaspoon dried thyme
1 teaspoon dried oregano
1 teaspoon dried basil
1 teaspoon cayenne pepper
Sea salt and ground black pepper, to taste

Directions

Toss all the ingredients in a lightly greased Air Fryer basket. Secure the air-frying lid.

Choose the "Roast" mode and cook the pork at 360 degrees F for 55 minutes, turning it over halfway through the cooking time.

Serve warm and enjoy!

Per serving: Calories: 301; Fat: 13g; Carbs: 1.6g; Protein: 37g; Sugars: 0.6g; Fiber: 0.5g

131. Wine-Braised Pork Belly [PC]

(Ready in about 25 minutes | Servings 6)

Ingredients

1 ½ pounds pork belly (1-inch thick)
1 cup roasted vegetable broth
4 garlic cloves, minced
2 tablespoons soy sauce
1/4 cup white wine

Directions

Score the pork belly and place all the ingredients in the inner pot of your Instant Pot Dup Crisp; secure the pressure-cooking lid.

Pressure cook for 20 minutes at High pressure. Once cooking is complete, use a natural pressure release; carefully remove the lid.

Bon appétit!

Per serving: Calories: 606; Fat: 61g; Carbs: 2g; Protein: 11.3g; Sugars: 1.1g; Fiber: 0.2g

132. Classic Dinner Rolls [AF]

(Ready in about 20 minutes | Servings 4)

Ingredients

1 pound ground pork
Sea salt and freshly ground black pepper, to taste
1 teaspoon red pepper flakes, crushed
1/2 cup scallions, chopped
2 garlic cloves, minced
1 tablespoon olive oil
1 tablespoon soy sauce
8 dinner rolls, split

Directions

In a mixing bowl, thoroughly combine the pork, spices, scallions, garlic, olive oil, and soy sauce. Form the mixture into four patties.

Place the patties in a lightly greased Air Fryer basket. Secure the air-frying lid.

Air fry the patties at 380 degrees F for about 15 minutes or until cooked through; make sure to turn them over halfway through the cooking time.

Serve the patties in dinner rolls and enjoy!

Per serving: Calories: 499; Fat: 31.6g; Carbs: 28.2g; Protein: 24.5g; Sugars: 2g; Fiber: 2.6g

133. Pork Chops with Red Wine [PC]

(Ready in about 20 minutes | Servings 4)

Ingredients

2 tablespoons butter
1 ½ pounds sirloin pork chops
2 garlic cloves, minced
1 small leek, sliced
1 cup chicken bone broth
1/4 cup red wine
2 tablespoons tomato sauce

Directions

Preheat your Instant Pot Duo Crisp on the "Sauté" function; once hot, melt the butter and cook the sirloin pork chops for approximately 4 minutes, turning them over to ensure even cooking.

Stir in the remaining ingredients and secure the pressure-cooking lid.

Pressure cook for 15 minutes at High pressure. Once cooking is complete, use a natural pressure release; carefully remove the lid. Enjoy!

Per serving: Calories: 317; Fat: 13.2g; Carbs: 5.5g; Protein: 40.3g; Sugars: 2g; Fiber: 0.9g

134. Easy Sausage Sandwich [AF]

(Ready in about 20 minutes | Servings 3)

Ingredients

1 pound sweet Italian sausage
6 white bread slices
2 teaspoons mustard

Directions

Place the sausage in a lightly greased Air fryer basket. Secure the air-frying lid.

Air fry the sausage at 370 degrees F for approximately 15 minutes, tossing the basket halfway through the cooking time.

Assemble the sandwiches with the bread, mustard, and sausage, and serve immediately. Bon appétit!

Per serving: Calories: 407; Fat: 14.5g; Carbs: 31.8g; Protein: 28.8g; Sugars: 7.6g; Fiber: 6.6g

135. Pork Loin Roast [PC]

(Ready in about 30 minutes | Servings 4)

Ingredients

2 teaspoons olive oil
1 pound pork loin roast, chopped
2 garlic cloves, minced
1 medium leek, chopped
1 chicken stock cube
1 cup water
1 teaspoon stone-ground mustard
1 pound asparagus, trimmed

Directions

Press the "Sauté" button and heat the olive oil; sear the pork for approximately 4 minutes or until no longer pink.

Add in the garlic, leek, chicken stock, water, and mustard; secure the pressure-cooking lid.

Pressure cook for 20 minutes at High pressure. Once cooking is complete, use a quick pressure release; carefully remove the lid.

Then, fold in the asparagus and press the "Sauté" button again; continue to cook for 2 minutes.

Serve warm and enjoy!

Per serving: Calories: 256; Fat: 12.4g; Carbs: 8.5g; Protein: 27.4g; Sugars: 3.1g; Fiber: 2.2g

136. Glazed Pork Belly [AF]

(Ready in about 20 minutes | Servings 6)

Ingredients

1 ½ pounds pork belly, cut into pieces
1/4 cup tomato sauce
1 tablespoon tamari sauce
2 tablespoons dark brown sugar
1 teaspoon garlic, minced
Sea salt and ground black pepper, to season

Directions

Toss all the ingredients in the Air Fryer basket. Secure the air-frying lid.

Air fry the pork belly at 400 degrees F for about 17 minutes, shaking the basket halfway through the cooking time.

Bon appétit!

Per serving: Calories: 603; Fat: 60.1g; Carbs: 3.3g; Protein: 11.1g; Sugars: 1.7g; Fiber: 0.8g

137. Southern Pork Chops [PC+AF]

(Ready in about 25 minutes | Servings 4)

Ingredients

2 tablespoons butter
1 pound rib chops
1 teaspoon garlic, minced
1 tablespoon Italian seasoning
Sea salt and freshly ground pepper, to taste
1/2 cup chicken broth
1/2 cup dry white wine
1/2 cup heavy cream
1/2 cup Parmesan cheese, grated

Directions

Melt the butter on the "Sauté" mode; now, sear the pork chops for approximately 4 minutes per side.

Add in the garlic, Italian seasoning, salt, black pepper, chicken broth, and wine; stir to combine and secure the pressure-cooking lid.

Pressure cook for 6 minutes at High pressure. Once cooking is complete, use a quick pressure release; carefully remove the lid.

Add in the cream and cheese, secure the air-frying lid. Air fry at 380 degrees F for about 15 minutes or until cooked through.

Bon appétit!

Per serving: Calories: 521; Fat: 44.4g; Carbs: 4.7g; Protein: 23.6g; Sugars: 1.1g; Fiber: 0.3g

138. Herbed Sausage with Brussels Sprouts [AF]

(Ready in about 20 minutes | Servings 4)

Ingredients

1 pound sausage links, uncooked
1 pound Brussels sprouts, halved
1 teaspoon dried thyme
1 teaspoon dried rosemary
1 teaspoon dried parsley flakes
1 teaspoon garlic powder

Directions

Place the sausage and Brussels sprouts in a lightly greased Air Fryer basket. Secure the air-frying lid.

Air fry the sausage and Brussels sprouts at 380 degrees F for approximately 15 minutes, tossing the basket halfway through the cooking time.

Bon appétit!

Per serving: Calories: 444; Fat: 35.9g; Carbs: 11.6g; Protein: 20.1g; Sugars: 2.5g; Fiber: 4.4g

139. Hungarian Pork Stew (Pörkölt) [PC]

(Ready in about 40 minutes | Servings 4)

Ingredients

2 tablespoons olive oil
2 pounds pork shoulder, diced
1 onion, chopped
2 garlic cloves, finely chopped
1 bell peppers, sliced
1 chili pepper, sliced
1 tablespoon paprika
1/2 cup tomato puree
2 cups chicken bone broth

Directions

Preheat your Instant Pot Duo Crisp on the "Sauté" function; heat the oil and sear the pork until lightly browned on all sides.

Stir in the remaining ingredients and secure the pressure-cooking lid.

Pressure cook for 35 minutes at High pressure. Once cooking is complete, use a quick pressure release; carefully remove the lid.

Bon appétit!

Per serving: Calories: 420; Fat: 20.8g; Carbs: 9.5g; Protein: 46.3g; Sugars: 4.2g; Fiber: 2g

140. Easy Bacon Salad [AF]

(Ready in about 20 minutes | Servings 5)

Ingredients

1 pound bacon, cut into thick slices
1 head lettuce, torn into leaves
1 tablespoon fresh chive, chopped
1 tablespoon fresh tarragon, chopped
1 tablespoon fresh parsley, chopped
2 tablespoons freshly squeezed lemon juice
2 garlic cloves, minced
Coarse sea salt and ground black pepper, to taste
1 teaspoon red pepper flakes, crushed
2 cups bread cubes

Directions

Place the bacon in the Air Fryer basket. Secure the air-frying lid.

Then, cook the bacon at 400 degrees F for approximately 10 minutes, tossing the basket halfway through the cooking time; reserve.

Air fry the bread cubes at 390 degrees F for approximately 6 minutes or until the bread is toasted.

Toss the remaining ingredients in a salad bowl; top your salad with the bacon and croutons. Bon appétit!

Per serving: Calories: 419; Fat: 36.3g; Carbs: 10.3g; Protein: 13.4g; Sugars: 2.5g; Fiber: 1g

141. Dijon Picnic Ham [PC]

(Ready in about 20 minutes | Servings 4)

Ingredients

2 pounds picnic ham
1 apple, cored and diced
1 teaspoon Dijon mustard
2 tablespoons maple syrup
1 cup chicken bone broth

Directions

Place all the ingredients in the inner pot of your Instant Pot Duo Crisp; secure the pressure-cooking lid.

Pressure cook for 15 minutes at High pressure. Once cooking is complete, use a natural pressure release; carefully remove the lid. Bon appétit!

Per serving: Calories: 546; Fat: 26.1g; Carbs: 15.2g; Protein: 59g; Sugars: 13.1g; Fiber: 1.2g

142. Garlicky Pork Butt [AF]

(Ready in about 1 hour | Servings 4)

Ingredients

1 ½ pounds pork butt
1 teaspoon butter, melted
2 garlic cloves, pressed
2 tablespoons fresh rosemary, chopped
Coarse sea salt and freshly ground black pepper, to taste

Directions

Toss all the ingredients in a lightly greased Air Fryer basket. Secure the air-frying lid.

Air fry the pork at 360 degrees F for 55 minutes, turning it over halfway through the cooking time. Serve warm and enjoy!

Per serving: Calories: 338; Fat: 22g; Carbs: 0.6g; Protein: 29.7g; Sugars: 0.2g; Fiber: 0.2g

PORK

143. Italian-Style Pork Soup [PC]

(Ready in about 35 minutes | Servings 4)

Ingredients

2 teaspoons olive oil
1 ½ pounds rib pork chops
1 celery stalk, diced
1 tablespoon Italian herb mix
1 bay laurel
2 cups chicken consommé
2 cups water

Directions

Heat the olive oil on the "Sauté" function; sear the rib pork chops for about 4 minutes, stirring periodically to ensure even cooking.

Add the other ingredients to the inner pot of your Instant Pot Duo Crisp; stir to combine and secure the pressure-cooking lid.

Pressure cook for 30 minutes at High pressure. Once cooking is complete, use a quick pressure release; carefully remove the lid. Bon appétit!

Per serving: Calories: 276; Fat: 11.4g; Carbs: 0.1g; Protein: 39.5g; Sugars: 0.1g; Fiber: 0.1g

144. The Best Pork Roast Ever [AF]

(Ready in about 55 minutes | Servings 4)

Ingredients

1 ½ pounds center-cut pork roast
1 tablespoon olive oil
Sea salt and freshly ground black pepper, to taste
1 teaspoon garlic powder
1 teaspoon hot paprika
1/2 teaspoon dried parsley flakes
1/2 teaspoon dried rosemary

Directions

Toss all the ingredients in a lightly greased Air Fryer basket. Secure the air-frying lid.

Choose the "Roast" mode. Cook the pork at 360 degrees F for 55 minutes, turning it over halfway through the cooking time.

Serve warm and enjoy!

Per serving: Calories: 330; Fat: 14.3g; Carbs: 1g; Protein: 37.4g; Sugars: 0g; Fiber: 0.3g

145. Rustic Pork with Prunes [PC]

(Ready in about 35 minutes | Servings 4)

Ingredients

1 tablespoon butter, at room temperature
2 pounds pork butt, diced
1 medium-sized leek, chopped
2 cloves garlic, minced
1 sweet potato, peeled and diced
1 bay laurel
2 cups roasted vegetable broth
2 ounces prunes

Directions

Preheat your Instant Pot Duo Crisp on the "Sauté" mode; now, melt the butter and cook the pork for approximately 4 minutes, stirring constantly to ensure even browning.

Stir in the remaining ingredients and secure the pressure-cooking lid.

Pressure cook for 30 minutes at High pressure. Once cooking is complete, use a natural pressure release; carefully remove the lid.

Serve in individual bowls and enjoy!

Per serving: Calories: 387; Fat: 15.9g; Carbs: 14.2g; Protein: 43.5g; Sugars: 2.2g; Fiber: 2g

146. Pork Chops with Onions [AF]

(Ready in about 20 minutes | Servings 4)

Ingredients

1 ½ pounds pork loin chops, boneless
2 tablespoons olive oil
1/2 teaspoon cayenne pepper
1 teaspoon garlic powder
Sea salt and ground black pepper, to taste
1 onion, cut into wedges

Directions

Place all the ingredients in a lightly greased Air Fryer basket. Secure the air-frying lid.

Air fry the pork loin chops at 400 degrees F for 15 minutes, turning them over halfway through the cooking time.

Bon appétit!

Per serving: Calories: 358; Fat: 18.8g; Carbs: 8g; Protein: 37.7g; Sugars: 4.8g; Fiber: 1g

147. Penne Pasta with Pork Sausage [PC]

(Ready in about 15 minutes | Servings 4)

Ingredients

1 pound Italian pork sausage
1 tablespoon olive oil
1/2 cup chicken bone broth
1 cup marinara sauce
1 tablespoon Italian seasoning mix
6 ounces penne pasta

Directions

Dump all the ingredients into the inner pot of your Instant Pot Duo Crisp; gently stir to combine and secure the pressure-cooking lid.

Pressure cook for 12 minutes at High pressure. Once cooking is complete, use a quick pressure release; carefully remove the lid. Bon appétit!

Per serving: Calories: 603; Fat: 40g; Carbs: 42g; Protein: 21.1g; Sugars: 2.8g; Fiber: 6.1g

148. Center Cut Rib Roast [AF]

(Ready in about 55 minutes | Servings 4)

Ingredients

1 ½ pounds pork center cut rib roast
2 teaspoons butter, melted
1 teaspoon red chili powder
1 teaspoon paprika
1 teaspoon garlic powder
1/2 teaspoon onion powder
Sea salt and ground black pepper, to taste
2 tablespoons tamari sauce

Directions

Toss all the ingredients in a lightly greased Air Fryer basket. Secure the air-frying lid.

Choose the "Roast" mode. Cook the pork at 360 degrees F for 55 minutes, turning it over halfway through the cooking time.

Serve warm and enjoy!

Per serving: Calories: 383; Fat: 17.8g; Carbs: 3.2g; Protein: 49.4g; Sugars: 1g; Fiber: 1.1g

149. Saucy Montreal-Style Pork [PC]

(Ready in about 45 minutes | Servings 4)

Ingredients

2 tablespoons olive oil
1 ½ pounds pork loin roast
1 teaspoon garlic, pressed
1 tablespoon Montreal seasoning mix
1 cup vegetable broth
1/4 cup tomato sauce

Directions

Press the "Sauté" button to preheat your Instant Pot Duo Crisp. Heat the olive oil and sear the pork for about 4 minutes.

Stir in the remaining ingredients and secure the pressure-cooking lid.

Pressure cook for 40 minutes at High pressure. Once cooking is complete, use a quick pressure release; carefully remove the lid.

Shred the pork and serve warm. Bon appétit!

Per serving: Calories: 324; Fat: 14.3g; Carbs: 5g; Protein: 39.3g; Sugars: 2g; Fiber: 1.3g

150. Mexican Tacos de Carnitas [AF]

(Ready in about 1 hour | Servings 4)

Ingredients

2 ancho chilis, seeded and minced
2 garlic cloves, chopped
1 tablespoon olive oil
Kosher salt and freshly ground black pepper, to season
1 teaspoon dried Mexican oregano
1 ½ pounds pork butt
4 corn tortillas, warmed

Directions

Toss all the ingredients, except for the tortillas, in a lightly greased Air Fryer basket. Secure the air-frying lid.

Air fry the pork butt at 360 degrees F for 55 minutes, turning it over halfway through the cooking time.

Using two forks, shred the pork and serve in tortillas with toppings of choice. Serve immediately!

Per serving: Calories: 538; Fat: 34.2g; Carbs: 11.3g; Protein: 44.1g; Sugars: 0.2g; Fiber: 1.6g

151. Italian-Style Pork Sausage [PC]

(Ready in about 15 minutes | Servings 5)

Ingredients

1 tablespoon olive oil
1 ½ pounds pork sausage
1/2 cup marinara sauce
1/2 cup roasted vegetable broth
2 teaspoons garlic, minced
1 tablespoon Italian herb mix

Directions

Dump all the ingredients into the inner pot of your Instant Pot Duo Crisp; gently stir to combine and secure the pressure-cooking lid.

Select the "Manual" mode and cook for 13 minutes at High pressure. Once cooking is complete, use a quick pressure release; carefully remove the lid.

Bon appétit!

Per serving: Calories: 506; Fat: 45.4g; Carbs: 3.2g; Protein: 19.9g; Sugars: 1.1g; Fiber: 0.5g

152. Cuban Pork Sandwiches [AF]

(Ready in about 1 hour | Servings 4)

Ingredients

1 ½ pounds pork butt
1 teaspoon stone-ground mustard
1/2 teaspoon ground cumin
2 cloves garlic, crushed
Kosher salt and freshly ground black pepper, to season
1/2 teaspoon ground allspice
2 tablespoons fresh pineapple juice
2 ounces Swiss cheese, sliced
16 ounces Cuban bread loaf, sliced

Directions

Toss all the ingredients, except for the cheese and bread, in a lightly greased Air Fryer basket. Secure the air-frying lid.

Air fry the pork butt at 360 degrees F for 55 minutes, turning it over halfway through the cooking time.

Using two forks, shred the pork; assemble your sandwiches with cheese and bread. Serve warm and enjoy!

Per serving: Calories: 684; Fat: 28.3g; Carbs: 57.8g; Protein: 45.1g; Sugars: 7.8g; Fiber: 4.7g

153. Rustic Pork Stew [PC]

(Ready in about 20 minutes | Servings 4)

Ingredients

2 ounces bacon, diced
1 pound ground pork
1 onion, chopped
2 garlic cloves, minced
1 cup tomato soup
1 cup chicken bone north
1 tablespoon fresh parsley, chopped
1 tablespoon fresh cilantro, chopped

Directions

Press the "Sauté" button to preheat your Instant Pot Duo Crisp. Then, cook the bacon, stirring and crumbling with a fork, until crisp.

Fold in the other ingredients and secure the pressure-cooking lid.

Pressure cook for 15 minutes at High pressure. Once cooking is complete, use a natural pressure release; carefully remove the lid.

Bon appétit!

Per serving: Calories: 338; Fat: 23.7g; Carbs: 5.2g; Protein: 22.6g; Sugars: 2.2g; Fiber: 1.2g

154. Dad's Bourbon Ribs [AF]

(Ready in about 40 minutes | Servings 5)

Ingredients

2 pounds Country-style ribs
1/4 cup Sriracha sauce
2 tablespoons bourbon
1 tablespoon honey
1 teaspoon stone-ground mustard

Directions

Toss all the ingredients in a lightly greased Air Fryer basket. Secure the air-frying lid.

Cook the pork ribs at 350 degrees F for 35 minutes, turning them over halfway through the cooking time. Bon appétit!

Per serving: Calories: 371; Fat: 21.6g; Carbs: 4.4g; Protein: 35.4g; Sugars: 3.8g; Fiber: 0.3g

155. Italian-Style Cheeseburger Casserole [PC+AF]

(Ready in about 20 minutes | Servings 5)

Ingredients

2 tablespoons olive oil
1 pound ground pork
7 ounces penne pasta
1 onion, chopped
2 garlic cloves, minced
1 cup marinara sauce
1/2 cup cream cheese
2 eggs, beaten

Directions

Place the olive oil, ground pork, pasta, onion, garlic, and marinara sauce in the inner pot of your Instant Pot Duo Crisp. Secure the pressure-cooking lid.

Pressure cook for 10 minutes at High pressure. Once cooking is complete, use a natural pressure release; carefully remove the lid.

Mix the cheese and egg until well combined; top your casserole with the cheese mixture.

Secure the air-frying lid. Choose the "Broil" function and cook at 400 degrees F for about 8 minutes or until golden brown. Bon appétit!

Per serving: Calories: 548; Fat: 34.1g; Carbs: 38.2g; Protein: 23.3g; Sugars: 3.8g; Fiber: 5.7g

156. Sweet Brats with Brussels Sprouts [AF]

(Ready in about 20 minutes | Servings 4)

Ingredients

1 pound bratwurst
1 pound Brussels sprouts
1 large onion, cut into wedges
1 teaspoon garlic, minced
1 tablespoon mustard
2 tablespoons honey

Directions

Toss all the ingredients in a lightly greased Air Fryer basket. Secure the air-frying lid.

Air fry the sausage at 380 degrees F for approximately 10 minutes, tossing the basket halfway through the cooking time.

Add in the Brussels sprouts and continue cooking for a further 5 minutes. Bon appétit!

Per serving: Calories: 438; Fat: 30.3g; Carbs: 25g; Protein: 18.7g; Sugars: 12g; Fiber: 5.1g

157. Spicy Pork Bowls [PC+AF]

(Ready in about 20 minutes | Servings 4)

Ingredients

2 tablespoons sesame oil
1 cup green onions, sliced
2 garlic cloves, minced
1 pound ground pork
1 medium-sized tomato, peeled and crushed
1 cup beef stock
1 teaspoon chili powder
2 tablespoons brown sugar
2 tablespoons fish sauce

Directions

Heat the sesame oil on the "Sauté" function. Once hot, cook the green onions, garlic, and pork for about 3 minutes, crumbling with a fork.

Stir in the tomato, beef stock, and chili powder, and secure the pressure-cooking lid.

Pressure cook for 10 minutes at High pressure. Once cooking is complete, use a natural pressure release; carefully remove the lid.

Add in the brown sugar and fish sauce. Secure the air-frying lid. Choose the "Broil" function and let it caramelize for about 8 minutes.

Serve in individual bowls and enjoy!

Per serving: Calories: 394; Fat: 31.1g; Carbs: 7.3g; Protein: 20.2g; Sugars: 5.8g; Fiber: 1.2g

158. Easy Crispy Pork Cutlets [AF]

(Ready in about 20 minutes | Servings 4)

Ingredients

1 ½ pounds pork cutlets
Seasoned salt and ground black pepper, to taste
1 cup tortilla chips, crushed
1/2 teaspoon cayenne pepper
2 tablespoons olive oil

Directions

Toss the pork cutlets with the remaining ingredients; place them in a lightly oiled Air Fryer basket. Secure the air-frying lid.

Air fry the pork cutlets at 400 degrees F for 15 minutes, turning them over halfway through the cooking time. Bon appétit!

Per serving: Calories: 480; Fat: 25.1g; Carbs: 18.2g; Protein: 43.7g; Sugars: 0.8g; Fiber: 1.4g

159. Grandma's Hot Ribs [PC]

(Ready in about 40 minutes | Servings 4)

Ingredients

1 ½ pounds country-style ribs
1 cup barbecue sauce
2 tablespoons brown sugar
2 tablespoons champagne vinegar
1 teaspoon hot sauce

Directions

Place all the ingredients in the inner pot of your Instant Pot Duo Crisp; secure the pressure-cooking lid.

Pressure cook for 35 minutes at High pressure. Once cooking is complete, use a quick pressure release; carefully remove the lid. Bon appétit!

Per serving: Calories: 387; Fat: 15.9g; Carbs: 14.2g; Protein: 43.5g; Sugars: 2.2g; Fiber: 2g

160. Holiday Pork with Crackling [PC+AF]

(Ready in about 50 minutes | Servings 5)

Ingredients

4 tablespoons beer
1 tablespoon garlic, crushed
1 teaspoon paprika
Sea salt and ground black pepper, to taste
2 pounds pork loin

Directions

Press the "Sauté" button to preheat your Instant Pot Duo Crisp. Heat the olive oil and sear the pork for about 4 minutes.

Stir in the remaining ingredients and secure the pressure-cooking lid.

Pressure cook for 30 minutes at High pressure. Once cooking is complete, use a quick pressure release; carefully remove the lid.

Secure the air-frying lid. Choose the "Broil" function and cook the pork for 10 minutes more.

Enjoy!

Per serving: Calories: 315; Fat: 15.2g; Carbs: 2.1g; Protein: 39.1g; Sugars: 0.5g; Fiber: 0.3g

161. Chunky Pork and Hash Brown Bake [PC]

(Ready in about 15 minutes | Servings 6)

Ingredients

2 tablespoons olive oil
1 pound sweet potato, diced
1 onion, sliced
2 garlic cloves, minced
1 pound ground pork
1/2 pound sausage, crumbled
1 teaspoon smoked paprika
1 cup chicken bone broth

Directions

Dump all the ingredients into the inner pot of your Instant Pot Duo Crisp. Secure the pressure-cooking lid.

Pressure cook for 10 minutes at High pressure. Once cooking is complete, use a natural pressure release; carefully remove the lid.

Bon appétit!

Per serving: Calories: 438; Fat: 32.7g; Carbs: 14.2g; Protein: 20.6g; Sugars: 0.7g; Fiber: 1.8g

162. Herbed Pork with Bell Peppers [AF]

(Ready in about 20 minutes | Servings 4)

Ingredients

1 ½ pounds center-cut rib chops
2 bell peppers, seeded and sliced
2 tablespoons olive oil
1/2 teaspoon mustard powder
Kosher salt and freshly ground black pepper, to taste
1 teaspoon fresh rosemary, chopped
1 teaspoon fresh basil, chopped

Directions

Toss all the ingredients in a lightly greased Air Fryer basket. Secure the air-frying lid.

Cook the pork chops and bell peppers at 400 degrees F for 15 minutes, turning them over halfway through the cooking time.

Bon appétit!

Per serving: Calories: 359; Fat: 22.2g; Carbs: 2.2g; Protein: 35.7g; Sugars: 1.1g; Fiber: 0.5g

163. Dad's Pork Salad [PC]

(Ready in about 20 minutes | Servings 4)

Ingredients

1 ½ cups water
1 tablespoon lemon juice
1 pound pork shanks, sliced
Sea salt and ground black pepper, to taste
1 teaspoon Dijon mustard
1/4 cup extra-virgin olive oil
2 tablespoons white wine vinegar
1 bell pepper, seeded and sliced
1 cucumber, sliced
1 large-sized tomato, sliced

Directions

Place the water, lemon juice, and steamer basket in the inner pot; next, lower the pork shanks into the steamer basket.

Secure the pressure-cooking lid. Choose the "Steam" mode and cook for 15 minutes at High pressure. Once cooking is complete, use a quick pressure release; carefully remove the lid.

Chop the pork and toss it with the remaining ingredients. Gently toss until everything is well combined.

Bon appétit!

Per serving: Calories: 288; Fat: 18.3g; Carbs: 2.7g; Protein: 25.6g; Sugars: 1.3g; Fiber: 0.5g

164. Country-Style Crispy Ribs [PC+AF]

(Ready in about 40 minutes | Servings 5)

Ingredients

2 pounds Country-style ribs
Coarse sea salt and ground black pepper, to taste
1 teaspoon smoked paprika
1 teaspoon mustard powder
1 tablespoon butter, melted
1 teaspoon chili sauce
4 tablespoons dry red wine

Directions

Place all the ingredients in the inner pot of your Instant Pot Duo Crisp; secure the pressure-cooking lid.

Pressure cook for 35 minutes at High pressure. Once cooking is complete, use a quick pressure release; carefully remove the lid.

Secure the air-frying lid. Choose the "Broil" function and cook for 5 minutes more or until crisp.

Bon appétit!

Per serving: Calories: 374; Fat: 23.8g; Carbs: 1.4g; Protein: 35.4g; Sugars: 0.6g; Fiber: 0.4g

165. Sticky Leg Steaks with Pineapple [PC]

(Ready in about 20 minutes | Servings 6)

Ingredients

3 pounds leg of pork steak
1/2 medium pineapple, peeled and sliced
2 tablespoons honey
1 cup vegetable broth
1/2 cup dry white wine
Kosher salt and ground white pepper, to taste

Directions

Lower the pork into the inner pot of your Instant Pot Duo Crisp; top with pineapple and honey; pour in the broth wine.

After that, season the pork with the salt and ground white pepper; secure the pressure-cooking lid.

Pressure cook for 15 minutes at High pressure. Once cooking is complete, use a natural pressure release; carefully remove the lid.

Bon appétit!

Per serving: Calories: 332; Fat: 9.6g; Carbs: 7g; Protein: 51.2g; Sugars: 6.7g; Fiber: 0.4g

166. Old-Fashioned Breakfast Patties [AF]

(Ready in about 20 minutes | Servings 4)

Ingredients

1 pound sausage patties
1 tablespoon mustard
1 teaspoon cayenne pepper
1 teaspoon jalapeno pepper, minced

Directions

Place all the ingredients in a lightly greased Air fryer basket. Secure the air-frying lid.

Air fry the sausage at 370 degrees F for approximately 15 minutes, tossing the basket halfway through the cooking time. Bon appétit!

Per serving: Calories: 393; Fat: 35.7g; Carbs: 1.5g; Protein: 16.3g; Sugars: 0.2g; Fiber: 0.4g

167. Mexican-Style Pork Carnitas [PC]

(Ready in about 45 minutes | Servings 5)

Ingredients

1 tablespoon lard, room temperature
2 pounds pork tenderloin
1 teaspoon garlic powder
1 teaspoon onion powder
1 teaspoon mustard powder
1 cup barbecue sauce
1 cup vegetable broth

Directions

Press the "Sauté" button to preheat your Instant Pot Duo Crisp; melt the lard and sear the pork for about 4 minutes.

Stir in the remaining ingredients and secure the pressure-cooking lid.

Pressure cook for 40 minutes at High pressure. Once cooking is complete, use a quick pressure release; carefully remove the lid.

Shred the pork and serve warm. Bon appétit!

Per serving: Calories: 334; Fat: 7.3g; Carbs: 24.5g; Protein: 39.3g; Sugars: 19g; Fiber: 0.7g

168. Sherry and Lime Glazed Ham [AF]

(Ready in about 1 hour | Servings 4)

Ingredients

1 ½ pounds ham
1/4 cup sherry wine
2 tablespoons dark brown sugar
2 tablespoons freshly squeezed lime juice
1 tablespoon stone-ground mustard
A pinch of grated nutmeg
1/2 teaspoon ground cloves
1/4 teaspoon ground cardamom
1/2 teaspoon ground black pepper, to taste

Directions

In a mixing bowl, whisk all the remaining ingredients to make the glaze.

Wrap the ham in a piece of aluminum foil and lower it into the Air Fryer basket. Now, cook the ham at 375 degrees F for about 30 minutes.

Remove top foil and choose the "Broil" function; continue to cook an additional 15 minutes, coating the ham with the glaze every 5 minutes.

Bon appétit!

Per serving: Calories: 470; Fat: 30.3g; Carbs: 1.6g; Protein: 45.7g; Sugars: 0.4g; Fiber: 0.4g

169. BBQ Spare Ribs [PC]

(Ready in about 40 minutes | Servings 5)

Ingredients

2 pounds spare ribs, trimmed
Kosher salt and freshly ground black pepper, to taste
1 shallot, cut into wedges
1 cup barbeque sauce
1/2 cup chicken bone broth

Directions

Place all the ingredients in the inner pot of your Instant Pot Duo Crisp; secure the pressure-cooking lid.

Pressure cook for 40 minutes at High pressure. Once cooking is complete, use a quick pressure release; carefully remove the lid.

Bon appétit!

Per serving: Calories: 487; Fat: 35.2g; Carbs: 8g; Protein: 35.3g; Sugars: 3.6g; Fiber: 1.7g

170. Crispy Bacon and Cauliflower Bites [AF]

(Ready in about 15 minutes | Servings 4)

Ingredients

1 pound bacon, cut into thick slices
1 pound cauliflower, cut into florets
1 tablespoon maple syrup
1 teaspoon paprika
Kosher salt and ground black pepper, to taste
2 cloves garlic, minced

Directions

Toss all the ingredients in the Air Fryer basket. Secure the air-frying lid.

Then, cook the bacon and cauliflower at 400 degrees F for approximately 12 minutes, turning them over halfway through the cooking time.

Serve immediately. Bon appétit!

Per serving: Calories: 512; Fat: 44.9g; Carbs: 11.8g; Protein: 16.7g; Sugars: 6.8g; Fiber: 2.7g

171. Pork Butt with Vegetables [PC]

(Ready in about 30 minutes | Servings 4)

Ingredients

1 ½ pounds pork butt
2 tablespoons olive oil
2 garlic cloves, minced
1 medium-sized leek, sliced
1 celery stalk, sliced
1 carrot, sliced

Directions

Place all the ingredients in the inner pot of your Instant Pot Duo Crisp; secure the pressure-cooking lid.

Pressure cook for 25 minutes at High pressure. Once cooking is complete, use a quick pressure release; carefully remove the lid. Bon appétit!

Per serving: Calories: 397; Fat: 27.8g; Carbs: 3.8g; Protein: 30.3g; Sugars: 0.9g; Fiber: 0.7g

172. Pork Butt Roast with Sage and Applesauce [AF]

(Ready in about 1 hour | Servings 5)

Ingredients

1 tablespoon olive oil
2 tablespoons soy sauce
2 pounds pork butt
Kosher salt and freshly ground black pepper, to taste
2 cloves garlic, smashed
2 sprigs fresh sage, chopped
1 cup applesauce

Directions

Toss all the ingredients, except for the applesauce, in a lightly greased Air Fryer basket. Secure the air-frying lid.

Cook the pork butt at 360 degrees F for 45 minutes, turning it over halfway through the cooking time.

Top the pork butt with the applesauce and choose the "Broil" function; continue cooking for a further 10 minutes.

Let it rest for a few minutes before slicing and serving. Bon appétit!

Per serving: Calories: 402; Fat: 26.2g; Carbs: 7.4g; Protein: 32.3g; Sugars: 5.8g; Fiber: 0.7g

173. Rustic Pork Soup [PC]

(Ready in about 40 minutes | Servings 4)

Ingredients

1 tablespoon lard
1 pound pork stew meat, diced
1 teaspoon onion powder
1 large carrot, trimmed and sliced
4 cups chicken bone broth
1 bay laurel

Directions

Melt the lard on the "Sauté" function; brown the pork for about 4 minutes, stirring periodically to ensure even cooking.

Add the other ingredients to the inner pot and stir to combine; secure the pressure-cooking lid.

Pressure cook for 35 minutes at High pressure. Once cooking is complete, use a quick pressure release; carefully remove the lid. Bon appétit!

Per serving: Calories: 247; Fat: 12.8g; Carbs: 1.5g; Protein: 29.3g; Sugars: 0.2g; Fiber: 0.2g

174. Herbed Breakfast Sausage [AF]

(Ready in about 20 minutes | Servings 4)

Ingredients

1 pound ground pork
1 small onion, chopped
1 garlic clove, minced
4 tablespoons tortilla chips, crushed
1 teaspoon fresh sage, minced
1 teaspoon fresh coriander, minced
1 tablespoon fresh parsley, minced
1 egg, beaten
1/2 teaspoon smoked paprika
Sea salt and freshly ground black pepper, to taste

Directions

In a mixing bowl, thoroughly combine all the ingredients. Form the mixture into four patties. Secure the air-frying lid.

Air fry the burgers at 380 degrees F for about 15 minutes or until cooked through; make sure to turn them over halfway through the cooking time. Bon appétit!

Per serving: Calories: 386; Fat: 28.7g; Carbs: 9.2g; Protein: 22.3g; Sugars: 1g; Fiber: 1.1g

175. Italian Meatballs with Marinara Sauce [PC]

(Ready in about 15 minutes | Servings 4)

Ingredients

1 pound ground pork
1 small onion, chopped
1 teaspoon garlic, minced
1/2 cup breadcrumbs
1 egg, whisked
Kosher salt and freshly ground black pepper, to taste
1 cup marinara sauce
1/2 cup chicken bone broth

Directions

Press the "Sauté" button to preheat your Instant Pot Duo Crisp. Then, brown the ground pork for about 3 minutes, crumbling with a wide spatula.

Stir in the onion and garlic and continue cooking for about 2 minutes or until they are tender and fragrant.

Add the breadcrumbs, egg, salt, and black pepper to the meatball mixture; shape the mixture into balls. Thoroughly combine the marinara sauce and broth in the inner pot; fold in the meatballs.

Secure the pressure-cooking lid. Pressure cook for 9 minutes at High pressure. Once cooking is complete, use a quick pressure release; carefully remove the lid. Bon appétit!

Per serving: Calories: 416; Fat: 27.4g; Carbs: 16.6g; Protein: 25.1g; Sugars: 4.3g; Fiber: 2.2g

176. Mediterranean-Style Pork Kebabs [AF]

(Ready in about 20 minutes | Servings 4)

Ingredients
- 1 pound pork tenderloin, cubed
- 1 pound bell peppers, diced
- 1 pound eggplant, diced
- 1 tablespoon olive oil
- 1 tablespoon parsley, chopped
- 1 tablespoon cilantro, chopped
- Sea salt and ground black pepper, to taste

Directions
Toss all the ingredients in a mixing bowl until well coated on all sides.

Thread the ingredients onto skewers and place them in the Air Fryer basket. Secure the air-frying lid.

Then, cook the skewers at 400 degrees F for approximately 15 minutes, turning them over halfway through the cooking time.

Bon appétit!

Per serving: Calories: 344; Fat: 16.3g; Carbs: 18g; Protein: 32.6g; Sugars: 10.1g; Fiber: 5.3g

177. Fall Off the Bone St Louis Style Ribs [PC]

(Ready in about 40 minutes | Servings 4)

Ingredients
- 1 ½ pounds St. Louis-style ribs
- 1 tablespoon granulated sugar
- 2 garlic cloves, minced
- 2 tablespoons soy sauce
- 1 cup tomato sauce
- Sea salt and ground black pepper, to taste

Directions
Stir all the ingredients into the inner pot of your Instant Pot Duo Crisp; gently stir to combine and secure the pressure-cooking lid.

Pressure cook for 35 minutes at High pressure. Once cooking is complete, use a quick pressure release; carefully remove the lid.

Bon appétit!

Per serving: Calories: 426; Fat: 21.7g; Carbs: 17.9g; Protein: 35.5g; Sugars: 10.7g; Fiber: 4.4g

178. Summer Pork Ribs [AF]

(Ready in about 40 minutes | Servings 4)

Ingredients
- 1 ½ pound baby back ribs
- 2 tablespoons olive oil
- 1 teaspoon smoked paprika
- 1 teaspoon garlic powder
- 1 teaspoon onion powder
- 1/2 teaspoon ground cumin
- 1 teaspoon mustard powder
- 1 teaspoon dried thyme
- Coarse sea salt and freshly cracked black pepper, to season

Directions
Toss all the ingredients in a lightly greased Air Fryer basket. Secure the air-frying lid.

Air fry the pork ribs at 350 degrees F for 35 minutes, turning them over halfway through the cooking time. Bon appétit!

Per serving: Calories: 440; Fat: 33.3g; Carbs: 1.8g; Protein: 33.7g; Sugars: 0.1g; Fiber: 0.4g

179. Pork with Green Beans [PC]

(Ready in about 10 minutes | Servings 5)

Ingredients
- 2 tablespoons butter
- 1 ½ pounds pork rib chops
- 1 tablespoon mirin
- 1 cup chicken bone broth
- 2 tablespoons orange juice
- 2 tablespoons honey
- 2 tablespoons balsamic vinegar
- 1 pound green beans, trimmed

Directions
Melt the butter on the "Sauté" function; once hot, sear the pork chops for 3 to 4 minutes per side or until no longer pink.

Add in the remaining ingredients and secure the pressure-cooking lid.

Pressure cook for 6 minutes at High pressure. Once cooking is complete, use a quick pressure release; carefully remove the lid.

Serve warm and enjoy!

Per serving: Calories: 288; Fat: 11.4g; Carbs: 15.5g; Protein: 31.4g; Sugars: 11.3g; Fiber: 2.5g

180. Asian-Style Back Ribs [PC+AF]

(Ready in about 40 minutes | Servings 4)

Ingredients
- 1 tablespoon sesame oil
- 1 ½ pounds back ribs
- 1/2 cup tomato sauce
- 1 tablespoon soy sauce
- 2 tablespoons agave syrup
- 2 tablespoons rice wine

Directions
Stir all the ingredients into the inner pot of your Instant Pot Duo Crisp; gently stir to combine and secure the pressure-cooking lid.

Pressure cook for 35 minutes at High pressure. Once cooking is complete, use a quick pressure release; carefully remove the lid.

Secure the air-frying lid. Press the "Broil" button and continue cooking an additional 5 minutes or until they reach around 195 degrees F.

Bon appétit!

Per serving: Calories: 470; Fat: 30.2g; Carbs: 15.6g; Protein: 34.4g; Sugars: 12.1g; Fiber: 2g

BEEF

181. Roast Beef Sandwiches [PC]

(Ready in about 30 minutes | Servings 4)

Ingredients

- 2 tablespoons butter
- 1 ½ pounds beef rump roast
- Kosher salt and ground black pepper, to taste
- 1 teaspoon smoked paprika
- 4 cloves garlic, minced
- 4 tablespoons brandy
- 2 tablespoons Worcestershire sauce
- 1 cup beef broth
- 1 ciabatta loaf, cut into 4 pieces

Directions

Place all the ingredients, except for the ciabatta loaf, in the inner pot of your Instant Pot Duo Crisp; secure the pressure-cooking lid.

Pressure cook for 30 minutes at High pressure. Once cooking is complete, use a natural pressure release; carefully remove the lid.

Cut the beef into strips and assemble the sandwich with the ciabatta loaf. Bon appétit!

Per serving: Calories: 612; Fat: 20.4g; Carbs: 60.1g; Protein: 45.5g; Sugars: 2.4g; Fiber: 3.3g

182. Herbed Beef Eye Round Roast [AF]

(Ready in about 55 minutes | Servings 4)

Ingredients

- 1 ½ pounds beef eye round roast
- 1 tablespoon olive oil
- 1 onion, sliced
- Sea salt and ground black pepper, to taste
- 1 rosemary sprig
- 1 thyme sprig

Directions

Toss the beef with the olive oil, salt, and black pepper; place the beef in the Air Fryer basket.

Air fry the beef eye round roast at 390 degrees F for 45 minutes, turning it over halfway through the cooking time.

Top the beef with the onion, rosemary, and thyme. Continue to cook an additional 10 minutes. Enjoy!

Per serving: Calories: 286; Fat: 13.6g; Carbs: 1.2g; Protein: 35.1g; Sugars: 0.6g; Fiber: 0.1g

183. Asian-Style Beef Bowl [PC]

(Ready in about 35 minutes | Servings 4)

Ingredients

- 1 ½ pounds top sirloin steak
- 1 large onion, diced
- 3 cloves garlic, minced
- 1/4 cup soy sauce
- 1 bell pepper, diced
- 1 pound Chinese cabbage, cut into wedges
- 2 cups jasmine rice, cooked

Directions

Place the beef, onion, garlic, soy sauce, and bell pepper in the inner pot of your Instant Pot Duo Crisp; secure the pressure-cooking lid.

Pressure cook for 30 minutes at High pressure. Once cooking is complete, use a quick pressure release; carefully remove the lid.

Add in the Chinese cabbage and continue cooking for a further 3 minutes. Spoon the beef mixture over hot jasmine rice and enjoy!

Per serving: Calories: 586; Fat: 26.5g; Carbs: 43.3g; Protein: 41.9g; Sugars: 7.1g; Fiber: 3.3g

184. Homemade Beef Burgers [AF]

(Ready in about 20 minutes | Servings 3)

Ingredients

- 3/4 pound ground beef
- 2 cloves garlic, minced
- 1 small onion, chopped
- Kosher salt and ground black pepper, to taste
- 3 hamburger buns

Directions

Mix the beef, garlic, onion, salt, and black pepper until everything is well combined. Form the mixture into three patties. Secure the air-frying lid.

Air fry the burgers at 380 degrees F for about 15 minutes or until cooked through; make sure to turn them over halfway through the cooking time.

Serve your burgers on the prepared buns and enjoy!

Per serving: Calories: 392; Fat: 16.6g; Carbs: 32.3g; Protein: 28.1g; Sugars: 5.3g; Fiber: 1.8g

185. French Au Jus [PC]

(Ready in about 45 minutes | Servings 5)

Ingredients

- 2 pounds top sirloin, sliced
- 1 packet Au Jus mix
- 2 cups water

Directions

Place all the ingredients in the inner pot of your Instant Pot Duo Crisp; secure the pressure-cooking lid.

Pressure cook for 40 minutes at High pressure. Once cooking is complete, use a quick pressure release; carefully remove the lid.

Bon appétit!

Per serving: Calories: 269; Fat: 10.7g; Carbs: 0.5g; Protein: 37.4g; Sugars: 0.1g; Fiber: 0.8g

186. Skirt Steak Sliders [AF]

(Ready in about 20 minutes | Servings 4)

Ingredients

- 1 ½ pounds skirt steak
- 1 teaspoon steak dry rub
- 1/2 teaspoon cayenne pepper
- Sea salt and ground black pepper, to taste
- 2 tablespoons olive oil
- 2 tablespoons Dijon mustard
- 8 Hawaiian buns

Directions

Toss the beef with the spices and olive oil; place the beef in the Air Fryer basket. Secure the air-frying lid.

Cook the beef at 400 degrees F for 15 minutes, turning it over halfway through the cooking time.

Cut the beef into slices and serve them with mustard and Hawaiian buns. Bon appétit!

Per serving: Calories: 544; Fat: 20.7g; Carbs: 44g; Protein: 44g; Sugars: 6.1g; Fiber: 2.3g

187. Wine-Braised Sirloin Steak [PC]

(Ready in about 45 minutes | Servings 5)

Ingredients

1 tablespoon butter
2 pounds sirloin steak, sliced
1 Spanish pepper, deseeded and chopped
2 garlic cloves, crushed
1 onion, chopped
1 tablespoon fresh rosemary, chopped
1 cup dry red wine
1 cup beef stock

Directions

Melt the butter on the "Sauté" function. After that, cook the steaks for approximately 5 minutes or until no longer pink on all sides.

Add in the remaining ingredients and secure the pressure-cooking lid.

Pressure cook for 40 minutes at High pressure. Once cooking is complete, use a quick pressure release; carefully remove the lid.

Serve warm and enjoy!

Per serving: Calories: 323; Fat: 16.5g; Carbs: 3.6g; Protein: 35.1g; Sugars: 1.4g; Fiber: 0.6g

188. Easy Paprika Steak [AF]

(Ready in about 15 minutes | Servings 5)

Ingredients

2 pounds flank steak
2 tablespoons olive oil
1 teaspoon paprika
Sea salt and ground black pepper, to taste

Directions

Toss the steak with the remaining ingredients; place the steak in the Air Fryer basket. Secure the air-frying lid.

Cook the steak at 400 degrees F for 12 minutes, turning over halfway through the cooking time.

Bon appétit!

Per serving: Calories: 299; Fat: 14.5g; Carbs: 02g; Protein: 38.5g; Sugars: 0g; Fiber: 0.2g

189. Kielbasa Beef Soup [PC]

(Ready in about 30 minutes | Servings 4)

Ingredients

1/2 pound Polish beef sausage, sliced
1 pound beef stew meat
1 yellow onion, chopped
1 bell pepper, seeded and chopped
2 carrots, chopped
1 celery stalk, chopped
4 cups beef stock
1 cup frozen corn

Directions

Sear the sausage and beef stew meat on the "Sauté" function until no longer pink on all sides.

Add in the onion, pepper, carrot, celery, and beef stock; secure the pressure-cooking lid.

Pressure cook for 20 minutes at High pressure. Once cooking is complete, use a quick pressure release; carefully remove the lid.

Fold in the frozen corn; let it stand in the residual heat for 5 minutes or until the corn is thoroughly warmed.

Ladle the soup into individual bowls and enjoy!

Per serving: Calories: 418; Fat: 23.2g; Carbs: 16g; Protein: 34.5g; Sugars: 4.2g; Fiber: 2.5g

190. Beef Breakfast Cups [AF]

(Ready in about 30 minutes | Servings 4)

Ingredients

Meatloaves:
1 pound ground beef
1/4 cup seasoned breadcrumbs
1/4 cup parmesan cheese, grated
1 small onion, minced
2 garlic cloves, pressed
1 egg, beaten
Sea salt and ground black pepper, to taste
Glaze:
4 tablespoons tomato sauce
1 tablespoon brown sugar
1 tablespoon Dijon mustard

Directions

Thoroughly combine all the ingredients for the meatloaves until everything is well combined.

Scrape the beef mixture into lightly oiled silicone cups and transfer them to the Air Fryer cooking basket. Secure the air-frying lid.

Cook the beef cups at 380 degrees F for 20 minutes.

In the meantime, mix the remaining ingredients for the glaze. Then, spread the glaze on the top of each muffin. Press the "Broil" button and continue to cook for another 5 minutes. Bon appétit!

Per serving: Calories: 355; Fat: 18.6g; Carbs: 14.2g; Protein: 25.7g; Sugars: 6.2g; Fiber: 2.3g

191. Herbed Top Sirloin Roast [PC]

(Ready in about 45 minutes | Servings 4)

Ingredients

1 tablespoon butter
2 pounds top sirloin
1 tablespoon steak seasoning mix
2 tablespoons olive oil
1 ½ cups vegetable broth
4 garlic cloves, sliced
1 tablespoon parsley, chopped
1 sprig thyme, chopped
2 sprigs rosemary, chopped
1 onion, peeled and diced

Directions

Press the "Sauté" button to preheat your Instant Pot Duo Crisp; then, melt the butter and sear the beef for about 4 minutes until no longer pink.

Stir in the remaining ingredients and secure the pressure-cooking lid.

Pressure cook for 40 minutes at High pressure. Once cooking is complete, use a quick pressure release; carefully remove the lid.

Bon appétit!

Per serving: Calories: 441; Fat: 23.1g; Carbs: 9.1g; Protein: 47.8g; Sugars: 5g; Fiber: 1.1g

192. Tangy and Herby London Broil [AF]

(Ready in about 30 minutes + marinating time | Servings 4)

Ingredients

1 pound London broil
Kosher salt and ground black pepper, to taste
2 tablespoons olive oil
1 small lemon, freshly squeezed
3 cloves garlic, minced
1 tablespoon fresh parsley, chopped
1 tablespoon fresh coriander, chopped

Directions

Toss the beef with the remaining ingredients and let it marinate for an hour.

Place the beef in a lightly oiled Air Fryer cooking basket and discard the marinade.

Choose the "Roast" button; cook the beef at 400 degrees F for 28 minutes, turning it over halfway through the cooking time.

Bon appétit!

Per serving: Calories: 227; Fat: 13.6g; Carbs: 27g; Protein: 23.8g; Sugars: 0.9g; Fiber: 0.3g

193. Bœuf à la Bourguignonne [PC]

(Ready in about 45 minutes | Servings 4)

Ingredients

2 ounces bacon, diced
1 large onion, sliced
4 cloves garlic, minced
1 ½ pounds beef stew meat, cut into bite-sized pieces
1 carrot, sliced
1 cup dry red wine
1 ½ cups roasted vegetable broth
1/2 cup tomato sauce
2 bay leaves

Directions

Preheat your Instant Pot Duo Crisp on the "Sauté" function; then, sear the bacon, stirring and crumbling with a fork, until crisp.

Then, sweat the onion and garlic until just tender and aromatic.

Add in the remaining ingredients and gently stir to combine; secure the pressure-cooking lid.

Pressure cook for 35 minutes at High pressure. Once cooking is complete, use a natural pressure release for 10 minutes; carefully remove the lid.

Bon appétit!

Per serving: Calories: 388; Fat: 16.5g; Carbs: 12.7g; Protein: 39g; Sugars: 6g; Fiber: 2.7g

194. Rump Roast with Red Wine [PC]

(Ready in about 55 minutes | Servings 4)

Ingredients

1 ½ pounds rump roast
2 tablespoons olive oil
Sea salt and ground black pepper, to taste
1 teaspoon Italian seasoning mix
1 onion, sliced
2 cloves garlic, peeled
1/4 cup red wine

Directions

Toss the rump roast with the remaining ingredients; place the rump roast in the inner pot of your Instant Pot Duo Crisp.

Secure the pressure-cooking lid. Choose the "Sous Vide" mode and cook for 3 hours. Once cooking is complete, use a quick pressure release; carefully remove the lid.

Press the "Broil" button and cook for 5 to 6 minutes or until it's done to your liking.

Bon appétit!

Per serving: Calories: 297; Fat: 16.9g; Carbs: 0.7g; Protein: 35.1g; Sugars: 0.2g; Fiber: 0.1g

195. Beef and Bacon Mac and Cheese [PC+AF]

(Ready in about 45 minutes | Servings 5)

Ingredients

2 tablespoons bacon bits
1 onion, diced
2 cloves garlic, crushed
8 ounces penne pasta
1 ½ pounds ground chuck
1 tablespoon Cajun seasoning mix
2 tomatoes, crushed
1 cup chicken bone broth
1 cup mozzarella cheese, shredded

Directions

Press the "Sauté" button and crisp up the bacon bits. After that, cook the onion and garlic in the bacon drippings for about 3 minutes.

Add in the pasta, ground chuck, Cajun seasoning mix, tomatoes, and broth. Gently stir to combine and secure the pressure-cooking lid.

Pressure cook for 35 minutes at High pressure. Once cooking is complete, use a quick pressure release; carefully remove the lid.

Top the casserole with mozzarella cheese and cover with the air-frying lid; let it cook for 5 minutes or until the cheese melts.

Bon appétit!

Per serving: Calories: 396; Fat: 6.5g; Carbs: 42.3g; Protein: 44.9g; Sugars: 2.6g; Fiber: 6.7g

196. Summer Beef Brisket [AF]

(Ready in about 1 hour 10 minutes | Servings 4)

Ingredients

1 ½ pounds beef brisket
1/4 cup barbecue sauce
2 tablespoons soy sauce

Directions

Toss the beef with the remaining ingredients; place the beef in the Air Fryer basket. Secure the air-frying lid.

Cook the beef at 390 degrees F for 15 minutes, turn the beef over and turn the temperature to 360 degrees F.

Continue to cook the beef for 55 minutes more. Bon appétit!

Per serving: Calories: 391; Fat: 26.7g; Carbs: 9.5g; Protein: 25.1g; Sugars: 7g; Fiber: 0.3g

197. Beef and Mushroom Casserole [PC]

(Ready in about 25 minutes | Servings 4)

Ingredients

2 tablespoons butter, divided
1 onion, chopped
3 cloves garlic, minced
1 pound cremini mushrooms, sliced
8 ounces egg noodles
1 pound beef steaks, cut into strips
1/2 cup dry white wine
1 cup beef broth
1 bay leaf
Sea salt and ground black pepper, to taste

Directions

Melt the butter on the "Sauté" function and cook the onion until it has softened.

Stir the other ingredients into the inner pot of your Instant Pot Duo Crisp; secure the pressure-cooking lid.

Pressure cook for 20 minutes at High pressure. Once cooking is complete, use a quick pressure release; carefully remove the lid.

Bon appétit!

Per serving: Calories: 507; Fat: 17.6g; Carbs: 48.2g; Protein: 37.8g; Sugars: 5.1g; Fiber: 3.9g

198. T-Bone Steak Salad [AF]

(Ready in about 15 minutes | Servings 5)

Ingredients

2 pounds T-bone steak
1 teaspoon garlic powder
Sea salt and ground black pepper, to taste
2 tablespoons lime juice
1/4 cup extra-virgin olive oil
1 bell pepper, seeded and sliced
1 red onion, sliced
1 tomato, diced

Directions

Toss the steak with the garlic powder, salt, and black pepper; place the steak in the Air Fryer cooking basket. Secure the air-frying lid.

Cook the steak at 400 degrees F for 12 minutes, turning it over halfway through the cooking time.

Cut the steak into slices and add in the remaining ingredients. Serve at room temperature or well-chilled.

Bon appétit!

Per serving: Calories: 316; Fat: 16g; Carbs: 3.7g; Protein: 38.1g; Sugars: 1.8g; Fiber: 0.7g

199. Italian Osso Buco [PC]

(Ready in about 45 minutes | Servings 5)

Ingredients

2 tablespoons olive oil
2 pounds beef shank, sliced
1 tablespoon dried porcini mushrooms, dehydrated
2 carrots, trimmed and sliced
1 large onion, sliced
1/2 cup dry white wine
2 cups vegetable broth
1/2 cup tomato puree

Directions

Press the "Sauté" button and heat the olive oil; sear the beef shanks for about 4 minutes or until no longer pink.

Stir in the remaining ingredients and secure the pressure-cooking lid.

Pressure cook for 40 minutes at High pressure. Once cooking is complete, use a quick pressure release; carefully remove the lid.

Serve in individual bowls. Bon appétit!

Per serving: Calories: 327; Fat: 15.1g; Carbs: 5.7g; Protein: 42.8g; Sugars: 2.5g; Fiber: 1.1g

200. Butter and Brandy Roast [AF]

(Ready in about 55 minutes | Servings 4)

Ingredients

1 ½ pounds rump roast
Ground black pepper and kosher salt, to taste
1 teaspoon paprika
2 tablespoons olive oil
1/4 cup brandy
2 tablespoons cold butter

Directions

Toss the rump roast with the black pepper, salt, paprika, olive oil, and brandy; place the rump roast in a lightly oiled Air Fryer cooking basket.

Secure the air-frying lid.

Cook the rump roast at 390 degrees F for 50 minutes, turning it over halfway through the cooking time.

Serve with cold butter and enjoy!

Per serving: Calories: 390; Fat: 22.4g; Carbs: 1.4g; Protein: 35.1g; Sugars: 0.6g; Fiber: 0.4g

201. Montreal-Style Beef [PC]

(Ready in about 40 minutes | Servings 5)

Ingredients

2 pounds beef top sirloin
1 tablespoon Montreal seasoning mix
1 shallot, cut into wedges
1 bell pepper, sliced
2 garlic cloves, chopped
1 cup beef bone broth

Directions

Place all the ingredients in the inner pot of your Instant Pot Duo Crisp; secure the pressure-cooking lid.

Pressure cook for 35 minutes at High pressure. Once cooking is complete, use a quick pressure release; carefully remove the lid.

Bon appétit!

Per serving: Calories: 279; Fat: 10.6g; Carbs: 6.2g; Protein: 39.8g; Sugars: 2.8g; Fiber: 1.1g

202. Filet Mignon with Herbs [AF]

(Ready in about 15 minutes | Servings 4)

Ingredients

1 ½ pounds filet mignon
Sea salt and ground black pepper, to taste
2 tablespoons olive oil
1 teaspoon dried rosemary
1 teaspoon dried thyme
1 teaspoon dried basil
2 cloves garlic, minced

Directions

Toss the beef with the remaining ingredients; place the beef in the Air Fryer cooking basket.

Secure the air-frying lid.

Cook the beef at 400 degrees F for 14 minutes, turning it over halfway through the cooking time.

Enjoy!

Per serving: Calories: 385; Fat: 26g; Carbs: 3.2g; Protein: 36.1g; Sugars: 0.5g; Fiber: 0.3g

203. Traditional Irish Beef Stew [PC]

(Ready in about 30 minutes | Servings 4)

Ingredients

1 tablespoon tallow, at room temperature
1 pound chuck roast, cubed
1 onion, chopped
4 garlic cloves, minced
2 carrots, sliced
2 cups Brussels sprouts, trimmed
2 cups beef broth
1/2 cup ale beer
1/4 cup tomato paste
1 bay laurel

Directions

Melt the tallow on the "Sauté" function; cook the chuck roast cubes for about 5 minutes, stirring periodically with a wide spatula.

Add in the other ingredients gently stir to combine, and secure the pressure-cooking lid.

Pressure cook for 20 minutes at High pressure. Once cooking is complete, use a natural pressure release; carefully remove the lid.

Ladle the soup into individual bowls and enjoy!

Per serving: Calories: 316; Fat: 16g; Carbs: 13.1g; Protein: 30.5g; Sugars: 4.6g; Fiber: 3g

204. Chinese-Style Beef [AF]

(Ready in about 55 minutes | Servings 4)

Ingredients

1 ½ pounds beef tenderloin, sliced
2 tablespoons sesame oil
1 teaspoon Five-spice powder
2 garlic cloves, minced
1 teaspoon fresh ginger, peeled and grated
2 tablespoons soy sauce

Directions

Toss the beef tenderloin with the remaining ingredients; then place it in the Air Fryer cooking basket.

Secure the air-frying lid.

Cook the beef tenderloin at 400 degrees F for 20 minutes, turning it over halfway through the cooking time.

Enjoy!

Per serving: Calories: 326; Fat: 18.7g; Carbs: 3g; Protein: 35.7g; Sugars: 1.6g; Fiber: 0.3g

205. Smoked Beef Brisket [PC]

(Ready in about 1 hour | Servings 5)

Ingredients

2 ½ pounds corned beef brisket
1 onion, cut into wedges
2 bell peppers, quartered
2 garlic cloves, chopped
1 teaspoon liquid smoke
1/4 cup honey
1 cup tomato sauce
1/2 cup beef stock

Directions

Add all the ingredients to the inner pot of your Instant Pot Duo Crisp; secure the pressure-cooking lid.

Pressure cook for 55 minutes at High pressure. Once cooking is complete, use a natural pressure release; carefully remove the lid.

Bon appétit!

Per serving: Calories: 587; Fat: 35.1g; Carbs: 32g; Protein: 35.6g; Sugars: 23g; Fiber: 4.1g

206. Classic Roast Beef [PC+AF]

(Ready in about 50 minutes | Servings 4)

Ingredients

1 ½ pounds eye round roast
4 cloves garlic, peeled and thinly sliced
2 tablespoons olive oil
Kosher salt and ground black pepper, to taste

Directions

Pierce the beef with a sharp knife and insert the garlic slices into the holes.

Toss the meat with the oil, salt, and black pepper and transfer it to the inner pot; secure the pressure-cooking lid.

Pressure cook for 40 minutes at High pressure. Once cooking is complete, use a quick pressure release; carefully remove the lid.

Secure the air-frying lid. Choose the "Roast" function and cook at 390 degrees F for 10 minutes, turning it over halfway through the cooking time.

Enjoy!

Per serving: Calories: 301; Fat: 11.5g; Carbs: 3g; Protein: 38.1g; Sugars: 0.8g; Fiber: 0.4g

207. Pearl Barley and Round Beef Soup [PC]

(Ready in about 25 minutes | Servings 4)

Ingredients

1 ½ pounds beef round roast, slice into strips
2 tablespoons olive oil
1 onion, chopped
1 cup dry red wine
1 cup tomato puree
2 cups beef broth
2 medium carrots, sliced
1 stalk celery, sliced
1/2 cup pearl barley

Directions

Add all the ingredients to the inner pot of your Instant Pot Duo Crisp; secure the pressure-cooking lid.

Pressure cook for 22 minutes at High pressure. Once cooking is complete, use a quick pressure release; carefully remove the lid.

Ladle your soup into serving bowls and enjoy!

Per serving: Calories: 432; Fat: 17.5g; Carbs: 28g; Protein: 38g; Sugars: 4.4g; Fiber: 5.7g

208. Decadent Coulotte Roast [AF]

(Ready in about 55 minutes | Servings 5)

Ingredients

2 pounds Coulotte roast
2 tablespoons butter
Kosher salt and ground black pepper, to taste
1 teaspoon ground allspice
1 teaspoon garlic, minced

Directions

Toss the beef with the remaining ingredients; place the beef in the Air Fryer cooking basket.

Secure the air-frying lid.

Cook the beef at 390 degrees F for 55 minutes, turning it over halfway through the cooking time.

Enjoy!

Per serving: Calories: 300; Fat: 15.5g; Carbs: 1.2g; Protein: 37.1g; Sugars: 0.4g; Fiber: 0.2g

209. Ribeye Steak Salad [PC]

(Ready in about 40 minutes | Servings 4)

Ingredients

1 ½ pounds boneless ribeye steak, slice into strips
2 cups water
2 bay leaves
1 rosemary sprig
2 thyme sprigs
1 bay leaf
2 tablespoons apple cider vinegar
1/4 cup extra-virgin olive oil
1 red onion, thinly sliced
1 Greek cucumber, sliced
1 tomato, sliced
3 ounces Feta cheese, crumbled

Directions

Add the boneless ribeye steak, water, bay leaves, rosemary, thyme, and bay leaf to the inner pot of your Instant Pot Duo Crisp; secure the pressure-cooking lid.

Pressure cook for 35 minutes at High pressure. Once cooking is complete, use a quick pressure release; carefully remove the lid.

Place the beef in a salad bowl along with the vinegar, olive oil, onion, Greek cucumber, and tomato. Toss to combine and top your salad with the crumbled Feta cheese.

Serve at room temperature or well-chilled. Enjoy!

Per serving: Calories: 423; Fat: 24.2g; Carbs: 1.3g; Protein: 48.7g; Sugars: 1.1g; Fiber: 0.1g

210. Italian Sausage with Baby Potatoes [AF]

(Ready in about 20 minutes | Servings 4)

Ingredients

8 baby potatoes, scrubbed and halved
4 smoked beef sausages
1 teaspoon Italian seasoning mix

Directions

Toss all the ingredients in a lightly oiled Air Fryer cooking basket.

Secure the air-frying lid.

Cook the sausage and potatoes at 400 degrees F for 15 minutes, tossing the basket halfway through the cooking time.

Serve warm and enjoy!

Per serving: Calories: 625; Fat: 33g; Carbs: 62.1g; Protein: 20.7g; Sugars: 2.6g; Fiber: 7.4g

211. London Broil Medley [PC]

(Ready in about 40 minutes | Servings 5)

Ingredients

2 tablespoons sesame oil
2 pounds London broil, sliced
2 garlic cloves, minced
1/2 pound Vidalia onions
1/4 cup tamari sauce
1/2 cup vegetable broth

Directions

Press the "Sauté" button and heat the sesame oil. Then, sear the London broil until no longer pink on all sides.

Add in the remaining ingredients and secure the pressure-cooking lid.

Pressure cook for 35 minutes at High pressure. Once cooking is complete, use a quick pressure release; carefully remove the lid.

Serve warm and enjoy!

Per serving: Calories: 317; Fat: 19g; Carbs: 1.4g; Protein: 38.2g; Sugars: 0.5g; Fiber: 0.3g

212. Broccoli and Beef Fritters [AF]

(Ready in about 20 minutes | Servings 4)

Ingredients

1 pound beef
1/2 pound broccoli, minced
1 small onion, chopped
2 garlic cloves, minced
Sea salt and ground black pepper, to taste
1 tablespoon tamari sauce

Directions

In a mixing bowl, thoroughly combine all the ingredients. Shape the mixture into four patties.

Place the patties in the Air fryer basket. Secure the air-frying lid.

Cook the burgers at 380 degrees F for about 15 minutes or until cooked through; make sure to turn them over halfway through the cooking time.

Serve the warm patties with a topping of choice. Bon appétit!

Per serving: Calories: 252; Fat: 14.7g; Carbs: 7g; Protein: 24.1g; Sugars: 2.4g; Fiber: 2.1g

213. Saucy Beef Brisket [PC]

(Ready in about 1 hour 25 minutes | Servings 5)

Ingredients

2 tablespoons olive oil
2 ½ pounds beef brisket
1 teaspoon mustard seeds
1 teaspoon fennel seeds
1 teaspoon mixed peppercorns, whole
1 teaspoon smoked paprika
3 cloves garlic, chopped
1/2 cup beef stock
1 cup apple juice

Directions

Press the "Sauté" button to preheat your Instant Pot Duo Crisp; heat the olive oil until sizzling.

Now, cook the beef for approximately 4 minutes per side. Add in the other ingredients and secure the pressure-cooking lid.

Pressure cook for 70 minutes at High pressure. Once cooking is complete, use a natural pressure release for about 10; carefully remove the lid.

Bon appétit!

Per serving: Calories: 527; Fat: 39.5g; Carbs: 7.1g; Protein: 33.6g; Sugars: 4.8g; Fiber: 0.6g

214. Ribeye Steak with Herbed Butter [AF]

(Ready in about 15 minutes | Servings 5)

Ingredients

2 pounds ribeye steaks, bone-in
Kosher salt and freshly ground black pepper, to taste
3 tablespoons butter
1 tablespoon fresh basil, minced
1 tablespoon fresh parsley, minced
2 tablespoons fresh scallions, minced
2 cloves garlic, minced
Kosher salt and freshly ground black pepper, to taste

Directions

Toss the steak with the salt and black pepper; place the steak in a lightly oiled Air Fryer cooking basket. Secure the air-frying lid.

Cook the steak at 400 degrees F for 12 minutes, turning it over halfway through the cooking time.

In the meantime, mix the butter with the remaining ingredients and place it in the refrigerator until well-chilled.

Serve the warm steak with the chilled herb butter and enjoy!

Per serving: Calories: 316; Fat: 18.1g; Carbs: 0.7g; Protein: 37.1g; Sugars: 0.1g; Fiber: 0.1g

215. Easy Beef Curry [PC]

(Ready in about 30 minutes | Servings 4)

Ingredients

1 pound beef top blade steak, cut into bite-sized pieces
2 tablespoons butter, melted
1 cup tomato sauce
1/2 cup chicken bone broth
1 tablespoon fish sauce
2 cloves garlic, pressed
1 bay laurel
1/2 teaspoon whole black peppercorns
2 tablespoons curry powder

Directions

Add all the ingredients to the inner pot of your Instant Pot Duo Crisp; gently stir to combine and secure the pressure-cooking lid.

Pressure cook for 25 minutes at High pressure. Once cooking is complete, use a natural pressure release; carefully remove the lid.

Serve your curry into individual bowls and enjoy!

Per serving: Calories: 339; Fat: 15.3g; Carbs: 16g; Protein: 32.4g; Sugars: 7.4g; Fiber: 5.7g

216. Beef Scotch Tender Steak [AF]

(Ready in about 55 minutes | Servings 4)

Ingredients

1 ½ pounds Scotch tender
2 garlic cloves, pressed
1 tablespoon stone-ground mustard
2 tablespoons balsamic vinegar
2 tablespoons soy sauce
2 tablespoons olive oil
1 teaspoon garlic powder
Kosher salt and ground black pepper, to taste

Directions

Toss the Scotch tender with the remaining ingredients; place the Scotch tender in the Air Fryer cooking basket.

Secure the air-frying lid.

Cook the Scotch tender at 390 degrees F for 55 minutes, turning it over halfway through the cooking time.

Enjoy!

Per serving: Calories: 339; Fat: 19.3g; Carbs: 4.8g; Protein: 36.4g; Sugars: 2.8g; Fiber: 0.5g

217. Buttery Garlicky Steaks [PC+AF]

(Ready in about 45 minutes | Servings 5)

Ingredients

2 tablespoons butter
2 garlic cloves, minced
2 ½ pounds flank steaks
2 sprigs thyme
1 cup chicken bone broth

Directions

Press the "Sauté" button and melt the butter. Sear the steak for about 5 minutes, turning it periodically to ensure even cooking.

Then, sauté the garlic in the pan drippings for 40 seconds or so. Add in the remaining ingredients and secure the pressure-cooking lid.

Pressure cook for 40 minutes at High pressure. Once cooking is complete, use a quick pressure release; carefully remove the lid.

Enjoy!

Per serving: Calories: 361; Fat: 16.2g; Carbs: 1g; Protein: 49.2g; Sugars: 0g; Fiber: 0.1g

218. Ground Beef and Mushroom Cups [AF]

(Ready in about 30 minutes | Servings 4)

Ingredients

1 pound ground beef
1 egg, beaten
1 teaspoon Dijon mustard
Sea salt and ground black pepper, to taste
1/2 onion, minced
1/2 cup mushrooms
1/4 cup seasoned bread crumbs
1 teaspoon Italian seasoning mix
1/2 cup ketchup

Directions

Thoroughly combine all the ingredients, except for the ketchup; mix until everything is well combined.

Scrape the beef mixture into lightly oiled silicone cups and transfer them to the Air Fryer cooking basket.

Secure the air-frying lid. Cook your muffins at 380 degrees F for 20 minutes.

Then, spread ketchup on top of each muffin and press the "Broil" button; continue cooking for another 5 minutes.

Bon appétit!

Per serving: Calories: 305; Fat: 17.1g; Carbs: 12.5g; Protein: 25.6g; Sugars: 8.1g; Fiber: 0.8g

219. Beef Peppery Salad [PC]

(Ready in about 35 minutes | Servings 5)

Ingredients

1 ½ pounds rib-eye steaks, cut small chunks
1 beef bouillon cube
1 cup water
1 bell pepper, sliced
1 red chili pepper, chopped
2 garlic cloves, minced
1 large tomato, diced
1/4 cup extra-virgin olive oil
2 teaspoons fresh lime juice
Sea salt and ground black pepper, to taste

Directions

Put the steaks, bouillon cube, and water into the inner pot of your Instant Pot Duo Crisp. Secure the pressure-cooking lid.

Pressure cook for 30 minutes at High pressure. Once cooking is complete, use a quick pressure release; carefully remove the lid.

Place the beef along with the remaining ingredients in a salad bowl. Toss to combine well and serve well-chilled.

Per serving: Calories: 410; Fat: 32.6g; Carbs: 4.5g; Protein: 25.8g; Sugars: 2.3g; Fiber: 1g

220. Classic Beef Parmigiana [AF]

(Ready in about 20 minutes | Servings 4)

Ingredients

1 pound filet mignon
Sea salt and ground black pepper, to season
1 teaspoon red pepper flakes
1 teaspoon rosemary, finely chopped
2 tablespoons olive oil
1 cup parmesan cheese, preferably freshly grated

Directions

Toss the filet mignon with the salt, black pepper, red pepper, rosemary, and olive oil; place the filet mignon in the Air Fryer cooking basket.

Secure the air-frying lid.

Cook the filet mignon at 400 degrees F for 14 minutes, turning it over halfway through the cooking time.

Top with the cheese and continue cooking an additional 4 minutes or until the cheese is melted and bubbly.

Enjoy!

Per serving: Calories: 382; Fat: 26.5g; Carbs: 4.9g; Protein: 31.1g; Sugars: 0.6g; Fiber: 0.2g

221. Beef Sausage with Yellow Potatoes [PC]

(Ready in about 10 minutes | Servings 4)

Ingredients

1 pound beef sausage, sliced
1 pound yellow potatoes, peeled and diced
1 cup vegetable broth
2 bay leaves

Directions

Simply throw all the ingredients into the inner pot; gently stir to combine and secure the pressure-cooking lid.

Pressure cook for 8 minutes at High pressure. Once cooking is complete, use a quick pressure release; carefully remove the lid.

Serve warm and enjoy!

Per serving: Calories: 429; Fat: 30.2g; Carbs: 22.6g; Protein: 15.8g; Sugars: 0.8g; Fiber: 2.6g

222. Aromatic Porterhouse Steak [AF]

(Ready in about 15 minutes | Servings 4)

Ingredients

1 ½ pounds Porterhouse steak
1 tablespoon olive oil
Kosher salt and ground black pepper, to taste
1/2 teaspoon cayenne pepper
1 teaspoon dried parsley
1 teaspoon dried oregano
1/2 teaspoon dried basil
2 tablespoons butter
2 garlic cloves, minced

Directions

Toss the steak with the remaining ingredients; place the steak in the Air Fryer cooking basket.

Secure the air-frying lid.

Cook the steak at 400 degrees F for 12 minutes, turning it over halfway through the cooking time.

Bon appétit!

Per serving: Calories: 326; Fat: 19.6g; Carbs: 1.9g; Protein: 35.6g; Sugars: 0.6g; Fiber: 0.4g

223. Pakistani Karahi Keema [PC]

(Ready in about 15 minutes | Servings 5)

Ingredients

1 tablespoon sesame oil
1 onion, chopped
2 cloves garlic, minced
1 ½ pounds ground chuck
1 pound white potatoes, peeled and diced
1 red chili pepper, minced
1 tablespoon fresh ginger, grated
1 teaspoon garam masala
2 cups beef bone broth

Directions

Choose the "Sauté" function and heat the oil; once hot, cook the onion, garlic, and ground meat until the vegetables are tender and the meat is no longer pink.

Stir in the remaining ingredients and secure the pressure-cooking lid.

Pressure cook for 10 minutes at High pressure. Once cooking is complete, use a quick pressure release; carefully remove the lid.

Bon appétit!

Per serving: Calories: 382; Fat: 20.2g; Carbs: 21.5g; Protein: 28g; Sugars: 2.3g; Fiber: 2.4g

224. Rosemary Garlicky Steak [AF]

(Ready in about 20 minutes | Servings 4)

Ingredients

1 pound ribeye steak, bone-in
2 tablespoons butter, room temperature
2 garlic cloves, minced
Sea salt and ground black pepper, to taste
2 rosemary sprigs, leaves picked, chopped

Directions

Toss the ribeye steak with the butter, garlic, salt, black pepper, and rosemary; place the steak in the Air Fryer cooking basket.

Secure the air-frying lid.

Cook the ribeye steak at 400 degrees F for 15 minutes, turning it over halfway through the cooking time.

Bon appétit!

Per serving: Calories: 263; Fat: 17.8g; Carbs: 3.7g; Protein: 22.7g; Sugars: 0.5g; Fiber: 0.2g

225. Asian-Style Round Steak [PC]

(Ready in about 35 minutes | Servings 4)

Ingredients

2 tablespoons sesame oil
1 ½ pounds top round steak, cut into chunks
1 onion, chopped
1 teaspoon garlic-ginger paste
1 tablespoon Chinese five-spice powder
1 teaspoon mixed whole peppercorns
1 cup vegetable broth
2 tablespoons soy sauce
2 tablespoons tomato paste

Directions

Heat the sesame oil on the "Sauté" function; brown the top round steak until no longer pink.

Add in the onion, garlic-ginger paste, Chinese five-spice powder, whole peppercorns, vegetable broth, soy sauce, tomato paste; secure the pressure-cooking lid.

Pressure cook for 30 minutes at High pressure. Once cooking is complete, use a quick pressure release; carefully remove the lid.

Ladle the soup into individual bowls and enjoy!

Per serving: Calories: 393; Fat: 21.8g; Carbs: 6.6g; Protein: 40.1g; Sugars: 3.8g; Fiber: 1.1g

226. Roast Beef with Mediterranean Herbs [AF]

(Ready in about 55 minutes | Servings 4)

Ingredients

1 ½ pounds bottom round roast
2 tablespoons olive oil
2 garlic cloves, minced
1 teaspoon rosemary
1 teaspoon parsley
1 teaspoon oregano
Sea salt and freshly ground black pepper

Directions

Toss the beef with the spices, garlic, and olive oil; place the beef in the Air Fryer cooking basket.

Secure the air-frying lid.

Cook the roast beef at 390 degrees F for 50 minutes, turning it over halfway through the cooking time.

Cut the beef into slices and serve them with dinner rolls. Bon appétit!

Per serving: Calories: 301; Fat: 16.7g; Carbs: 0.4g; Protein: 35.4g; Sugars: 0.1g; Fiber: 0.1g

227. Saucy Top Sirloin [PC]

(Ready in about 40 minutes | Servings 5)

Ingredients

1 tablespoon lard
2 pounds top sirloin
Sea salt and freshly ground black pepper, to taste
1 teaspoon smoked paprika
2 cloves garlic, minced
1 bay leaf
2 sprigs thyme
1 onion, peeled and sliced
1 cup beef broth

Directions

Press the "Sauté" button and melt the lard; once hot, cook the beef until no longer pink.

Stir in the remaining ingredients and secure the pressure-cooking lid.

Pressure cook for 35 minutes at High pressure. Once cooking is complete, use a quick pressure release; carefully remove the lid.

Bon appétit!

Per serving: Calories: 275; Fat: 13.5g; Carbs: 1g; Protein: 37.5g; Sugars: 0.1g; Fiber: 0.2g

228. Grandma's Classic Meatloaf [AF]

(Ready in about 30 minutes | Servings 4)

Ingredients

1 ½ pounds ground chuck
1 egg, beaten
2 tablespoons olive oil
4 tablespoons crackers, crushed
1/2 cup shallots, minced
2 garlic cloves, minced
1 tablespoon fresh rosemary, chopped
1 tablespoon fresh thyme, chopped
Sea salt and ground black pepper, to taste

Directions

Thoroughly combine all the ingredients until everything is well combined.

Scrape the beef mixture into a lightly oiled baking pan and transfer it to the Air Fryer cooking basket.

Secure the air-frying lid.

Air fry your meatloaf at 390 degrees F for 25 minutes. Bon appétit!

Per serving: Calories: 373; Fat: 23.1g; Carbs: 5g; Protein: 36.8g; Sugars: 1.4g; Fiber: 0.6g

229. Greek-Style Beef Bowl [PC]

(Ready in about 45 minutes | Servings 5)

Ingredients

1 tablespoon butter
2 ½ pounds beef shanks, sliced
2 garlic cloves, minced
1 medium onion, sliced
1 zucchini, sliced
1 tablespoon Mediterranean seasoning mix
1 cup beef stock
1/2 cup dry white wine
1 tomato, chopped

Directions

Press the "Sauté" button to preheat your Instant Pot Duo Crisp and melt the butter. Once hot, cook the beef for 4 to 5 minutes, stirring periodically to ensure even browning.

Add in the remaining ingredients and secure the pressure-cooking lid.

Pressure cook for 40 minutes at High pressure. Once cooking is complete, use a quick pressure release; carefully remove the lid.

Enjoy!

Per serving: Calories: 359; Fat: 13.5g; Carbs: 2.8g; Protein: 52.1g; Sugars: 0.9g; Fiber: 0.6g

230. Dijon and Paprika Steak [AF]

(Ready in about 15 minutes | Servings 4)

Ingredients

1 ½ pounds chuck eye steak
2 tablespoons olive oil
1 teaspoon paprika
1 tablespoon Dijon mustard
Kosher salt and ground black pepper, to taste

Directions

Toss the steak with the remaining ingredients; place the steak in the Air Fryer cooking basket.

Secure the air-frying lid.

Cook the steak at 400 degrees F for 12 minutes, turning it over halfway through the cooking time.

Bon appétit!

Per serving: Calories: 300; Fat: 17.5g; Carbs: 0.5g; Protein: 35.1g; Sugars: 0.1g; Fiber: 0.4g

231. Spicy Cube Steak [PC]

(Ready in about 45 minutes | Servings 5)

Ingredients

2 tablespoons olive oil
2 pounds cube steak, sliced
1 cup vegetable broth
2 tablespoons soy sauce
1 tablespoon fish sauce
1 tablespoon sriracha
4 cloves garlic, minced

Directions

Heat the olive oil on the "Sauté" mode. Cook the steaks for approximately 5 minutes or until no longer pink on all sides.

Add in the remaining ingredients and secure the pressure-cooking lid.

Pressure cook for 40 minutes at High pressure. Once cooking is complete, use a quick pressure release; carefully remove the lid.

Serve warm and enjoy!

Per serving: Calories: 333; Fat: 18.5g; Carbs: 2.6g; Protein: 39.2g; Sugars: 1.4g; Fiber: 0.2g

232. Easy Mini Meatloaves [AF]

(Ready in about 25 minutes | Servings 4)

Ingredients

1 pound ground chuck
1 tablespoon olive oil
1 small-sized onion, chopped
2 garlic cloves, minced
1/4 cup breadcrumbs
1 egg, beaten
Sea salt and ground black pepper, to taste
1/2 cup ketchup

Directions

Thoroughly combine all the ingredients, except for the ketchup; mix until everything is well combined.

Scrape the beef mixture into a lightly oiled muffin tin and transfer it to the Air Fryer cooking basket.

Cook your meatloaves at 380 degrees F for 20 minutes. Then, spread the ketchup over top the meatloaves.

Press the "Broil" button and continue cooking for another 5 minutes.

Bon appétit!

Per serving: Calories: 603; Fat: 40g; Carbs: 42g; Protein: 21.1g; Sugars: 2.8g; Fiber: 6.1g

233. Mexican Meatball Soup (Albondigas Soup) [PC]

(Ready in about 35 minutes | Servings 4)

Ingredients

1 ½ pounds ground chuck
1/4 cup tortilla chips, crushed
1/4 cup Cotija cheese, crumbled
Sea salt and ground black pepper, to taste
4 cups vegetable broth
1 onion, chopped
1 cup salsa, medium or hot
1 teaspoon Mexican oregano

Directions

Mix the ground chuck, tortilla chips, cheese, salt, and black pepper. Shape the mixture into 1-inch meatballs.

Meanwhile, add the vegetable broth to the inner pot and press the "Sauté" button; bring it to a boil.

Add the prepared meatballs to the boiling broth, along with the other ingredients. Secure the pressure-cooking lid.

Pressure cook your soup for 30 minutes at High pressure. Once cooking is complete, use a quick pressure release; carefully remove the lid.

Enjoy!

Per serving: Calories: 363; Fat: 17.3g; Carbs: 10.6g; Protein: 42.4g; Sugars: 4.4g; Fiber: 2g

234. Mustard and Ketchup Glazed Beef [PC+AF]

(Ready in about 1 hour 10 minutes | Servings 4)

Ingredients

1 ½ pounds beef brisket
2 tablespoons tomato ketchup
1 tablespoon brown mustard
1 teaspoon chili powder
2 tablespoons salt
1 teaspoon garlic powder
1 teaspoon onion powder
1 tablespoon ground black pepper
1 tablespoon brown sugar

Directions

Toss the beef with the remaining ingredients; place the beef in the inner pot. Secure the pressure-cooking lid.

Pressure cook for 60 minutes at High pressure. Once cooking is complete, use a natural pressure release for about 10; carefully remove the lid.

Secure the air-frying lid and choose the "Broil" function.

Continue to cook the beef for a further 10 minutes or until cooked through. Bon appétit!

Per serving: Calories: 362; Fat: 25.6g; Carbs: 5.9g; Protein: 25.8g; Sugars: 2.8g; Fiber: 1.1g

235. Philly Cheesesteak Quiche [PC+AF]

(Ready in about 35 minutes | Servings 4)

Ingredients

1 tablespoon tallow
1 pound beef flank steak, finely sliced
1 large onion, chopped
2 garlic cloves, minced
1 cup tomato soup
Sea salt and ground black pepper, to taste
1/2 cup Greek yogurt
2 eggs, whole
1 cup Cheddar cheese, shredded

Directions

Press the "Sauté" button and melt the tallow. Once hot, cook the beef flank steak for about 3 minutes, stirring occasionally to ensure even browning.

Stir in the onion and garlic; continue cooking for 1 to 2 minutes or until just tender and aromatic; add in the tomato soup, salt, and black pepper; secure the pressure-cooking lid.

Pressure cook for 20 minutes at High pressure. Once cooking is complete, use a quick pressure release; carefully remove the lid.

In a mixing bowl, whisk the yogurt and eggs. Spoon the egg mixture onto your casserole; top with shredded Cheddar cheese.

Secure the air-frying lid; let it cook for 5 to 6 minutes or until thoroughly cooked.

Bon appétit!

Per serving: Calories: 407; Fat: 23.2g; Carbs: 8.5g; Protein: 37.2g; Sugars: 4.7g; Fiber: 1.3g

236. Mustard Garlic Beef Shoulder [AF]

(Ready in about 55 minutes | Servings 4)

Ingredients

1 ½ pounds beef shoulder
Sea salt and ground black pepper, to taste
1 teaspoon cayenne pepper
1/2 teaspoon ground cumin
2 tablespoons olive oil
2 cloves garlic, minced
1 teaspoon Dijon mustard
1 onion, cut into slices

Directions

Toss the beef with the spices, garlic, mustard, and olive oil; place the beef in a lightly oiled Air Fryer cooking basket. Secure the air-frying lid.

Cook the beef at 390 degrees F for 45 minutes, turning it over halfway through the cooking time.

Add in the onion and continue to cook an additional 10 minutes. Bon appétit!

Per serving: Calories: 309; Fat: 16.2g; Carbs: 2.2g; Protein: 36.1g; Sugars: 0.8g; Fiber: 0.4g

237. Autumn Braised Beef [PC]

(Ready in about 1 hour | Servings 4)

Ingredients

1 ½ pounds corned beef brisket
1/2 cup apple cider
1/2 cup cream of onion soup
1 tablespoon fish sauce
2 tablespoons brown sugar

Directions

Add all the ingredients to the inner pot of your Instant Pot Duo Crisp; gently stir to combine and secure the pressure-cooking lid.

Pressure cook for 55 minutes at High pressure. Once cooking is complete, use a natural pressure release; carefully remove the lid.

Bon appétit!

Per serving: Calories: 379; Fat: 26.1g; Carbs: 7.8g; Protein: 25.8g; Sugars: 5.4g; Fiber: 0.5g

238. Sticky Glazed Short Loin [AF]

(Ready in about 15 minutes | Servings 5)

Ingredients

2 pounds short loin, sliced
2 tablespoons butter, room temperature
1 tablespoon dark brown sugar
1 teaspoon coarse sea salt
1 teaspoon ground black pepper
1 teaspoon cayenne pepper
1 teaspoon ground coriander

Directions

Toss the short loin with the remaining ingredients; place the short loin in the Air Fryer cooking basket.

Secure the air-frying lid.

Cook the short loin at 400 degrees F for 14 minutes, turning it over halfway through the cooking time. Bon appétit!

Per serving: Calories: 315; Fat: 14g; Carbs: 6.5g; Protein: 41.1g; Sugars: 5.1g; Fiber: 0.2g

239. Rib-Eye Steak with Mushrooms [PC]

(Ready in about 35 minutes | Servings 5)

Ingredients

1 tablespoon butter
1 ½ pounds rib-eye steak, cut into small chunks
4 garlic cloves, crushed
1 pound mushrooms, sliced
1 cup beef broth

Directions

Press the "Sauté" button and melt the butter. Sear the steak for about 5 minutes, turning it periodically to ensure even browning.

Then, cook the garlic and mushrooms in the pan drippings for 1 to 2 minutes.

Pour in the broth and gently stir to combine; secure the pressure-cooking lid.

Pressure cook for 25 minutes at High pressure. Once cooking is complete, use a quick pressure release; carefully remove the lid. Enjoy!

Per serving: Calories: 398; Fat: 31.2g; Carbs: 3.7g; Protein: 27.3g; Sugars: 1.8g; Fiber: 1g

240. Gyro Style Shredded Beef [AF]

(Ready in about 1 hour 10 minutes | Servings 4)

Ingredients

1 ½ pounds beef brisket
2 tablespoons olive oil
Sea salt and freshly ground black pepper, to season
1 teaspoon dried oregano
1 teaspoon mustard powder
1/2 teaspoon ground cumin
2 cloves garlic, minced
2 tablespoons chives, chopped
2 tablespoons cilantro, chopped

Directions

Toss the beef brisket with the remaining ingredients; now, place the beef brisket in the Air Fryer cooking basket.

Secure the air-frying lid.

Cook the beef brisket at 390 degrees F for 15 minutes, turn the beef over and reduce the temperature to 360 degrees F.

Continue to cook the beef brisket for approximately 55 minutes or until cooked through.

Shred the beef with two forks and serve with toppings of choice. Bon appétit!

Per serving: Calories: 403; Fat: 32.3g; Carbs: 1.2g; Protein: 25.1g; Sugars: 0.1g; Fiber: 0.3g

POULTRY

241. Chicken Noodle Soup [PC]

(Ready in about 20 minutes | Servings 4)

Ingredients

1 tablespoon lard, at room temperature
1 pound chicken drumettes
Sea salt and ground black pepper, to taste
1 cup leek, chopped
5 cups chicken broth
6 ounces egg noodles

Directions

Melt the lard on the "Sauté" function until hot and sizzling. Once hot, sear the chicken drumettes for about 2 minutes on each side.

Add the remaining ingredients to the inner pot.

Pressure cook for 15 minutes at High pressure. Once cooking is complete, use a natural pressure release; carefully remove the lid.

Bon appétit!

Per serving: Calories: 385; Fat: 10.2g; Carbs: 35.9g; Protein: 35.7g; Sugars: 2.5g; Fiber: 2g

242. Easy Chicken Nuggets [AF]

(Ready in about 13 minutes | Servings 4)

Ingredients

1 ½ pounds chicken tenders
1 tablespoon olive oil
1 egg, whisked
1 teaspoon fresh parsley, minced
1 teaspoon garlic, minced
Sea salt and black pepper, to taste
1 cup breadcrumbs

Directions

Pat the chicken dry with kitchen towels.

In a bowl, thoroughly combine the oil, egg, parsley, garlic, salt, and black pepper.

Dip the chicken tenders into the egg mixture. Then, roll the chicken over the breadcrumbs. Secure the air-frying lid.

Air fry the chicken tenders at 360 degrees F for 10 minutes, shaking the basket halfway through the cooking time.

Bon appétit!

Per serving: Calories: 347; Fat: 10.4g; Carbs: 20.8g; Protein: 39.4g; Sugars: 2.2g; Fiber: 1.4g

243. Authentic Teriyaki Chicken [PC]

(Ready in about 30 minutes | Servings 4)

Ingredients

1 tablespoon sesame oil
1 ½ pounds chicken drumettes
1/2 cup scallions, chopped
1/4 cup dark soy sauce
1/4 cup rice wine
1 teaspoon ginger-garlic paste
Sea salt and ground black pepper, to taste
1 tablespoon corn starch

Directions

Press the "Sauté" button and heat the oil; once hot, sear the chicken drumettes for approximately 3 minutes on each side or until no longer pink.

Stir in the remaining ingredients and secure the pressure-cooking lid.

Pressure cook for 25 minutes at High pressure. Once cooking is complete, use a quick pressure release; carefully remove the lid.

Bon appétit!

Per serving: Calories: 284; Fat: 11.1g; Carbs: 8.2g; Protein: 36.5g; Sugars: 4.1g; Fiber: 1g

244. Homemade Chicken Burgers [AF]

(Ready in about 20 minutes | Servings 3)

Ingredients

3/4 pound chicken, ground
1/4 cup tortilla chips, crushed
1/4 cup Parmesan cheese, grated
1 egg, beaten
2 tablespoons onion, minced
2 garlic cloves, minced
1 tablespoon BBQ sauce

Directions

Mix all the ingredients until everything is well combined. Form the mixture into three patties.

Secure the air-frying lid.

Air fry the burgers at 380 degrees F for about 17 minutes or until cooked through; make sure to turn them over halfway through the cooking time.

Bon appétit!

Per serving: Calories: 373; Fat: 23.8g; Carbs: 11.7g; Protein: 27g; Sugars: 0.8g; Fiber: 0.9g

245. Thai Spicy Duck Soup [PC]

(Ready in about 25 minutes | Servings 4)

Ingredients

1 tablespoon olive oil
2 scallion stalks, thinly sliced
2 garlic cloves, minced
1 pound duck, whole with bones
1 cup chicken consommé
3 cups water
1 tablespoon Thai chili sauce

Directions

Place all the ingredients in the inner pot of your Instant Pot Duo Crisp; secure the pressure-cooking lid.

Pressure cook your soup for 20 minutes at High pressure. Once cooking is complete, use a natural pressure release; carefully remove the lid.

Bon appétit!

Per serving: Calories: 304; Fat: 21.3g; Carbs: 4.3g; Protein: 23g; Sugars: 0.4g; Fiber: 0.3g

246. Roasted Chicken Salad [AF]

(Ready in about 20 minutes | Servings 3)

Ingredients

1 pound chicken breast
2 tablespoons scallions, chopped
1 carrot, shredded
1/2 cup mayonnaise
1 tablespoon mustard
Sea salt and ground black pepper, to taste

Directions

Pat the chicken dry with kitchen towels. Place the chicken in a lightly oiled cooking basket.

Secure the air-frying lid. Cook the chicken at 380 degrees F for 12 minutes, turning them over halfway through the cooking time.

Chop the chicken breasts and transfer it to a salad bowl; add in the remaining ingredients and toss to combine well. Bon appétit!

Per serving: Calories: 373; Fat: 23.8g; Carbs: 11.7g; Protein: 27g; Sugars: 0.8g; Fiber: 1g

247. BBQ Chicken Legs [PC]

(Ready in about 35 minutes | Servings 6)

Ingredients

2 pounds chicken legs
1 cup BBQ sauce
Sea salt and ground black pepper, to season
2 tablespoons ghee
1/4 cup honey
2 garlic cloves, crushed

Directions

Place all the ingredients in the inner pot of your Instant Pot Duo Crisp and secure the pressure-cooking lid.

Pressure cook for 30 minutes at High pressure. Once cooking is complete, use a quick pressure release; carefully remove the lid. Bon appétit!

Per serving: Calories: 286; Fat: 10.9g; Carbs: 15.6g; Protein: 29.9g; Sugars: 13.7g; Fiber: 0.9g

248. Traditional Tacos Dorados [AF]

(Ready in about 20 minutes | Servings 5)

Ingredients

3/4 pound chicken breasts, boneless and skinless
Kosher salt and ground black pepper, to taste
1/2 teaspoon red chili powder
5 small corn tortillas
5 ounces Cotija cheese, crumbled

Directions

Pat the chicken dry with kitchen towels. Toss the chicken breasts with the salt, pepper, and red chili powder.

Secure the air-frying lid.

Cook the chicken at 380 degrees F for 12 minutes, turning them over halfway through the cooking time.

Place the shredded chicken and cheese on one end of each tortilla. Roll them up tightly and transfer them to a lightly oiled Air Fryer basket.

Press the "Bake" button and bake your taquitos at 360 degrees F for 6 minutes. Bon appétit!

Per serving: Calories: 256; Fat: 13g; Carbs: 14.2g; Protein: 20.4g; Sugars: 2.8g; Fiber: 1.7g

249. Chicken Breasts with Garlic and Wine [PC]

(Ready in about 25 minutes | Servings 4)

Ingredients

2 tablespoons olive oil
1 ½ pounds chicken breasts, skinless and boneless
Sea salt and ground black pepper
4 garlic cloves, crushed
1 cup chicken stock
1/2 cup white wine
1 bay laurel

Directions

Place all the ingredients in the inner pot of your Instant Pot Duo Crisp; secure the pressure-cooking lid.

Pressure cook the chicken breast for 20 minutes at High pressure. Once cooking is complete, use a natural pressure release; carefully remove the lid.

Bon appétit!

Per serving: Calories: 374; Fat: 22.9g; Carbs: 2.4g; Protein: 37.3g; Sugars: 0.9g; Fiber: 0.2g

250. Classic Balsamic Chicken [AF]

(Ready in about 25 minutes | Servings 4)

Ingredients

1 ½ pounds chicken drumettes
2 tablespoons olive oil
2 tablespoons balsamic vinegar
Kosher salt and ground black pepper, to taste

Directions

Toss the chicken drumettes with the remaining ingredients. Secure the air-frying lid.

Air fry the chicken drumettes at 380 degrees F for 22 minutes, turning them over halfway through the cooking time.

Bon appétit!

Per serving: Calories: 265; Fat: 11.4g; Carbs: 2.4g; Protein: 34.4g; Sugars: 1.8g; Fiber: 0.2g

251. Smothered Turkey Cutlets [PC]

(Ready in about 25 minutes | Servings 5)

Ingredients

2 tablespoons olive oil
2 pounds turkey breast, slice into cutlets
1 tablespoon poultry seasoning mix
1 sprig rosemary
1 sprig thyme
1 leek, cut into thick slices
1 cup cream of celery soup

Directions

Press the "Sauté" button and heat the olive oil until sizzling; now, sear the turkey cutlets for about 4 minutes or until they are no longer pink.

Stir in the remaining ingredients. Secure the pressure-cooking lid.

Pressure cook for 20 minutes at High pressure. Once cooking is complete, use a natural pressure release; carefully remove the lid.

Bon appétit!

Per serving: Calories: 366; Fat: 19.3g; Carbs: 4.9g; Protein: 47.9g; Sugars: 0.7g; Fiber: 0.6g

252. Dijon Barbecued Turkey [AF]

(Ready in about 1 hour 5 minutes | Servings 5)

Ingredients

2 tablespoons olive oil
Sea salt and freshly cracked black pepper, to taste
1 tablespoon Dijon mustard
1 tablespoon hot sauce
1 teaspoon smoked paprika
1 teaspoon dried basil
1 teaspoon dried thyme
2 pounds turkey breast, bone-in

Directions

In a mixing bowl, thoroughly combine the olive oil, salt, black pepper, mustard, hot sauce, paprika, basil, and thyme.

Rub the mixture all over the turkey breast. Secure the air-frying lid.

Ari fry the turkey breast at 350 degrees F for 1 hour, turning them over every 20 minutes. Bon appétit!

Per serving: Calories: 342; Fat: 18g; Carbs: 1.6g; Protein: 40.3g; Sugars: 0.6g; Fiber: 0.6g

253. Chicken Macaroni Soup [PC]

(Ready in about 15 minutes | Servings 4)

Ingredients

1 pound chicken breasts, boneless and cut into 1-inch pieces
1 onion, chopped
4 cups vegetable broth
4 ounces macaroni
1 cup extra-sharp cheddar cheese, grated

Directions

Place the chicken, onion, broth and macaroni in the inner pot of your Instant Pot Duo Crisp; gently stir to combine.

Pressure cook for 10 minutes at High pressure. Once cooking is complete, use a natural pressure release; carefully remove the lid.

Fold in the cheddar cheese and stir until the cheese melts. Bon appétit!

Per serving: Calories: 465; Fat: 21.3g; Carbs: 25.2g; Protein: 39g; Sugars: 2.3g; Fiber: 1.4g

254. Stuffed Chicken Breasts [AF]

(Ready in about 25 minutes | Servings 4)

Ingredients

1 pound chicken breasts, boneless, skinless, cut into four pieces
2 tablespoons sundried tomatoes, chopped
1 garlic clove, minced
2 ounces mozzarella cheese, crumbled
Sea salt and ground black pepper, to taste
1 tablespoon olive oil

Directions

Flatten the chicken breasts with a mallet.

Stuff each piece of chicken with the sundried tomatoes, garlic, and cheese. Roll them up and secure with toothpicks.

Season the chicken with the salt and pepper and drizzle the olive oil over them.

Place the stuffed chicken in the Air Fryer cooking basket. Secure the air-frying lid.

Cook the chicken at 400 degrees F for about 20 minutes, turning them over halfway through the cooking time.

Bon appétit!

Per serving: Calories: 257; Fat: 13.9g; Carbs: 2.7g; Protein: 28.3g; Sugars: 1.4g; Fiber: 0.6g

255. Classic Turkey Soup [PC]

(Ready in about 25 minutes | Servings 4)

Ingredients

1 pound turkey, whole with bones
1 medium onion, chopped
2 carrots, chopped
1 celery stalk, chopped
1 bay laurel
Sea salt and ground black pepper, to taste
1 cup chicken consommé
3 cups water

Directions

Place all the ingredients in the inner pot of your Instant Pot Duo Crisp; secure the pressure-cooking lid.

Pressure cook the soup for 20 minutes at High pressure. Once cooking is complete, use a natural pressure release; carefully remove the lid.

Bon appétit!

Per serving: Calories: 267; Fat: 18.3g; Carbs: 6.6g; Protein: 17.3g; Sugars: 3.2g; Fiber: 1.6g

256. Mom's Famous Chicken Fingers [AF]

(Ready in about 20 minutes | Servings 4)

Ingredients

- 1 egg, whisked
- 1/2 cup all-purpose flour
- 1 teaspoon garlic powder
- 1 teaspoon cayenne pepper
- Sea salt and ground black pepper, to taste
- 1/4 cup breadcrumbs
- 1/4 cup parmesan cheese, grated
- 1 ½ pounds chicken breast boneless, skinless and cut into strips

Directions

Mix the egg and flour in a shallow bowl. In a separate bowl, whisk the garlic powder, cayenne pepper, salt, black pepper, breadcrumbs, and parmesan cheese.

Dip the chicken breasts into the egg mixture. Then, roll the chicken breasts over the breadcrumb mixture. Secure the air-frying lid.

Air fry the chicken at 380 degrees F for 12 minutes, turning them over halfway through the cooking time.

Bon appétit!

Per serving: Calories: 475; Fat: 28.6g; Carbs: 14.4g; Protein: 36.4.1g; Sugars: 0.8g; Fiber: 0.8g

257. Chunky Turkey Soup [PC]

(Ready in about 25 minutes | Servings 4)

Ingredients

- 2 teaspoons olive oil
- 3/4 pound ground turkey
- 1 onion, chopped
- 2 garlic cloves, chopped
- 1 tablespoon poultry seasoning mix
- 4 cups chicken bone broth

Directions

Stir all the ingredients into the inner pot of your Instant Pot Duo Crisp; secure the pressure-cooking lid.

Pressure cook for 20 minutes at High pressure. Once cooking is complete, use a quick pressure release; carefully remove the lid.

Bon appétit!

Per serving: Calories: 239; Fat: 14.6g; Carbs: 4.7g; Protein: 21.9g; Sugars: 1.4g; Fiber: 0.6g

258. Restaurant-Style Fried Chicken [AF]

(Ready in about 15 minutes + marinating time | Servings 4)

Ingredients

- 1 pound chicken breast halves
- Sea salt and ground black pepper, to taste
- 1 cup buttermilk
- 1 cup all-purpose flour
- 1/2 teaspoon onion powder
- 1 teaspoon garlic powder
- 1 teaspoon smoked paprika

Directions

Toss together the chicken pieces, salt, and black pepper in a large bowl to coat. Stir in the buttermilk until the chicken is coated on all sides. Place the chicken in your refrigerator for about 6 hours.

In a shallow bowl, thoroughly combine the flour, onion powder, garlic powder, and smoked paprika.

Then, dredge the chicken in the seasoned flour; shake off any excess and transfer them to a lightly oiled Air Fryer basket. Secure the air-frying lid.

Cook the chicken breasts at 380 degrees F for 12 minutes, turning them over halfway through the cooking time. Enjoy!

Per serving: Calories: 266; Fat: 3.9g; Carbs: 26.7g; Protein: 28.1g; Sugars: 3g; Fiber: 0.8g

259. Hungarian Chicken Stew (Gulyás) [PC]

(Ready in about 25 minutes | Servings 4)

Ingredients

- 2 teaspoons lard
- 2 pounds chicken legs
- 1 tablespoon paprika
- 1 large-sized onion, thinly sliced
- 1 teaspoon fresh garlic, minced
- 2 large-sized carrots, sliced
- 1/2 cup dry red wine
- 2 cups chicken bone broth
- 1 cup tomato sauce

Directions

Press the "Sauté" button and melt the lard; then, sear the chicken until no longer pink, turning them periodically to ensure even cooking.

Stir in the other ingredients and secure the pressure-cooking lid.

Pressure cook your goulash for 20 minutes at High pressure. Once cooking is complete, use a natural pressure release; carefully remove the lid. Bon appétit!

Per serving: Calories: 409; Fat: 12.8g; Carbs: 18.6g; Protein: 48.3g; Sugars: 9.1g; Fiber: 5.3g

260. Ground Turkey Sliders [AF]

(Ready in about 25 minutes | Servings 4)

Ingredients

- 1 pound turkey, ground
- 1 tablespoon olive oil
- 1 avocado, peeled, pitted and chopped
- 2 garlic cloves, minced
- 1/2 cup breadcrumbs
- Kosher salt and ground black pepper, to taste
- 8 small rolls

Directions

Mix the turkey, olive oil, avocado, garlic, breadcrumbs, salt, and black pepper until everything is well combined. Form the mixture into eight small patties.

Secure the air-frying lid.

Cook the patties at 380 degrees F for about 20 minutes or until cooked through; make sure to turn them over halfway through the cooking time.

Serve your patties in the prepared rolls and enjoy!

Per serving: Calories: 509; Fat: 22.4g; Carbs: 48g; Protein: 31.6g; Sugars: 6.7g; Fiber: 5g

261. Thai Spicy Chicken Bowl [PC]

(Ready in about 15 minutes | Servings 4)

Ingredients

1 tablespoon sesame oil
1 pound chicken breasts, diced
1 red bell pepper, thinly sliced
1 small onion, thinly sliced
2 cloves garlic, minced
1 Bird-eye chili, minced
Kosher salt and ground black pepper, to taste
1 cup white rice

Directions

Press the "Sauté" button and heat the olive oil.

Once hot, sear the chicken breasts for about 5 minutes or until no longer pink. Stir the remaining ingredients into the inner pot. Secure the pressure-cooking lid.

Pressure cook for 6 minutes at High pressure. Once cooking is complete, use a quick pressure release; carefully remove the lid. Bon appétit!

Per serving: Calories: 414; Fat: 14.3g; Carbs: 41.1g; Protein: 27.3g; Sugars: 1.9g; Fiber: 2g

262. Spicy Chicken Breasts [AF]

(Ready in about 15 minutes + marinating time | Servings 4)

Ingredients

1 pound chicken breasts, boneless, skinless
1/2 cup rice wine
1 tablespoon stone-ground mustard
1 teaspoon garlic, minced
1 teaspoon black peppercorns, whole
1 teaspoon chili powder
1/4 teaspoon sea salt, or more to taste

Directions

Place the chicken, wine, mustard, garlic, and whole peppercorns in a ceramic bowl. Cover the bowl and let the chicken marinate for about 3 hours in your refrigerator.

Discard the marinade and place the chicken breasts in the Air Fryer cooking basket. Secure the air-frying lid.

Cook the chicken breasts at 380 degrees F for 12 minutes, turning them over halfway through the cooking time.

Season the chicken with the chili powder and salt. Serve immediately and enjoy!

Per serving: Calories: 206; Fat: 11g; Carbs: 1g; Protein: 24.2g; Sugars: 0.4g; Fiber: 0.2g

263. Shredded Chicken Sliders [PC]

(Ready in about 25 minutes | Servings 4)

Ingredients

2 teaspoons butter, at room temperature
1 pound chicken legs, skinless and boneless
1 tablespoon poultry seasoning blend
1 cup roasted vegetable broth
4 brioche burger buns, lightly toasted

Directions

Melt the butter on the "Sauté" function. Then, brown the chicken for approximately 5 minutes.

Add in the poultry seasoning blend and vegetable broth. Secure the pressure-cooking lid.

Pressure cook for 15 minutes at High pressure. Once cooking is complete, use a natural pressure release; carefully remove the lid.

Shred the meat and serve on the lightly toasted brioche burger buns. Bon appétit!

Per serving: Calories: 460; Fat: 24.5g; Carbs: 32.6g; Protein: 25.9g; Sugars: 16.3g; Fiber: 1g

264. Lemony Turkey Wings [AF]

(Ready in about 45 minutes | Servings 5)

Ingredients

2 pounds turkey wings
2 tablespoons olive oil
1/2 teaspoon garlic powder
1/2 teaspoon onion powder
1 teaspoon poultry seasoning mix
2 tablespoons fresh parsley, roughly chopped
1 lemon, cut into slices

Directions

Toss the turkey wings with the olive oil, garlic powder, onion powder, and poultry seasoning mix.

Secure the air-frying lid.

Cook the turkey wings at 400 degrees F for 40 minutes, turning them over halfway through the cooking time.

Let the turkey rest for 10 minutes before carving and serving. Garnish the turkey wings with the parsley and lemon slices. Bon appétit!

Per serving: Calories: 411; Fat: 27.8g; Carbs: 1.3g; Protein: 36.5g; Sugars: 0.3g; Fiber: 0.2g

265. Classic BBQ Turkey [PC]

(Ready in about 20 minutes | Servings 4)

Ingredients

2 tablespoons olive oil
1 ½ pounds turkey tenderloins
1 tablespoon poultry seasoning mix
1 cup BBQ sauce
Sea salt and ground black pepper, to taste

Directions

Press the "Sauté" button and heat the oil; now, sear the turkey tenderloin for about 4 minutes or until tender and translucent.

Stir in the remaining ingredients. Secure the pressure-cooking lid.

Pressure cook for 15 minutes at High pressure. Once cooking is complete, use a natural pressure release; carefully remove the lid. Bon appétit!

Per serving: Calories: 336; Fat: 16.5g; Carbs: 6.6g; Protein: 38.5g; Sugars: 3.3g; Fiber: 1.5g

266. Duck a l'Orange [AF]

(Ready in about 45 minutes | Servings 4)

Ingredients
1 pound duck legs
1/4 cup orange sauce
Sea salt and red pepper flakes, crushed

Directions
Toss the duck legs with the remaining ingredients. Secure the air-frying lid.

Cook the duck legs at 400 degrees F for 40 minutes, turning them over halfway through the cooking time.

Bon appétit!

Per serving: Calories: 471; Fat: 44.1g; Carbs: 2.9g; Protein: 13.3.1g; Sugars: 2.1g; Fiber: 0.3g

267. Chicken Tenderloin with Feta Cheese [PC]

(Ready in about 20 minutes | Servings 4)

Ingredients
1 ½ pounds chicken tenderloin
1 cup chicken broth
1/4 cup orange juice
Sea salt and ground black pepper, to taste
1 teaspoon Greek oregano
1 tablespoon Dijon mustard
2 ounces feta cheese, crumbled

Directions
Place the chicken tenderloin, broth, orange juice, salt, black pepper, oregano, and mustard. Secure the pressure-cooking lid.

Pressure cook for 10 minutes at High pressure. Once cooking is complete, use a quick pressure release; carefully remove the lid.

Top the chicken with feta cheese and enjoy!

Per serving: Calories: 338; Fat: 10.1g; Carbs: 4.3g; Protein: 53g; Sugars: 2.4g; Fiber: 0.5g

268. Fried Chicken Wings [AF]

(Ready in about 15 minutes | Servings 2)

Ingredients
3/4 pound chicken wings, boneless
1 tablespoon butter, room temperature
1/2 teaspoon garlic powder
1/2 teaspoon shallot powder
1/2 teaspoon mustard powder

Directions
Toss the chicken wings with the remaining ingredients. Secure the air-frying lid.

Air fry the chicken wings at 380 degrees F for 18 minutes, turning them over halfway through the cooking time.

Bon appétit!

Per serving: Calories: 265; Fat: 11.7g; Carbs: 0.5g; Protein: 37.5g; Sugars: 0.5g; Fiber: 0.9g

269. Murgh Kari (Indian Chicken Curry) [PC]

(Ready in about 20 minutes | Servings 4)

Ingredients
2 teaspoons butter
1 shallot, chopped
1 ½ pounds chicken tenderloin, cut into bite-sized pieces
1 teaspoon ginger-garlic paste
1/2 teaspoon ground cumin
1 teaspoon curry powder
Kosher salt and freshly ground black pepper, to taste
1 cup dahi (Indian yogurt)

Directions
Preheat your Instant Pot Duo Crisp on the "Sauté" function.

Melt the butter and cook the shallot and chicken tenderloins for about 3 minutes or until the shallot is fragrant and the chicken is no longer pink.

Add in the ginger-garlic paste and spices. Secure the pressure-cooking lid.

Pressure cook for 12 minutes at High pressure. Once cooking is complete, use a quick pressure release; carefully remove the lid.

Pour in the Indian yogurt and stir until well combined. Taste and adjust the seasonings.

Bon appétit!

Per serving: Calories: 413; Fat: 27.8g; Carbs: 2.6g; Protein: 36.2g; Sugars: 1.1g; Fiber: 0.4g

270. Authentic German Schweineschnitzel [AF]

(Ready in about 25 minutes | Servings 3)

Ingredients
1 ½ pounds turkey thighs, skinless, boneless
1 egg, beaten
1/2 cup all-purpose flour
1/2 cup seasoned breadcrumbs
1/2 teaspoon red pepper flakes, crushed
Sea salt and ground black pepper, to taste
1 tablespoon olive oil

Directions
Flatten the turkey thighs with a mallet.

Whisk the egg in a shallow bowl. Place the flour in a second bowl.

Then, in a third shallow bowl, place the breadcrumbs, red pepper, salt, and black pepper. Dip the turkey first in the flour, then, in the beaten egg, and roll them in the breadcrumb mixture.

Place the breaded turkey thighs in the Air Fryer basket. Mist your schnitzel with the olive oil and transfer it to the cooking basket.

Secure the air-frying lid. Cook the schnitzel at 380 degrees F for 22 minutes, turning it over halfway through the cooking time.

Bon appétit!

Per serving: Calories: 579; Fat: 27.4g; Carbs: 30.3g; Protein: 51g; Sugars: 2g; Fiber: 1.6g

271. Spicy Turkey Bolognese [PC]

(Ready in about 15 minutes | Servings 4)

Ingredients

1 tablespoon olive oil
1 pound turkey, ground
1 large-sized onion, finely minced
3 garlic cloves, minced
1 Italian pepper, seeded and chopped
1 red chili pepper, seeded and chopped
1 cup tomato puree
1 cup chicken bone broth
1 tablespoon Italian herb blend
1/2 cup red wine

Directions

Press the "Sauté" button and heat the oil; brown the ground turkey for about 3 minutes, crumbling it with a fork.

Stir in the remaining ingredients and secure the pressure-cooking lid.

Pressure cook for 8 minutes at High pressure. Once cooking is complete, use a quick pressure release; carefully remove the lid.

Bon appétit!

Per serving: Calories: 420; Fat: 20.8g; Carbs: 12.5g; Protein: 44.8g; Sugars: 6g; Fiber: 2.3g

272. Pomegranate-Glazed Duck [AF]

(Ready in about 45 minutes | Servings 5)

Ingredients

2 pounds duck breasts
1 tablespoon butter, melted
2 tablespoons pomegranate molasses
2 tablespoons miso paste
1 teaspoon garlic, minced
1 teaspoon ginger, peeled and minced
1 teaspoon Five-spice powder

Directions

Pat the duck breasts dry with paper towels. Toss the duck breast with the remaining ingredients. Secure the air-frying lid.

Cook the duck breasts at 330 degrees F for 15 minutes, turning them over halfway through the cooking time.

Turn the heat to 350 degrees F; continue to cook for about 15 minutes or until cooked through.

Let it rest for 10 minutes before carving and serving. Bon appétit!

Per serving: Calories: 356; Fat: 11.7g; Carbs: 23.5g; Protein: 38.8g; Sugars: 15g; Fiber: 5.1g

273. Traditional Chicken Chili [PC]

(Ready in about 20 minutes | Servings 4)

Ingredients

2 tablespoons olive oil
1 large onion, chopped
3 garlic cloves, chopped
1 habanero pepper, chopped
1 ½ pounds ground chicken
1 teaspoon dried Mexican oregano
1 ½ cups vegetable broth
1 cup canned red kidney beans

Directions

Press the "Sauté" button and heat the olive oil; once hot, sauté the onion and garlic for about 2 minutes or until they have softened.

Stir the pepper, ground chicken, oregano, and broth into the inner pot; secure the pressure-cooking lid.

Pressure cook for 12 minutes at High pressure. Once cooking is complete, use a quick pressure release; carefully remove the lid.

Add in the canned beans, secure the lid once again, and let it sit in the residual heat until warmed through. Serve hot and enjoy!

Per serving: Calories: 395; Fat: 21.2g; Carbs: 15.5g; Protein: 35.6g; Sugars: 3.5g; Fiber: 3.7g

274. Chicken Fillets with Peppers [AF]

(Ready in about 20 minutes | Servings 4)

Ingredients

1 pound chicken fillets
2 tablespoons butter
2 bell peppers, seeded and sliced
1 teaspoon garlic, minced
Sea salt and ground black pepper, to taste
1 teaspoon red pepper flakes

Directions

Toss the chicken fillets with the butter and place them in the Air Fryer basket. Top the chicken with bell peppers, garlic, salt, black pepper, and red pepper flakes.

Secure the air-frying lid.

Cook the chicken and peppers at 380 degrees F for 15 minutes, tossing the basket halfway through the cooking time.

Serve warm and enjoy!

Per serving: Calories: 305; Fat: 22.8g; Carbs: 2.3g; Protein: 21.6g; Sugars: 1.1g; Fiber: 0.4g

275. Colorful Chicken Salad [PC]

(Ready in about 15 minutes | Servings 4)

Ingredients

1 ½ pounds chicken tenderloin
1 cup water
1 cup iceberg lettuce, shredded
1 red bell pepper, sliced
1 carrot, shredded
1 cup cherry tomatoes, halved
1 medium red onion, thinly sliced
2 tablespoons olive oil
1 tablespoon fresh lemon juice

Directions

Place the water and steamer basket in the inner pot of your Instant Pot Duo Crisp; then, lower the chicken tenderloin into the steamer basket.

Pressure cook for 10 minutes at High pressure. Once cooking is complete, use a quick pressure release; carefully remove the lid.

Chop the chicken and toss it with the remaining ingredients.

Bon appétit!

Per serving: Calories: 285; Fat: 11.2g; Carbs: 8.9g; Protein: 35.6g; Sugars: 6.5g; Fiber: 1.5g

POULTRY

276. Spicy Ranch Chicken [AF]

(Ready in about 25 minutes | Servings 4)

Ingredients

1/2 cup all-purpose flour
1 tablespoon Ranch seasoning mix
1 pound chicken drumsticks
1 tablespoon hot sauce
Sea salt and ground black pepper, to taste

Directions

Pat the chicken drumsticks dry with paper towels. Toss the chicken drumsticks with the remaining ingredients and place them in the Air Fryer basket.

Secure the air-frying lid.

Cook the chicken drumsticks at 370 degrees F for 20 minutes, turning them over halfway through the cooking time.

Bon appétit!

Per serving: Calories: 309; Fat: 17.2g; Carbs: 13.4g; Protein: 22.8g; Sugars: 0.4g; Fiber: 0.8g

277. Decadent Duck with Prunes [PC]

(Ready in about 35 minutes | Servings 4)

Ingredients

2 tablespoons olive oil
1 pound whole duck
1/2 cup prunes
2 tablespoons maple syrup
1/2 teaspoon cayenne pepper
Sea salt and freshly ground black pepper, to taste

Directions

Press the "Sauté" button and heat the oil; sear the duck for about 4 minutes or until no longer pink.

Stir in the remaining ingredients and secure the pressure-cooking lid.

Pressure cook for 30 minutes at High pressure. Once cooking is complete, use a quick pressure release; carefully remove the lid.

Bon appétit!

Per serving: Calories: 382; Fat: 24.2g; Carbs: 21.4g; Protein: 20.4g; Sugars: 6.2g; Fiber: 0.1g

278. Italian-Style Turkey Breasts [AF]

(Ready in about 1 hour 5 minutes | Servings 4)

Ingredients

1 tablespoon butter, room temperature
Kosher salt and ground black pepper, to taste
1 teaspoon cayenne pepper
1 teaspoon Italian herb mix
1 pound turkey breast, bone-in

Directions

In a mixing bowl, thoroughly combine the butter, salt, black pepper, cayenne pepper, and herb mix.

Rub the mixture all over the turkey breast and place it in the Air Fryer basket. Secure the air-frying lid.

Cook the turkey breast at 350 degrees F for 1 hour, turning them over every 20 minutes.

Bon appétit!

Per serving: Calories: 210; Fat: 10.1g; Carbs: 1.3g; Protein: 25.1g; Sugars: 0.6g; Fiber: 0.4g

279. Chicken Cheese Pie [PC+AF]

(Ready in about 20 minutes | Servings 4)

Ingredients

2 tablespoons olive oil
1 small onion, chopped
2 cloves garlic, crushed
1 pound chicken breasts, diced
1 cup chicken broth
1/2 cup breadcrumbs
2 tablespoons butter, room temperature
1/2 cup Colby cheese, shredded

Directions

Press the "Sauté" button to preheat your Instant Pot Duo Crisp; now, heat the olive oil and sauté the onion and garlic for about 2 minutes or until they have softened.

Stir the chicken breasts and broth into the inner pot of your Instant Pot Duo Crisp; secure the pressure-cooking lid.

Pressure cook for 12 minutes at High pressure. Once cooking is complete, use a quick pressure release; carefully remove the lid.

Mix the breadcrumbs, butter, and cheese. Top the chicken with the breadcrumb mixture.

Secure the air-frying lid and cook for 5 to 6 minutes more until the cheese melts. Bon appétit!

Per serving: Calories: 392; Fat: 28.2g; Carbs: 4.4g; Protein: 29g; Sugars: 1.2g; Fiber: 0.4g

280. Spicy Mustard Chicken Thighs [AF]

(Ready in about 25 minutes | Servings 4)

Ingredients

1 pound chicken thighs, bone-in
Sea salt and freshly ground black pepper, to taste
2 tablespoons olive oil
1 teaspoon stone-ground mustard
1/4 cup hot sauce

Directions

Pat the chicken dry with kitchen towels. Toss the chicken with the remaining ingredients.

Secure the air-frying lid.

Air fry the chicken at 380 degrees F for 22 minutes, turning them over halfway through the cooking time.

Bon appétit!

Per serving: Calories: 317; Fat: 25.4g; Carbs: 1.5g; Protein: 19.1g; Sugars: 0.6g; Fiber: 1g

281. Apple Maple Turkey Tenderloin [PC]

(Ready in about 25 minutes | Servings 5)

Ingredients

2 tablespoons olive oil
2 pounds turkey tenderloin
1 tablespoon poultry seasoning mix
1 cup chicken bone broth
1 apple, peeled and diced
2 tablespoons maple syrup

Directions

Press the "Sauté" button to heat the olive oil until sizzling; once hot, brown your turkey for approximately 4 minutes per side or until they are no longer pink.

Add in the remaining ingredients and stir to combine; secure the pressure-cooking lid.

Pressure cook for 20 minutes at High pressure. Once cooking is complete, use a quick pressure release; carefully remove the lid. Bon appétit!

Per serving: Calories: 369; Fat: 12.3g; Carbs: 11.6g; Protein: 51.6g; Sugars: 8.7g; Fiber: 1.7g

282. Greek Chicken Fillets [AF]

(Ready in about 15 minutes | Servings 4)

Ingredients

1 ½ pounds chicken fillets
1 tablespoon olive oil
1 teaspoon garlic, minced
1 tablespoon Greek seasoning mix
1/2 teaspoon red pepper flakes, crushed
Sea salt and ground black pepper, to taste

Directions

Pat the chicken dry with paper towels. Toss the chicken fillets with the remaining ingredients and place them in the Air Fryer basket.

Secure the air-frying lid.

Cook the chicken fillets at 380 degrees F for 12 minutes, turning them over halfway through the cooking time.

Bon appétit!

Per serving: Calories: 227; Fat: 13.4g; Carbs: 0.2g; Protein: 23.4g; Sugars: 0.2g; Fiber: 1g

283. Chicken Tikka Masala [PC]

(Ready in about 25 minutes | Servings 4)

Ingredients

2 tablespoons ghee
1 ½ pounds chicken legs, boneless and skinless
1 onion, chopped
2 garlic cloves, minced
1 teaspoon fresh ginger, peeled and grated
1 teaspoon garam masala
1 teaspoon turmeric powder
Kosher salt and ground black pepper, to taste

Directions

Press the "Sauté" button to preheat your Instant Pot Duo Crisp; melt the ghee and sear the chicken for about 4 minutes or until golden brown.

Add the other ingredients to the inner pot and secure the pressure-cooking lid.

Pressure cook for 20 minutes at High pressure. Once cooking is complete, use a quick pressure release; carefully remove the lid. Bon appétit!

Per serving: Calories: 276; Fat: 13g; Carbs: 3.6g; Protein: 33.3g; Sugars: 1.2g; Fiber: 0.7g

284. Saucy Turkey Wings [AF]

(Ready in about 45 minutes + marinating time | Servings 5)

Ingredients

2 pounds turkey wings, bone-in
2 garlic cloves, minced
1 small onion, chopped
1 tablespoon Dijon mustard
1/2 cup red wine
Sea salt and ground black pepper, to taste
1 teaspoon poultry seasoning

Directions

Place the turkey wings, garlic, onion, mustard, and wine in a ceramic bowl. Cover the bowl and let the turkey marinate in your refrigerator overnight.

Discard the marinade and toss the turkey wings with the salt, black pepper, and poultry seasoning.

Secure the air-frying lid.

Air fry the turkey wings at 400 degrees F for 40 minutes, turning them over halfway through the cooking time. Bon appétit!

Per serving: Calories: 377; Fat: 22.5g; Carbs: 3.2g; Protein: 37.4g; Sugars: 1.3g; Fiber: 0.6g

285. Turkey and Sweet Potato Stew [PC]

(Ready in about 25 minutes | Servings 4)

Ingredients

2 tablespoons lard
1 ½ pounds turkey drumsticks, skinless and boneless
1 onion, chopped
2 garlic cloves, minced
1/2 pound sweet potato, peeled and diced
1 cup tomatoes, pureed
1/2 cup vegetable broth
Sea salt and black pepper, to taste

Directions

Press the "Sauté" button to preheat your Instant Pot Duo Crisp; melt the lard and sear the turkey drumsticks for about 3 minutes per side.

Add in the remaining ingredients, gently stir to combine, and secure the pressure-cooking lid.

Pressure cook for 20 minutes at High pressure. Once cooking is complete, use a quick pressure release; carefully remove the lid. Bon appétit!

Per serving: Calories: 328; Fat: 13.5g; Carbs: 14.5g; Protein: 37.3g; Sugars: 2.6g; Fiber: 2.1g

286. Butter Paprika Chicken Cutlets [AF]

(Ready in about 20 minutes | Servings 4)

Ingredients

1 pound chicken breasts, boneless, skinless, cut into 4 pieces
1 tablespoon butter, melted
1 teaspoon smoked paprika
Kosher salt and ground black pepper, to taste
1 teaspoon garlic powder

Directions

Flatten the chicken breasts to 1/4-inch thickness. Toss the chicken breasts with the remaining ingredients.

Place the chicken breasts in the Air Fryer basket. Secure the air-frying lid.

Cook the chicken at 380 degrees F for 12 minutes, turning them over halfway through the cooking time.

Bon appétit!

Per serving: Calories: 229; Fat: 13.8g; Carbs: 1.9g; Protein: 24.1g; Sugars: 0.6g; Fiber: 0.4g

287. Duck Breast with Herbs and Wine [PC]

(Ready in about 35 minutes | Servings 4)

Ingredients

2 tablespoons olive oil
1 ½ pounds duck breast
Sea salt and ground black pepper, to taste
1 teaspoon fresh thyme
1 teaspoon fresh cilantro
1 teaspoon fresh rosemary
1/2 cup dry white wine
1/2 cup chicken broth

Directions

Press the "Sauté" button and heat the oil; sear the duck breast for about 4 minutes or until no longer pink.

Stir in the remaining ingredients. Secure the pressure-cooking lid.

Pressure cook for 30 minutes at High pressure. Once cooking is complete, use a quick pressure release; carefully remove the lid.

Bon appétit!

Per serving: Calories: 283; Fat: 14.2g; Carbs: 1.5g; Protein: 34.1g; Sugars: 1g; Fiber: 0.8g

288. Thai-Style Chicken Drumettes [AF]

(Ready in about 25 minutes | Servings 3)

Ingredients

1 pound chicken drumettes, bone-in
Sea salt and freshly ground black pepper, to taste
1/4 cup Thai hot sauces
2 tablespoons sesame oil
1 teaspoon tamari sauce

Directions

Toss the chicken drumettes with the remaining ingredients.

Place the chicken breasts in the Air Fryer basket. Secure the air-frying lid.

Air fry the chicken drumettes at 380 degrees F for 22 minutes, turning them over halfway through the cooking time.

Bon appétit!

Per serving: Calories: 260; Fat: 13.3g; Carbs: 0.5g; Protein: 31.2g; Sugars: 0.4g; Fiber: 0.5g

289. Smothered Chicken Fillets [PC]

(Ready in about 20 minutes | Servings 4)

Ingredients

1 ½ pounds chicken fillets
1 cup vegetable broth
Kosher salt and ground black pepper, to taste
1 teaspoon paprika
6 ounces button mushrooms, sliced
1 cup heavy cream

Directions

Press the "Sauté" button to preheat your Instant Pot Duo Crisp; sear the chicken for approximately 3 minutes per side or until it is lightly browned.

Add the broth, salt, black pepper, paprika, and mushrooms to the inner pot. Secure the pressure-cooking lid.

Pressure cook for 12 minutes at High pressure. Once cooking is complete, use a quick pressure release; carefully remove the lid.

Fold in the heavy cream, stir, and serve warm. Bon appétit!

Per serving: Calories: 494; Fat: 37.3g; Carbs: 3.8g; Protein: 35.3g; Sugars: 2.3g; Fiber: 1g

290. Easy Chicken Drumsticks [AF]

(Ready in about 25 minutes | Servings 4)

Ingredients

4 chicken drumsticks, bone-in
1 tablespoon butter
1/2 teaspoon cayenne pepper
1 teaspoon Italian herb mix
Sea salt and ground black pepper, to taste

Directions

Pat the chicken drumsticks dry with paper towels. Toss the chicken drumsticks with the remaining ingredients.

Place the chicken breasts in the Air Fryer basket. Secure the air-frying lid.

Air fry the chicken drumsticks at 370 degrees F for 20 minutes, turning them over halfway through the cooking time.

Bon appétit!

Per serving: Calories: 235; Fat: 14.8g; Carbs: 0.3g; Protein: 23.2g; Sugars: 0.1g; Fiber: 0.3g

291. Hungarian Paprika Chicken [PC]

(Ready in about 25 minutes | Servings 4)

Ingredients

1 tablespoon lard
1 pound chicken legs, boneless skinless
1 medium yellow onion, chopped
2 cloves garlic, minced
1 bell pepper, seeded and chopped
1 chili pepper, seeded and chopped
1 stalk celery, chopped
Kosher salt and freshly ground black pepper, to taste
1 bay leaf
1 teaspoon paprika
3 cups chicken bone broth

Directions

Press the "Sauté" button and melt the lard; then, sear the chicken legs for about 4 minutes, turning periodically to ensure even browning.

Stir in the other ingredients and secure the pressure-cooking lid.

Pressure cook for 20 minutes at High pressure. Once cooking is complete, use a natural pressure release; carefully remove the lid.

Bon appétit!

Per serving: Calories: 484; Fat: 29.3g; Carbs: 6.5g; Protein: 45.3g; Sugars: 2.3g; Fiber: 0.9g

292. Roasted Turkey Legs [PC]

(Ready in about 45 minutes | Servings 4)

Ingredients

1 ½ pounds turkey legs
1 tablespoon butter, melted
1 teaspoon hot paprika
1 teaspoon garlic, pressed
Sea salt and ground black pepper, to taste
2 tablespoons scallions, chopped

Directions

Toss the turkey legs with the remaining ingredients, except for the scallions; secure the pressure-cooking lid.

Pressure cook for 20 minutes at High pressure. Once cooking is complete, use a natural pressure release; carefully remove the lid.

Add in scallions and press the "Roast" button.

Roast the turkey legs at 380 degrees F for 40 minutes, turning them over halfway through the cooking time.

Enjoy!

Per serving: Calories: 279; Fat: 14.4g; Carbs: 1.8g; Protein: 33.6g; Sugars: 0.7g; Fiber: 0.5g

293. Easy Chinese Chicken [PC]

(Ready in about 20 minutes | Servings 4)

Ingredients

2 teaspoons sesame oil
1 ½ pounds chicken drumettes
1/4 cup tamari sauce
1 teaspoon Chinese five-spice powder
1 tablespoon maple syrup
2 tablespoons cooking sake

Directions

Preheat your Instant Pot Duo Crisp on the "Sauté" mode and heat the sesame oil. Brown the chicken drumettes for about 3 minutes; turn them over and cook for 2 to 3 minutes longer.

Stir the remaining ingredients into the inner pot and secure the pressure-cooking lid.

Pressure cook for 15 minutes at High pressure. Once cooking is complete, use a quick pressure release; carefully remove the lid.

Serve warm and enjoy!

Per serving: Calories: 270; Fat: 6.8g; Carbs: 4.5g; Protein: 34.8g; Sugars: 3.6g; Fiber: 0.3g

294. Smoked Paprika and Butter Chicken Breasts [AF]

(Ready in about 15 minutes | Servings 4)

Ingredients

1 pound chicken breasts raw, boneless and skinless
1 tablespoon butter, room temperature
1 teaspoon garlic powder
Kosher salt and ground black pepper, to taste
1 teaspoon dried parsley flakes
1 teaspoon smoked paprika
1/2 teaspoon dried oregano

Directions

Pat the chicken dry with kitchen towels. Toss the chicken breasts with the remaining ingredients.

Place the chicken breasts in the Air Fryer basket. Secure the air-frying lid.

Cook the chicken at 380 degrees F for 12 minutes, turning them over halfway through the cooking time.

Bon appétit!

Per serving: Calories: 227; Fat: 13.4g; Carbs: 0.2g; Protein: 23.4g; Sugars: 0.2g; Fiber: 1g

295. Country-Style Duck with Walnuts [PC]

(Ready in about 35 minutes | Servings 5)

Ingredients

2 tablespoons olive oil
2 pounds whole duck
Sea salt and freshly ground black pepper, to taste
1/2 cup vegetable broth
1 shallot, sliced
1/4 cup maple syrup
1/2 cup walnut halves

Directions

Press the "Sauté" button and heat the oil; sear the duck for about 4 minutes or until no longer pink.

Stir in the remaining ingredients. Secure the pressure-cooking lid.

Pressure cook for 30 minutes at High pressure. Once cooking is complete, use a quick pressure release; carefully remove the lid.

Bon appétit!

Per serving: Calories: 541; Fat: 39g; Carbs: 12.3g; Protein: 33.6g; Sugars: 9.1g; Fiber: 0.7g

296. Chinese Duck with Hoisin Sauce [AF]

(Ready in about 40 minutes | Servings 3)

Ingredients
- 1 pound duck breast
- 1 tablespoon Hoisin sauce
- 1 tablespoon Five-spice powder
- Sea salt and black pepper, to taste
- 1/4 teaspoon ground cinnamon

Directions
Pat the duck breasts dry with paper towels. Toss the duck breast with the remaining ingredients.

Place the duck breasts in the Air Fryer basket. Secure the air-frying lid.

Cook the duck breast at 330 degrees F for 15 minutes, turning them over halfway through the cooking time.

Turn the heat to 350 degrees F; continue to cook for about 15 minutes or until cooked through.

Let it rest for 10 minutes before carving and serving. Bon appétit!

Per serving: Calories: 345; Fat: 23.2g; Carbs: 5.7g; Protein: 23.1g; Sugars: 2.3g; Fiber: 0.8g

297. Chicken Fillets with Wine [PC]

(Ready in about 15 minutes | Servings 4)

Ingredients
- 2 tablespoons butter
- 1 pound chicken fillets
- 1 tablespoon poultry seasoning mix
- 1/2 cup chicken stock
- 1/2 cup dry white wine

Directions
Press the "Sauté" button and melt the butter; once hot, sear the chicken for about 4 minutes on each side.

Stir in the seasoning mix, chicken stock, and wine. Secure the pressure-cooking lid.

Pressure cook for 8 minutes at High pressure. Once cooking is complete, use a natural pressure release; carefully remove the lid. Bon appétit!

Per serving: Calories: 211; Fat: 9.3g; Carbs: 1.5g; Protein: 23.9g; Sugars: 0.3g; Fiber: 0.2g

298. Garlic and Parm Chicken Wings [AF]

(Ready in about 25 minutes | Servings 3)

Ingredients
- 1 pound chicken wings, bone-in
- Sea salt and red pepper flakes, to taste
- 2 tablespoons olive oil
- 1/2 cup parmesan cheese, grated
- 2 cloves garlic, pressed

Directions
Pat the chicken dry with kitchen towels. Toss the chicken with the remaining ingredients.

Place the chicken wings in the Air Fryer basket. Secure the air-frying lid.

Air fry the chicken at 380 degrees F for 22 minutes, turning them over halfway through the cooking time.

Bon appétit!

Per serving: Calories: 349; Fat: 19.1g; Carbs: 4.4g; Protein: 38.3g; Sugars: 1.1g; Fiber: 0.3g

299. Sticky Chicken Wings [PC]

(Ready in about 25 minutes | Servings 4)

Ingredients
- 2 tablespoons olive oil
- 3 cloves garlic, minced
- 1 ½ pounds chicken wings
- 1 teaspoon paprika
- Sea salt and ground black pepper, to taste
- 2 tablespoons brown sugar
- 2 tablespoons soy sauce

Directions
Press the "Sauté" button to preheat your Instant Pot Duo Crisp; heat the olive oil and sear the chicken for about 5 minutes.

Stir the remaining ingredients into the inner pot. Secure the pressure-cooking lid.

Pressure cook for 15 minutes at High pressure. Once cooking is complete, use a quick pressure release; carefully remove the lid. Bon appétit!

Per serving: Calories: 322; Fat: 14.3g; Carbs: 8.1g; Protein: 38.3g; Sugars: 6.1g; Fiber: 0.6g

300. English Muffin with Chicken [AF]

(Ready in about 20 minutes | Servings 4)

Ingredients
- 1 pound chicken breasts
- 1 tablespoon olive oil
- Sea salt and black pepper, to taste
- 4 slices cheddar cheese
- 4 teaspoons yellow mustard
- 4 English muffins, lightly toasted

Directions
Pat the chicken dry with kitchen towels. Toss the chicken breasts with the olive oil, salt, and pepper.

Place the chicken wings in the Air Fryer basket. Secure the air-frying lid.

Cook the chicken at 380 degrees F for 12 minutes, turning them over halfway through the cooking time.

Shred the chicken using two forks and serve with cheese, mustard, and English muffins. Bon appétit!

Per serving: Calories: 439; Fat: 21g; Carbs: 26.2g; Protein: 35.3g; Sugars: 1g; Fiber: 2.8g

FISH & SEAFOOD

301. Authentic Fish Biryani [PC]

(Ready in about 10 minutes | Servings 4)

Ingredients

1 tablespoon peanut oil
1 yellow onion, peeled and chopped
1 teaspoon ginger-garlic paste
1 cup water
2 bouillon cubes
1 cup tomato puree
1 pound pollock fillets, sliced
1 cinnamon stick
1 teaspoon garam masala
3 cups basmati rice, cooked

Directions

Press the "Sauté" button to preheat your Instant Pot Duo Crisp; heat the peanut oil and sauté the onion for 2 to 3 minutes or until tender.

Add in the ginger-garlic paste and continue sautéing for 30 seconds or so. Add in the water, bouillon cubes, tomato puree, pollock, cinnamon, and garam masala.

Secure the pressure-cooking lid. Pressure cook for 7 minutes at High pressure. Once cooking is complete, use a quick pressure release; carefully remove the lid.

Serve hot Biryani over the cooked rice and enjoy!

Per serving: Calories: 318; Fat: 7.4g; Carbs: 43.3g; Protein: 18.8g; Sugars: 4.3g; Fiber: 3.2g

302. Calamari in Sherry Sauce [AF]

(Ready in about 10 minutes | Servings 4)

Ingredients

1 pound calamari, sliced into rings
2 tablespoons butter, melted
4 garlic cloves, smashed
2 tablespoons sherry wine
2 tablespoons fresh lemon juice
Coarse sea salt and ground black pepper, to taste
1 teaspoon paprika
1 teaspoon dried oregano

Directions

Toss all the ingredients in a lightly greased Air Fryer cooking basket. Secure the air-frying lid.

Cook your calamari at 400 degrees F for 5 minutes, tossing the basket halfway through the cooking time.

Bon appétit!

Per serving: Calories: 169; Fat: 7.5g; Carbs: 6.6g; Protein: 18.3g; Sugars: 1g; Fiber: 0.6g

303. Classic Codfish Curry [PC]

(Ready in about 15 minutes | Servings 4)

Ingredients

2 tablespoons butter
1 onion, sliced
2 garlic cloves, sliced
1 red chili pepper, sliced
1 cup vegetable broth
1 cup tomato, pureed
1 teaspoon curry powder
1 teaspoon ground cumin
1 cup coconut milk, unsweetened
1 ½ pounds codfish, cut into bite-size pieces
1 tablespoon fresh lemon juice

Directions

Press the "Sauté" button to preheat your Instant Pot Duo Crisp; melt the butter until hot and sauté the onion, garlic, and chili pepper for approximately 3 minutes or until they are tender and fragrant.

Add in the broth, tomato, curry, and cumin.

Secure the pressure-cooking lid. Pressure cook for 6 minutes at High pressure. Once cooking is complete, use a quick pressure release; carefully remove the lid.

Afterwards, add in the coconut milk and codfish; let it simmer on the "Sauté" function for about 5 minutes.

Ladle your curry into individual bowls, garnished with a few drizzles of the fresh lemon juice!

Per serving: Calories: 244; Fat: 9.1g; Carbs: 7g; Protein: 30.1g; Sugars: 4.9g; Fiber: 1g

304. Mahi-Mahi with Butter and Herbs [AF]

(Ready in about 15 minutes | Servings 4)

Ingredients

1 pound mahi-mahi fillets
2 tablespoons butter, at room temperature
2 tablespoons fresh lemon juice
Kosher salt and freshly ground black pepper, to taste
1 teaspoon smoked paprika
1 teaspoon garlic, minced
1 teaspoon dried basil
1 teaspoon dried oregano

Directions

Toss the fish fillets with the remaining ingredients and place them in a lightly oiled Air Fryer cooking basket.

Secure the air-frying lid.

Cook the fish fillets at 400 degrees F for about 14 minutes, turning them over halfway through the cooking time. Bon appétit!

Per serving: Calories: 248; Fat: 16.6g; Carbs: 1.4g; Protein: 21.3g; Sugars: 0.2g; Fiber: 0.3g

305. Halibut Fillets with Shallots [PC]

(Ready in about 10 minutes | Servings 4)

Ingredients

1 pound halibut fillets
2 tablespoons olive oil
2 sprigs fresh thyme
2 sprigs fresh rosemary
1 shallot, sliced
Sea salt and ground black pepper, to taste

Directions

Add 1 cup of water to the inner pot of your Instant Pot Duo Crisp; place the steamer rack in the inner pot.

Lower the halibut fillets onto the rack. Add the olive oil, herbs, shallot, salt, and black pepper; secure the pressure-cooking lid.

Pressure cook for 4 minutes at Low pressure. Once cooking is complete, use a quick pressure release; carefully remove the lid. Bon appétit!

Per serving: Calories: 295; Fat: 22.3g; Carbs: 6.4g; Protein: 17.5g; Sugars: 2.9g; Fiber: 1.4g

306. Swordfish Steaks with Cilantro [AF]

(Ready in about 15 minutes | Servings 4)

Ingredients

1 pound swordfish steaks
4 garlic cloves, peeled
4 tablespoons olive oil
2 tablespoons fresh lemon juice, more for later
1 tablespoon fresh cilantro, roughly chopped
1 teaspoon Spanish paprika
Sea salt and ground black pepper, to taste

Directions

Toss the swordfish steaks with the remaining ingredients and place them in a lightly oiled Air Fryer cooking basket.

Secure the air-frying lid.

Cook the swordfish steaks at 400 degrees F for about 10 minutes, turning them over halfway through the cooking time.

Bon appétit!

Per serving: Calories: 295; Fat: 21.7g; Carbs: 2.8g; Protein: 22.9g; Sugars: 0.8g; Fiber: 0.5g

307. Butter Paprika Salmon [PC]

(Ready in about 10 minutes | Servings 4)

Ingredients

2 tablespoons butter, room temperature
1 onion, chopped
1 pound salmon fillets
1 cup vegetable broth
1 teaspoon paprika
Sea salt and ground black pepper, to taste

Directions

Select the "Sauté" mode and melt the butter; cook the onion for about 3 minutes or until they are fragrant.

Add in the remaining ingredients and secure the pressure-cooking lid.

Pressure cook for 4 minutes at High pressure. Once cooking is complete, use a quick pressure release; carefully remove the lid. Enjoy!

Per serving: Calories: 226; Fat: 11.3g; Carbs: 2.8g; Protein: 24.5g; Sugars: 1.2g; Fiber: 0.5g

308. Authentic Mediterranean Calamari [AF]

(Ready in about 10 minutes | Servings 4)

Ingredients

1 cup all-purpose flour
1/2 cup tortilla chips, crushed
1 teaspoon mustard powder
1 tablespoon dried parsley
Sea salt and freshly ground black pepper, to taste
1 teaspoon cayenne pepper
2 tablespoons olive oil
1 pound calamari, sliced into rings

Directions

In a mixing bowl, thoroughly combine the flour, tortilla chips, spices, and olive oil. Mix to combine well.

Now, dip your calamari into the flour mixture to coat. Place the calamari in a lightly oiled Air Fryer cooking basket; now, secure the air-frying lid.

Cook your calamari at 400 degrees F for 5 minutes, turning them over halfway through the cooking time.

Bon appétit!

Per serving: Calories: 400; Fat: 13.1g; Carbs: 36.6g; Protein: 39.3g; Sugars: 0.3g; Fiber: 1.6g

309. Grouper Fillets with Vegetables [PC]

(Ready in about 10 minutes | Servings 5)

Ingredients

2 tablespoons peanut oil
1 yellow onion, thinly sliced
2 pounds grouper fillets
1 zucchini, sliced
1 carrot, sliced
1 cup marinara sauce
1 cup vegetable broth
Sea salt and ground black pepper, to taste

Directions

Select the "Sauté" mode and heat the peanut oil until sizzling; cook the onion for about 3 minutes or until they are fragrant.

Add in the remaining ingredients and secure the pressure-cooking lid.

Pressure cook for 4 minutes at High pressure. Once cooking is complete, use a quick pressure release; carefully remove the lid. Enjoy!

Per serving: Calories: 243; Fat: 7.6g; Carbs: 4.6g; Protein: 37.3g; Sugars: 2.5g; Fiber: 1.2g

310. Mackerel Fillets with Classic Chimichurri [AF]

(Ready in about 15 minutes | Servings 4)

Ingredients

1 tablespoon olive oil, or more to taste
1 ½ pounds mackerel fillets
Sea salt and ground black pepper, taste
2 tablespoons parsley
2 garlic cloves, minced
2 tablespoons fresh lime juice

Directions

Toss the fish fillets with the remaining ingredients and place them in a lightly oiled Air Fryer cooking basket.

Secure the air-frying lid.

Cook the fish fillets at 400 degrees F for about 14 minutes, turning them over halfway through the cooking time.

Bon appétit!

Per serving: Calories: 218; Fat: 6.8g; Carbs: 2.3g; Protein: 34.6g; Sugars: 0.8g; Fiber: 0.3g

FISH & SEAFOOD

311. Pancetta, Fish, and Cauliflower Stew [PC]

(Ready in about 15 minutes | Servings 4)

Ingredients

- 2 ounces pancetta, diced
- 1 yellow onion, chopped
- 1 teaspoon fresh garlic, minced
- 1 pound cauliflower florets
- 1 pound sea bass fillets, sliced
- 2 sprigs fresh rosemary
- 2 sprigs fresh thyme
- 1 cup dry white wine
- 2 cups chicken bone broth

Directions

Select the "Sauté" mode to preheat your Instant Pot Duo Crisp; now, cook the pancetta for about 2 minutes, crumbling with a fork; reserve.

Then, in the pan drippings, sauté the onion, garlic, and cauliflower florets for approximately 3 minutes or until the vegetables are tender and fragrant.

Add in the remaining ingredients and secure the pressure-cooking lid.

Pressure cook for 10 minutes at High pressure. Once cooking is complete, use a quick pressure release; carefully remove the lid. Bon appétit!

Per serving: Calories: 294; Fat: 11.2g; Carbs: 9.7g; Protein: 27.5g; Sugars: 4g; Fiber: 2.7g

312. Fried Garlicky Shrimp [AF]

(Ready in about 10 minutes | Servings 4)

Ingredients

- 1 ½ pounds raw shrimp, peeled and deveined
- 1 tablespoon olive oil
- 1 teaspoon garlic, minced
- 1 teaspoon cayenne pepper
- 1/2 teaspoon lemon pepper
- Sea salt, to taste

Directions

Toss all the ingredients in a lightly greased Air Fryer cooking basket. Secure the air-frying lid.

Air fry the shrimp at 400 degrees F for 6 minutes, tossing the basket halfway through the cooking time.

Bon appétit!

Per serving: Calories: 181; Fat: 4.3g; Carbs: 1.1g; Protein: 34.4g; Sugars: 0.3g; Fiber: 0.2g

313. Tuna Fillets with Tomatoes [PC]

(Ready in about 10 minutes | Servings 4)

Ingredients

- 1 pound tuna fillets
- 2 tablespoons olive oil
- 1 cup grape tomatoes
- Sea salt and ground black pepper, to taste
- 2 garlic cloves, sliced

Directions

Add 1 cup of water to the inner pot of your Instant Pot Duo Crisp; place a steamer rack in the inner pot.

Lower the tuna fillets onto the rack. Add the olive oil, tomatoes, salt, black pepper, and garlic; secure the pressure-cooking lid.

Choose the "Steam" mode and cook for 3 minutes at Low pressure. Once cooking is complete, use a quick pressure release; carefully remove the lid. Bon appétit!

Per serving: Calories: 256; Fat: 12.4g; Carbs: 8.3g; Protein: 27.1g; Sugars: 6g; Fiber: 0.5g

314. Restaurant-Style Fish Fingers [AF]

(Ready in about 15 minutes | Servings 4)

Ingredients

- 1/2 cup all-purpose flour
- 1 large egg
- 2 tablespoons buttermilk
- 1/2 cup crackers, crushed
- 1 teaspoon garlic powder
- Sea salt and ground black pepper, to taste
- 1/2 teaspoon cayenne pepper
- 1 pound tilapia fillets, cut into strips

Directions

In a shallow bowl, place the flour. Whisk the egg and buttermilk in the second bowl, and mix the crushed crackers and spices in the third bowl.

Dip the fish strips in the flour mixture, then in the whisked eggs; finally, roll the fish strips over the cracker mixture until they are well coated on all sides.

Arrange the fish sticks in the Air Fryer basket. Secure the air-frying lid.

Air fry the fish sticks at 400 degrees F for about 10 minutes, shaking the basket halfway through the cooking time. Bon appétit!

Per serving: Calories: 196; Fat: 3.5g; Carbs: 14.2g; Protein: 26.6g; Sugars: 1.1g; Fiber: 0.7g

315. Classic Seafood Hot Pot [PC]

(Ready in about 15 minutes | Servings 4)

Ingredients

- 2 ounces bacon, chopped
- 1 onion, chopped
- 2 garlic cloves minced
- 3 cups water
- 2 bouillon cubes
- 1 cup dry white wine
- 1 teaspoon dried thyme
- 1 teaspoon dried basil
- Sea salt and ground black pepper, to taste
- 1 teaspoon cayenne pepper
- 1/2 pound prawns, cleaned and deveined
- 1 pound clams, cleaned

Directions

Preheat your Instant Pot Duo Crisp on the "Sauté" mode; now, cook the bacon until crisp and reserve.

Then, sauté the onion and garlic in the bacon grease for about 3 minutes, stirring and adding a few tablespoons of water.

Add in the remaining ingredients. Secure the pressure-cooking lid.

Pressure cook for 7 minutes at High pressure. Once cooking is complete, use a quick pressure release; carefully remove the lid.

Serve your chowder into soup bowls, garnish with the reserved bacon, and enjoy!

Per serving: Calories: 233; Fat: 7.1g; Carbs: 8.6g; Protein: 30.5g; Sugars: 1.9g; Fiber: 0.9g

FISH & SEAFOOD

316. Dilled King Prawn Salad [AF]

(Ready in about 10 minutes | Servings 4)

Ingredients

1 ½ pounds king prawns, peeled and deveined
Coarse sea salt and ground black pepper, to taste
1 tablespoon fresh lemon juice
1 cup mayonnaise
1 teaspoon Dijon mustard
1 tablespoon fresh parsley, roughly chopped
1 teaspoon fresh dill, minced
1 shallot, chopped

Directions

Toss the prawns with the salt and black pepper in a lightly greased Air Fryer cooking basket.

Secure the air-frying lid.

Air fry the prawns at 400 degrees F for 6 minutes, tossing the basket halfway through the cooking time.

Add the prawns to a salad bowl; add in the remaining ingredients and stir to combine well.

Bon appétit!

Per serving: Calories: 341; Fat: 21.2g; Carbs: 2.3g; Protein: 34.7g; Sugars: 1g; Fiber: 0.5g

317. Beer Crab Bowl [PC]

(Ready in about 10 minutes | Servings 5)

Ingredients

1 ½ pounds crabs, cleaned and cracked
2 tablespoons butter
2 garlic cloves, minced
1 yellow onion, chopped
1 Spanish pepper, seeded and sliced
1 red chili pepper, seeded and sliced
1/2 cup ale beer
1 cup shellfish stock
1 lime, cut into wedges

Directions

Add all the ingredients, except for the lime, into the inner pot of your Instant Pot Duo Crisp.

Secure the pressure-cooking lid.

Pressure cook for 4 minutes at High pressure. Once cooking is complete, use a quick pressure release; carefully remove the lid.

Bon appétit!

Per serving: Calories: 213; Fat: 8.3g; Carbs: 5.1g; Protein: 26g; Sugars: 1.8g; Fiber: 0.6g

318. Halibut with Chives and Peppercorns [AF]

(Ready in about 15 minutes | Servings 4)

Ingredients

1 pound halibut steaks
1/4 cup butter
Sea salt, to taste
2 tablespoons fresh chives, chopped
1 teaspoon garlic, minced
1 teaspoon mixed peppercorns, ground

Directions

Toss the halibut steaks with the remaining ingredients and place them in a lightly oiled Air Fryer cooking basket.

Secure the air-frying lid.

Cook the halibut steaks at 400 degrees F for about 12 minutes, turning them over halfway through the cooking time. Bon appétit!

Per serving: Calories: 314; Fat: 27g; Carbs: 0.3g; Protein: 16.5g; Sugars: 0.1g; Fiber: 0.1g

319. Pasta and Tuna Casserole [PC+AF]

(Ready in about 20 minutes | Servings 4)

Ingredients

2 tablespoons olive oil
1 large-sized shallot, chopped
2 garlic cloves, minced
1 tablespoon fresh parsley, chopped
1 tablespoon fresh rosemary, chopped
8 ounces penne pasta, dry
1 pound tuna fillets, sliced
1 cup marinara sauce
1 cup chicken bone broth
1/2 cup parmesan cheese, grated
1/2 cup fresh breadcrumbs

Directions

Press the "Sauté" button and heat the olive oil. Once hot, sauté the shallot for approximately 3 minutes or until tender.

Stir in the garlic and continue sautéing for a further 30 seconds. Add in the parsley, rosemary, pasta, tuna, marinara sauce, and broth.

Secure the pressure-cooking lid. Pressure cook for 10 minutes at High pressure. Once cooking is complete, use a quick pressure release; carefully remove the lid.

Top with the cheese and breadcrumbs; cover with the air-frying lid and let it cook for 5 to 6 minutes or until the cheese melts.

Bon appétit!

Per serving: Calories: 524; Fat: 17.4g; Carbs: 54.7g; Protein: 37.1g; Sugars: 3.1g; Fiber: 7.8g

320. Fried Paprika and Chive Prawns [AF]

(Ready in about 10 minutes | Servings 4)

Ingredients

1 ½ pounds prawns, peeled and deveined
2 garlic cloves, minced
2 tablespoons fresh chives, chopped
1/2 cup whole-wheat flour
1/2 teaspoon sweet paprika
1 teaspoon hot paprika
Salt and freshly ground black pepper, to taste
2 tablespoons coconut oil
2 tablespoons lemon juice

Directions

Toss all the ingredients in a lightly greased Air Fryer cooking basket.

Secure the air-frying lid.

Cook the prawns at 400 degrees F for 9 minutes, tossing the basket halfway through the cooking time. Bon appétit!

Per serving: Calories: 261; Fat: 801g; Carbs: 12.1g; Protein: 35.4g; Sugars: 0.3g; Fiber: 2g

FISH & SEAFOOD

321. Fish and Vegetable Hot Pot [PC]

(Ready in about 15 minutes | Servings 4)

Ingredients

2 teaspoons butter, room temperature
2 garlic cloves, chopped
1 onion, chopped, thinly sliced
1 bell pepper, sliced
1 large carrot, sliced
1 celery stalk, chopped
1 cup tomato sauce
2 cups chicken broth
1 teaspoon fennel seeds
1 teaspoon mustard seeds
Sea salt and ground black pepper, to taste
1 pound pollock, cut into bite-sized pieces
4 ounces shrimp, deveined

Directions

Press the "Sauté" button to preheat your Instant Pot Duo Crisp; then, cook the onion, pepper, and garlic for about 2 minutes or until the vegetables have just softened.

Add in the carrot, celery, tomato sauce, broth, and spices. Secure the pressure-cooking lid.

Pressure cook for 7 minutes at High pressure. Once cooking is complete, use a quick pressure release; carefully remove the lid.

Fold in the pollock and shrimp; continue to cook on the "Sauté" mode for a further 5 minutes or until thoroughly heated.

Bon appétit!

Per serving: Calories: 215; Fat: 3.7g; Carbs: 17.4g; Protein: 24.5g; Sugars: 8.4g; Fiber: 4.8g

322. Fish and Avocado Pita [AF]

(Ready in about 15 minutes | Servings 4)

Ingredients

1 pound monkfish fillets
1 tablespoon olive oil
Sea salt and ground black pepper, to taste
Sea salt and ground black pepper, to taste
1 teaspoon cayenne pepper
4 tablespoons coleslaw
1 avocado, pitted, peeled and diced
1 tablespoon fresh parsley, chopped
4 (6-1/2 inch) Greek pitas, warmed

Directions

Toss the fish fillets with the olive oil; place them in a lightly oiled Air Fryer cooking basket.

Secure the air-frying lid.

Air fry the fish fillets at 400 degrees F for about 14 minutes, turning them over halfway through the cooking time.

Assemble your pitas with the chopped fish and remaining ingredients and serve warm. Bon appétit!

Per serving: Calories: 494; Fat: 24.3g; Carbs: 43.8g; Protein: 28.8g; Sugars: 3.8g; Fiber: 8.3g

323. American-Style Cioppino [PC]

(Ready in about 15 minutes | Servings 5)

Ingredients

2 tablespoons butter
1 large onion, chopped
2 cloves garlic, minced
2 fresh tomatoes, pureed
3 cups fish broth
1 sprig thyme
1 cup dry white wine
1 pound king prawns
12 large mussels, cleaned and debearded
1 ½ pounds halibut fillets, cut into bite-sized chunks

Directions

Melt the butter on the "Sauté" mode; then, cook the onion and garlic for about 2 minutes or until tender and fragrant.

Add in the remaining ingredients, except for the seafood, and gently stir to combine.

Secure the pressure-cooking lid. Pressure cook for 5 minutes at High pressure. Once cooking is complete, use a quick pressure release; carefully remove the lid.

Fold in the seafood and bring to a boil on the "Sauté" mode; continue to cook for 5 minutes or until they are cooked through.

Bon appétit!

Per serving: Calories: 429; Fat: 24.1g; Carbs: 7.5g; Protein: 44.5g; Sugars: 2.7g; Fiber: 1.1g

324. Sea Bass with Butter and Wine [AF]

(Ready in about 15 minutes | Servings 3)

Ingredients

2 tablespoons butter, room temperature
1 pound sea bass such
1/4 cup dry white wine
1/4 cup all-purpose flour
Sea salt and ground black pepper, to taste
1 teaspoon mustard seeds
1 teaspoon fennel seeds
2 cloves garlic, minced

Directions

Toss the fish with the remaining ingredients; place them in a lightly oiled Air Fryer cooking basket.

Secure the air-frying lid.

Air fry the fish at 400 degrees F for about 10 minutes, turning them over halfway through the cooking time.

Bon appétit!

Per serving: Calories: 294; Fat: 13.1g; Carbs: 10.7g; Protein: 31.8g; Sugars: 0.8g; Fiber: 0.9g

325. Seafood Salad with Olives and Cheese [PC]

(Ready in about 10 minutes + chilling time | Servings 4)

Ingredients

1/2 cup dry white wine
1 cup water
2 bay leaves
1 ½ pounds clams, cleaned
1 pound salmon
2 cloves garlic, minced
2 tablespoons fresh chives
2 cups iceberg lettuce, shredded
1 teaspoon oregano
1 Greek cucumber, thinly sliced
2 tablespoons fresh lemon juice
4 tablespoons extra-virgin olive oil
Sea salt and ground black pepper, to taste
2 ounces Kalamata olives
2 ounces feta cheese, crumbled

Directions

Add the wine, water, and bay leaves to the inner pot of your Instant Pot Duo Crisp. Lower a metal trivet into the inner pot.

Put the clams and salmon into the steamer basket and lower the basket onto the rack.

Secure the pressure-cooking lid. Choose the "Steam" program and cook for 3 minutes at Low pressure. Once cooking is complete, use a quick pressure release; carefully remove the lid.

Allow the steamed seafood to cool at room temperature.

Meanwhile, toss the other ingredients in a salad bowl; add in the reserved seafood and gently toss to combine. Enjoy!

Per serving: Calories: 415; Fat: 17.3g; Carbs: 10.6g; Protein: 51.5g; Sugars: 2.2g; Fiber: 1.3g

326. Mediterranean Calamari Parmigiano [AF]

(Ready in about 10 minutes | Servings 4)

Ingredients

1 ½ pounds small squid tubes
2 tablespoons butter, melted
1 chili pepper, chopped
2 garlic cloves, minced
1 teaspoon red pepper flakes
Sea salt and ground black pepper, to taste
1/4 cup dry white wine
2 tablespoons fresh lemon juice
1 teaspoon Mediterranean herb mix
2 tablespoons Parmigiano-Reggiano cheese, grated

Directions

Toss all the ingredients, except for the Parmigiano-Reggiano cheese, in a lightly greased Air Fryer cooking basket.

Secure the air-frying lid.

Cook your squid at 400 degrees F for 5 minutes, tossing the basket halfway through the cooking time.

Top the warm squid with cheese. Bon appétit!

Per serving: Calories: 267; Fat: 11.3g; Carbs: 9.3g; Protein: 29.8g; Sugars: 2g; Fiber: 0.4g

327. Creamy Codfish Pate [PC]

(Ready in about 10 minutes | Servings 8)

Ingredients

1 cup chicken broth
1/2 cup dry white wine
1 ½ pounds codfish
1 tablespoon stone-ground mustard
2 tablespoons crème fraîche
2 tablespoons butter, room temperature
1 teaspoon rosemary, chopped
1 teaspoon thyme, chopped
Sea salt and freshly ground black pepper

Directions

Add the broth and wine to the inner pot of your Instant Pot Duo Crisp; place the steamer rack in the inner pot.

Lower the codfish onto the rack; secure the pressure-cooking lid.

Choose the "Steam" mode and cook for 3 minutes at Low pressure. Once cooking is complete, use a quick pressure release; carefully remove the lid.

Place the fish along with the remaining ingredients in a blender or food processor; blend the mixture, adding the cooking liquid periodically. Bon appétit!

Per serving: Calories: 108; Fat: 5.6g; Carbs: 8.5g; Protein: 5.8g; Sugars: 2.4g; Fiber: 0.7g

328. Mackerel Fish Cakes [AF]

(Ready in about 15 minutes | Servings 4)

Ingredients

1 pound mackerel fillet, boneless and chopped
1 tablespoon olive oil
1/2 onion, chopped
2 garlic cloves, crushed
1 teaspoon hot paprika
1 tablespoon fresh cilantro, chopped
2 tablespoons fresh parsley, chopped
Sea salt and ground black pepper, to taste
4 English muffins, toasted

Directions

Mix all the ingredients, except for the English muffins, in a bowl. Shape the mixture into four patties and place them in a lightly oiled Air Fryer cooking basket.

Secure the air-frying lid.

Air fry the fish patties at 400 degrees F for about 14 minutes, turning them over halfway through the cooking time.

Serve on English muffins and enjoy!

Per serving: Calories: 404; Fat: 20.4g; Carbs: 28.4g; Protein: 26.6g; Sugars: 2.1g; Fiber: 3.3g

329. Asian-Style Mackerel [PC]

(Ready in about 10 minutes | Servings 4)

Ingredients

2 tablespoons ghee, room temperature
1 ½ pounds mackerel fillets
1 teaspoon garlic, minced
1/2 cup scallions, sliced
Coarse sea salt and red pepper flakes, to taste
4 tablespoons maple syrup
1 teaspoon stone-ground mustard
2 tablespoons soy sauce
1 cup chicken bone broth

Directions

Select the "Sauté" mode to preheat your Instant Pot Duo Crisp; melt the ghee and sauté the garlic and scallions for about 3 minutes or until they are tender and aromatic.

Add in the remaining ingredients and secure the pressure-cooking lid.

Pressure cook for 4 minutes at High pressure. Once cooking is complete, use a quick pressure release; carefully remove the lid. Enjoy!

Per serving: Calories: 326; Fat: 11.2g; Carbs: 17.7g; Protein: 36.9g; Sugars: 14.5g; Fiber: 0.7g

330. Fried Shrimp and Broccoli [AF]

(Ready in about 10 minutes | Servings 4)

Ingredients

1 pound raw shrimp, peeled and deveined
1/2 pound broccoli florets
1 tablespoon olive oil
1 garlic clove, minced
2 tablespoons freshly squeezed lemon juice
Coarse sea salt and ground black pepper, to taste
1 teaspoon paprika

Directions

Toss all the ingredients in a lightly greased Air Fryer cooking basket.

Secure the air-frying lid.

Cook the shrimp and broccoli at 400 degrees F for 6 minutes, tossing the basket halfway through the cooking time.

Bon appétit!

Per serving: Calories: 160; Fat: 4.2g; Carbs: 6g; Protein: 24.7g; Sugars: 1.8g; Fiber: 1.9g

331. Mussels Salad with Spinach [PC]

(Ready in about 10 minutes | Servings 4)

Ingredients

1 ½ pounds mussels, cleaned and beard removed
1 medium-sized onion, thinly sliced
1 garlic clove, crushed
2 tablespoons fresh lemon juice
1/4 cup extra-virgin olive oil
1 bell peppers, sliced
2 cups baby spinach
2 tablespoons fresh parsley, roughly chopped

Directions

Pour 1 cup of water into the inner pot of your Instant Pot Duo Crisp; now, place the metal rack in the inner pot.

Place the mussels in the steamer basket; lower the steamer basket onto the metal rack.

Secure the pressure-cooking lid. Choose the "Steam" mode and cook for 3 minutes at Low pressure. Once cooking is complete, use a quick pressure release; carefully remove the lid.

Stir the remaining ingredients into a salad bowl; add in the mussels and toss to combine. Serve well-chilled and enjoy!

Per serving: Calories: 278; Fat: 17.6g; Carbs: 8.9g; Protein: 21.3g; Sugars: 0.9g; Fiber: 0.6g

332. Mexican Cod Fish Tacos [AF]

(Ready in about 15 minutes | Servings 4)

Ingredients

1 pound codfish fillets
1 tablespoon olive oil
1 avocado, pitted, peeled and mashed
4 tablespoons mayonnaise
1 teaspoon mustard
1 shallot, chopped
1 habanero pepper, chopped
8 small corn tortillas

Directions

Toss the fish fillets with the olive oil; place them in a lightly oiled Air Fryer cooking basket.

Secure the air-frying lid.

Air fry the fish fillets at 400 degrees F for about 14 minutes, turning them over halfway through the cooking time.

Assemble your tacos with the chopped fish and remaining ingredients and serve warm. Bon appétit!

Per serving: Calories: 414; Fat: 21.9g; Carbs: 27.4g; Protein: 28.3g; Sugars: 1.6g; Fiber: 6.9g

333. Creole Sea Bass with Tomato [PC]

(Ready in about 10 minutes | Servings 4)

Ingredients

2 tablespoons olive oil
1 teaspoon garlic, minced
1 small-sized leek, sliced
1 ½ pounds sea bass fillets
Sea salt and ground black pepper, to taste
1 tablespoon Creole seasoning mix
1 cup vegetable broth
1 large-sized tomato, pureed

Directions

Select the "Sauté" mode to preheat your Instant Pot Duo Crisp; heat the olive oil and sauté the garlic and leeks for about 3 minutes or until they are tender.

Add in the remaining ingredients and secure the pressure-cooking lid.

Pressure cook for 4 minutes at High pressure. Once cooking is complete, use a quick pressure release; carefully remove the lid. Enjoy!

Per serving: Calories: 264; Fat: 10.7g; Carbs: 6.5g; Protein: 33.5g; Sugars: 2.7g; Fiber: 1.2g

334. Orange Roughy Fillets [AF]

(Ready in about 15 minutes | Servings 4)

Ingredients

1 pound orange roughy fillets
2 tablespoons butter
2 cloves garlic, minced
Sea salt and red pepper flakes, to taste

Directions

Toss the fish fillets with the remaining ingredients and place them in a lightly oiled Air Fryer cooking basket.

Secure the air-frying lid.

Air fry the fish fillets at 400 degrees F for about 10 minutes, turning them over halfway through the cooking time.

Bon appétit!

Per serving: Calories: 144; Fat: 6.7g; Carbs: 1.6g; Protein: 18.9g; Sugars: 0.8g; Fiber: 0.3g

335. Honey and Orange Tilapia [PC]

(Ready in about 10 minutes | Servings 4)

Ingredients

1/4 cup honey
1/4 cup fresh orange juice
2 tablespoons butter
2 tablespoons soy sauce
1 ½ pound tilapia fillet
1 cup chicken bone broth
Sea salt and cayenne pepper, to taste

Directions

Add all the ingredients to the inner pot of your Instant Pot Duo Crisp; secure the pressure-cooking lid.

Pressure cook for 4 minutes at High pressure. Once cooking is complete, use a quick pressure release; carefully remove the lid.

Enjoy!

Per serving: Calories: 324; Fat: 10.5g; Carbs: 22.5g; Protein: 36.5g; Sugars: 20.8g; Fiber: 0.4g

336. Sticky Trout Bites [AF]

(Ready in about 15 minutes | Servings 4)

Ingredients

1 pound trout, cut into sticks
1 tablespoon olive oil
2 tablespoons liquid honey
2 teaspoons apple cider vinegar
2 cloves garlic, minced
Sea salt and ground black pepper, to taste
1/2 teaspoon cayenne pepper

Directions

Toss all the ingredients in a lightly greased Air Fryer cooking basket.

Secure the air-frying lid.

Cook your fish at 390 degrees F for 12 minutes, tossing the basket halfway through the cooking time.

Bon appétit!

Per serving: Calories: 238; Fat: 10.9g; Carbs: 10.3g; Protein: 23.6g; Sugars: 9.2g; Fiber: 0.3g

337. Traditional Italian Brodetto [PC]

(Ready in about 20 minutes | Servings 4)

Ingredients

2 teaspoons olive oil
1 onion, chopped
2 large garlic cloves, minced
1 celery stalk, chopped
1 tablespoon Italian herb mix
Sea salt and ground black pepper, to taste
2 cups chicken broth
1/2 cup dry white wine
1 tomato, chopped
1 tablespoon capers, drained
1 ½ pounds halibut fillet, cut into cubes

Directions

Heat the olive oil on the "Sauté" mode and cook the onion and garlic for about 3 minutes or until tender and fragrant.

Add in the remaining ingredients, except for the fish.

Secure the pressure-cooking lid. Pressure cook for 7 minutes at High pressure. Once cooking is complete, use a quick pressure release; carefully remove the lid.

Fold in the halibut fish and let it cook on the "Sauté" mode for 5 minutes more or until cooked through. Bon appétit!

Per serving: Calories: 405; Fat: 26.7g; Carbs: 6.4g; Protein: 27.5g; Sugars: 3.1g; Fiber: 1.2g

338. Hot and Spicy Squid [AF]

(Ready in about 10 minutes | Servings 5)

Ingredients

1 ½ pounds squid, cut into pieces
1 chili pepper, chopped
1 small lemon, squeezed
2 tablespoons olive oil
1 tablespoon capers, drained
2 garlic cloves, minced
1 tablespoon coriander, chopped
2 tablespoons parsley, chopped
1 teaspoon sweet paprika
Sea salt and ground black pepper, to taste

Directions

Toss all the ingredients in a lightly greased Air Fryer cooking basket.

Secure the air-frying lid.

Air fry the squid at 400 degrees F for 5 minutes, tossing the basket halfway through the cooking time. Bon appétit!

Per serving: Calories: 205; Fat: 7.7g; Carbs: 8g; Protein: 24.9g; Sugars: 1.2g; Fiber: 0.6g

339. Asian Hong Shao Yu [PC]

(Ready in about 10 minutes | Servings 4)

Ingredients

1 tablespoon peanut oil
1 pound tuna fillets
1 onion, chopped
1 teaspoon ginger-garlic paste
1 cup dashi
1 teaspoon oyster sauce
2 tablespoons soy sauce
1 cup coconut milk, unsweetened
Sea salt and Szechuan pepper, to taste

FISH & SEAFOOD

Directions

Preheat your Instant Pot on the "Sauté" function; once hot, heat the oil and cook the onion for approximately 3 minutes or until they are fragrant and translucent.

Add in the remaining ingredients and secure the pressure-cooking lid.

Pressure cook for 4 minutes at High pressure. Once cooking is complete, use a quick pressure release; carefully remove the lid. Enjoy!

Per serving: Calories: 233; Fat: 7.4g; Carbs: 8.7g; Protein: 30.5g; Sugars: 6.3g; Fiber: 0.8g

340. Tangy Minty Swordfish [AF]

(Ready in about 15 minutes | Servings 4)

Ingredients

1 pound swordfish steaks
2 tablespoons olive oil
2 tablespoons fresh mint leaves, chopped
3 tablespoons fresh lemon juice
1 teaspoon garlic powder
1/2 teaspoon shallot powder
Sea salt and freshly ground black pepper, to taste

Directions

Toss the swordfish steaks with the remaining ingredients and place them in a lightly oiled Air Fryer cooking basket.

Secure the air-frying lid.

Air fry the swordfish steaks at 400 degrees F for about 10 minutes, turning them over halfway through the cooking time. Bon appétit!

Per serving: Calories: 229; Fat: 14.3g; Carbs: 1.4g; Protein: 22.4g; Sugars: 0.3g; Fiber: 0.3g

341. Herb Garlic Mussels [PC]

(Ready in about 10 minutes | Servings 4)

Ingredients

1/2 cup vegetable broth
1 cup dry white wine
A few saffron threads
1 thyme sprig
2 rosemary sprigs
2 pounds mussels, cleaned and beard removed
2 tablespoons butter
2 garlic cloves, finely chopped

Directions

Pour the broth and wine into the inner pot of your Instant Pot Duo Crisp; add in the saffron, thyme, and rosemary. Now, place the metal rack in the inner pot.

Place the mussels in the steamer basket; lower the steamer basket onto the metal rack.

Secure the pressure-cooking lid. Choose the "Steam" mode and cook for 3 minutes at Low pressure. Once cooking is complete, use a quick pressure release; carefully remove the lid. Reserve the steamed mussels.

Press the "Sauté" button and melt the butter until sizzling. Now, cook the garlic for 30 seconds or so; add in the cooking liquid and let the sauce cook to your desired thickness.

Stir the mussels into the sauce and enjoy!

Per serving: Calories: 304; Fat: 11.7g; Carbs: 10.5g; Protein: 27.8g; Sugars: 0.6g; Fiber: 0.2g

342. Thai-Style Sea Bass [AF]

(Ready in about 20 minutes | Servings 4)

Ingredients

1 ½ pounds sea bass fillet
2 tablespoons lemon juice
2 garlic cloves, minced
1/2 cup coconut, shredded
1/2 cup all-purpose flour
Coarse sea salt and ground black pepper, to taste
2 tomatoes, sliced

Directions

Toss the fish fillets with the lemon juice, garlic, coconut, flour, salt, and black pepper; place them in a lightly oiled Air Fryer cooking basket.

Secure the air-frying lid. Cook the fish fillets at 400 degrees F for about 8 minutes.

Turn them over and top with the tomatoes. Continue to cook for a further 8 minutes.

Bon appétit!

Per serving: Calories: 237; Fat: 3.6g; Carbs: 15.4g; Protein: 33.3g; Sugars: 1.8g; Fiber: 1.2g

343. Chilean Caldillo de Mariscos [PC]

(Ready in about 15 minutes | Servings 4)

Ingredients

2 tablespoons olive oil
1/2 cup shallots, sliced
2 cloves garlic, chopped
1 teaspoon chili pepper, chopped
1 anchovy fillet, chopped
Sea salt and ground black pepper, to taste
1 teaspoon smoked paprika
1 cup clam juice
1 cup tomato puree
1 cup white wine
1 pound halibut, cut into bite-sized pieces

Directions

Press the "Sauté" button and heat the olive oil; then, sauté the shallot for about 3 minutes or until tender. Add in the garlic and continue to sauté for 30 to 40 seconds or until aromatic.

Add in the remaining ingredients.

Secure the pressure-cooking lid. Pressure cook for 7 minutes at High pressure. Once cooking is complete, use a quick pressure release; carefully remove the lid.

Bon appétit!

Per serving: Calories: 338; Fat: 22.1g; Carbs: 14.6g; Protein: 18.6g; Sugars: 6.3g; Fiber: 22.9g

FISH & SEAFOOD

344. Fried Calamari Rings [AF]

(Ready in about 10 minutes | Servings 4)

Ingredients

2 cups all-purpose flour
1 cup beer
Sea salt and ground black pepper, to taste
2 teaspoons garlic powder
1 teaspoon dried parsley flakes
1 tablespoon olive oil
1 pound calamari rings

Directions

In a mixing bowl, thoroughly combine the flour, beer, spices, and olive oil. Mix to combine well.

Now, dip your calamari into the flour mixture to coat. Place them in a greased Air Fryer cooking basket.

Secure the air-frying lid.

Air fry your calamari at 400 degrees F for 5 minutes, turning them over halfway through the cooking time.

Bon appétit!

Per serving: Calories: 397; Fat: 5.5g; Carbs: 55.5g; Protein: 24.8g; Sugars: 0.8g; Fiber: 2g

345. Catfish and Mushroom Medley [PC]

(Ready in about 10 minutes | Servings 4)

Ingredients

2 tablespoon olive oil
1 onion, chopped
1 pound button mushrooms, sliced
1 ½ pounds catfish
2 tomatoes, pureed
1 cup chicken bone broth
1 tablespoon smoked paprika
1/2 teaspoon garlic powder
Sea salt and cayenne pepper, to taste

Directions

Choose the "Sauté" mode to preheat your Instant Pot Duo Crisp; heat the olive oil and sauté the onion for about 3 minutes or until translucent.

Add in the mushrooms and continue sautéing an additional 2 minutes or until your mushrooms release the liquid.

Add in the remaining ingredients and secure the pressure-cooking lid.

Pressure cook for 4 minutes at High pressure. Once cooking is complete, use a quick pressure release; carefully remove the lid.

Enjoy!

Per serving: Calories: 286; Fat: 19.3g; Carbs: 6.5g; Protein: 19.5g; Sugars: 1.2g; Fiber: 0.4g

346. Salmon Fillets with Lemon and Herbs [AF]

(Ready in about 15 minutes | Servings 4)

Ingredients

1 ½ pounds salmon fillets
2 sprigs fresh rosemary
1 tablespoon fresh basil
1 tablespoon fresh thyme
1 tablespoon fresh dill
1 small lemon, juiced
2 tablespoons olive oil
Sea salt and ground black pepper, to taste
1 teaspoon stone-ground mustard
2 cloves garlic, chopped

Directions

Toss the salmon with the remaining ingredients; place them in a lightly oiled Air Fryer cooking basket.

Secure the air-frying lid.

Air fry the salmon fillets at 380 degrees F for about 12 minutes, turning them over halfway through the cooking time.

Serve immediately and enjoy!

Per serving: Calories: 293; Fat: 14.7g; Carbs: 3.7g; Protein: 36.1g; Sugars: 0.8g; Fiber: 0.7g

347. Tilapia with Cremini Mushroom Sauce [PC]

(Ready in about 10 minutes | Servings 4)

Ingredients

2 tablespoons butter
2 garlic cloves, minced
1 shallot, chopped
1 pound cremini mushrooms, sliced
1 ½ pounds tilapia fillets
1/2 teaspoon dill weed
Sea salt and ground black pepper, to taste
1 tablespoon lime juice
1 cup fish broth

Directions

Select the "Sauté" mode to preheat your Instant Pot Duo Crisp; melt the butter and sauté the garlic, shallot, and mushrooms for about 3 minutes or until they are tender and fragrant.

Add in the remaining ingredients and secure the pressure-cooking lid.

Pressure cook for 4 minutes at High pressure. Once cooking is complete, use a quick pressure release; carefully remove the lid.

Enjoy!

Per serving: Calories: 259; Fat: 9.4g; Carbs: 6.3g; Protein: 39g; Sugars: 3.1g; Fiber: 1.5g

348. Spicy Fish Patties [AF]

(Ready in about 15 minutes | Servings 4)

Ingredients

1 pound tilapia fish fillets, chopped
1/2 cup breadcrumbs
4 tablespoons shallots, chopped
2 garlic cloves, minced
1 tablespoon olive oil
8 dinner rolls
8 slices Provolone cheese

Directions

Mix all the ingredients, except for the dinner rolls and cheese, in a bowl. Shape the mixture into four patties and place them in a lightly oiled Air Fryer cooking basket.

Secure the air-frying lid.

Air fry the fish patties at 400 degrees F for about 14 minutes, turning them over halfway through the cooking time.

Serve with cheese and hamburger buns. Enjoy!

Per serving: Calories: 508; Fat: 23.7g; Carbs: 31.3g; Protein: 42.4g; Sugars: 2.4g; Fiber: 2.6g

349. Salmon and Broccoli Quiche [PC+AF]

(Ready in about 25 minutes | Servings 4)

Ingredients

2 tablespoons butter
1 onion, chopped
8 ounces macaroni, dry
8 ounces broccoli florets
1 cup milk
1 cup chicken bone broth
1 tablespoon capers, drained
1 pound salmon fillets, diced
1/2 cup cream cheese, crumbled
1/2 cup cheddar cheese, grated

Directions

Press the "Sauté" button and melt the butter. Once hot, cook the onion for approximately 3 minutes, stirring periodically.

Add in the macaroni, broccoli florets, milk, chicken bone broth, capers, and salmon.

Secure the pressure-cooking lid. Pressure cook for 9 minutes at High pressure. Once cooking is complete, use a quick pressure release; carefully remove the lid.

Top your quiche with the cheese and cover with the air-frying lid; let it cook for 10 minutes longer or until heated through.

Bon appétit!

Per serving: Calories: 620; Fat: 28.7g; Carbs: 49.7g; Protein: 39.3g; Sugars: 6.9g; Fiber: 2.4g

350. American-Style Fried Shrimp [AF]

(Ready in about 15 minutes | Servings 4)

Ingredients

1 cup all-purpose flour
1 teaspoon Old Bay seasoning
Sea salt and lemon pepper, to taste
1/2 cup buttermilk
1 cup seasoned breadcrumbs
1 ½ pounds shrimp, peeled and deveined

Directions

In a shallow bowl, mix the flour, spices, and buttermilk. Place the seasoned breadcrumbs in a second bowl.

Dip the shrimp in the flour mixture, then in the breadcrumbs until they are well coated on all sides.

Arrange the shrimp in a well-greased Air Fryer cooking basket. Secure the air-frying lid.

Cook the shrimp at 400 degrees F for about 10 minutes, shaking the basket halfway through the cooking time.

Bon appétit!

Per serving: Calories: 381; Fat: 1.4g; Carbs: 45.2g; Protein: 39.8g; Sugars: 5.2g; Fiber: 5.4g

351. Herbed Fish Boil [PC]

(Ready in about 15 minutes | Servings 4)

Ingredients

2 tablespoons butter, melted
1 onion, chopped
2 garlic cloves, minced
1 pound salmon fillets, cut into bite-sized chunks
1 bell peppers, sliced
1 teaspoon dried basil
1 sprig thyme
2 sprigs rosemary
2 bay leaves
1 teaspoon curry paste
4 cups fish broth

Directions

Simply throw all the ingredients in the inner pot of your Instant Pot Duo Crisp. Secure the pressure-cooking lid.

Pressure cook for 10 minutes at High pressure. Once cooking is complete, use a quick pressure release; carefully remove the lid.

Ladle the fish boil into individual bowls and serve immediately. Enjoy!

Per serving: Calories: 285; Fat: 15.7g; Carbs: 5.5g; Protein: 29.1g; Sugars: 2g; Fiber: 1g

352. Sea Scallops with Rosemary and Wine [AF]

(Ready in about 10 minutes | Servings 4)

Ingredients

1 ½ pounds sea scallops
4 tablespoons butter, melted
1 tablespoon garlic, minced
Sea salt and ground black pepper, to season
2 rosemary sprigs, leaves picked and chopped
4 tablespoons dry white wine

Directions

Toss all the ingredients in a lightly greased Air Fryer cooking basket.

Secure the air-frying lid.

Air fry the scallops at 400 degrees F for 7 minutes, tossing the basket halfway through the cooking time.

Bon appétit!

Per serving: Calories: 318; Fat: 15.1g; Carbs: 11.1g; Protein: 32.7g; Sugars: 0.6g; Fiber: 0.4g

FISH & SEAFOOD

353. Spicy Tilapia Hot Pot [PC]

(Ready in about 15 minutes | Servings 4)

Ingredients

2 tablespoons butter
1 onion, chopped
1 Spanish pepper, seeded and sliced
1 red chili pepper, seeded and sliced
2 garlic cloves, cut in half, green shoots removed
2 anchovy fillets, soaked and drained
2 tomatoes, pureed
2 cups beef broth
2 bay leaves
1 ½ pounds tilapia, cut into bite-sized pieces
1/2 lemon, juiced

Directions

Melt the butter on the "Sauté" function and sauté the onion and Spanish pepper for about 3 minutes or until they are just tender.

Add in the chili pepper, garlic, anchovy fillets, tomatoes, broth, bay leaves, and tilapia. Secure the pressure-cooking lid.

Pressure cook for 10 minutes at High pressure. Once cooking is complete, use a quick pressure release; carefully remove the lid.

Ladle your stew into individual bowls, drizzle each serving with the fresh lemon juice, and enjoy!

Per serving: Calories: 272; Fat: 9.6g; Carbs: 8g; Protein: 38.3g; Sugars: 4.1g; Fiber: 1.6g

354. Tuna Steak Salad with Spinach [AF]

(Ready in about 15 minutes | Servings 4)

Ingredients

1 pound fresh tuna steak
Sea salt and ground black pepper, to taste
2 tablespoons fresh lemon juice
1 small onion, thinly sliced
1 carrot, julienned
2 cups baby spinach
2 tablespoons parsley, roughly chopped

Directions

Toss the fish with the salt and black pepper; place your tuna in a lightly oiled Air Fryer cooking basket.

Secure the air-frying lid.

Air fry your tuna at 400 degrees F for about 10 minutes, turning it over halfway through the cooking time.

Chop your tuna with two forks and add in the remaining ingredients; stir to combine and serve well-chilled. Bon appétit!

Per serving: Calories: 187; Fat: 5.7g; Carbs: 5.3g; Protein: 27.5g; Sugars: 2.3g; Fiber: 1.3g

355. Saucy Tilapia Fillets with Wine [PC]

(Ready in about 10 minutes | Servings 4)

Ingredients

1 cup chicken broth
1/2 cup white wine
2 bay leaves
1 pound tilapia fillets
2 tablespoons butter
1 onion, chopped
2 garlic cloves, minced
Sea salt and ground black pepper, to taste

Directions

Place the chicken broth, wine, and bay leaves in the inner pot of your Instant Pot Duo Crisp.

Lower a metal trivet into the inner pot of your Instant Pot Duo Crisp. Place a piece of aluminum foil on the trivet.

Lower the fish onto the trivet and secure the pressure-cooking lid.

Choose the "Steam" mode and cook for 3 minutes at Low pressure. Once cooking is complete, use a quick pressure release; carefully remove the lid. Reserve the fish and liquid.

Press the "Sauté" button and melt the butter until sizzling; cook the onion and garlic until tender. Add in the cooking liquid, salt, black pepper, and fish to the inner pot. Let it simmer for 3 minutes more.

Bon appétit!

Per serving: Calories: 199; Fat: 8.1g; Carbs: 4.7g; Protein: 24.7g; Sugars: 2.2g; Fiber: 0.7g

356. Italian Sausage-Stuffed Squid [AF]

(Ready in about 10 minutes | Servings 4)

Ingredients

2 tablespoons olive oil, divided, or as needed
1 small onion, chopped
2 cloves garlic, minced
1 tablespoon fresh parsley, chopped
1 small Italian pepper, chopped
Sea salt and ground black pepper, to taste
4 ounces beef sausage, crumbled
1 pound squid tubes, cleaned

Directions

In a mixing bowl, thoroughly combine the olive oil, onion, garlic, parsley, Italian pepper, salt, black pepper, and sausage.

Stuff the squid tubes with the sausage filling and secure them with toothpicks. Place them in a lightly oiled Air Fryer cooking basket.

Secure the air-frying lid.

Air fry the stuffed squid tubes at 400 degrees F for 5 minutes, turning them over halfway through the cooking time.

Bon appétit!

Per serving: Calories: 280; Fat: 13.7g; Carbs: 11.2g; Protein: 26.3g; Sugars: 1.8g; Fiber: 1.5g

FISH & SEAFOOD

357. Fish and Bacon Chowder [PC]

(Ready in about 20 minutes | Servings 4)

Ingredients

2 ounces bacon, diced
1 onion, finely chopped
1 pound potatoes, peeled and cubed
1 celery stalk, chopped
1 teaspoon garlic powder
1 teaspoon mustard powder
1 bay laurel
1 teaspoon lemon-pepper seasoning
1 pound tilapia fish, sliced
Coarse sea salt and ground white pepper, to taste
3 cups vegetable broth
1 cup fat-free evaporated milk

Directions

Preheat your Instant Pot on the "Sauté" mode and cook the bacon until crisp; reserve. Then, sauté the onion and potatoes in the bacon grease for about 3 minutes, stirring and adding a few tablespoons of water; reserve.

Add in the remaining ingredients, except for the evaporated milk, and gently stir to combine.

Secure the pressure-cooking lid. Pressure cook for 7 minutes at High pressure. Once cooking is complete, use a quick pressure release; carefully remove the lid.

Pour in the milk, cover, and let it sit in the residual heat for 5 minutes.

Serve your chowder into soup bowls, garnish with the reserved bacon, and enjoy!

Per serving: Calories: 238; Fat: 7g; Carbs: 31.7g; Protein: 10.9g; Sugars: 8.9g; Fiber: 3.6g

358. Sea Scallop and Baby Greens Bowl [AF]

(Ready in about 10 minutes | Servings 4)

Ingredients

1 ½ pounds sea scallops
Sea salt and ground black pepper, to taste
2 tablespoons olive oil
1 tablespoon balsamic vinegar
2 garlic cloves, minced
2 teaspoons fresh tarragon, minced
1 teaspoon Dijon mustard
1 cup mixed baby greens
1 small tomato, diced

Directions

Toss the scallops, salt, and black pepper in a lightly greased Air Fryer cooking basket.

Secure the air-frying lid.

Air fry the scallops at 400 degrees F for 7 minutes, tossing the basket halfway through the cooking time.

Toss the scallops with the remaining ingredients and serve at room temperature or well-chilled.

Bon appétit!

Per serving: Calories: 243; Fat: 10.2g; Carbs: 3.3g; Protein: 32.1g; Sugars: 1.8g; Fiber: 0.5g

359. Cod with Coconut Yogurt Sauce [PC]

(Ready in about 15 minutes | Servings 4)

Ingredients

2 tablespoons ghee, at room temperature
1 onion, chopped
1 teaspoon ginger-garlic paste
2 tomatoes, chopped
1 teaspoon turmeric powder
Sea salt and cayenne pepper
2 chicken bullions cubes
1 ½ pound cod fillets
1 cup water
1 cup coconut yogurt

Directions

Select the "Sauté" mode and melt the ghee; once hot, cook the onion for about 3 minutes or until they are tender and fragrant.

Add in the remaining ingredients, except for the coconut yogurt; secure the pressure-cooking lid.

Pressure cook for 4 minutes at High pressure. Once cooking is complete, use a quick pressure release; carefully remove the lid.

Fold in the yogurt, stir and secure the lid; let it sit in the residual heat for about 5 minutes or until heated through. Enjoy!

Per serving: Calories: 221; Fat: 8.3g; Carbs: 10.9g; Protein: 27.2g; Sugars: 5.4g; Fiber: 2.2g

360. Salmon Salad with Aleppo Pepper [AF]

(Ready in about 15 minutes | Servings 4)

Ingredients

1 pound salmon fillets
Sea salt and ground black pepper, to taste
2 tablespoons olive oil
2 garlic cloves, minced
1 bell pepper, sliced
1 shallot, chopped
1/2 cup Kalamata olives, pitted and sliced
1/2 lemon, juiced
1 teaspoon Aleppo pepper, minced

Directions

Toss the salmon fillets with the salt, black pepper, and olive oil; place them in a lightly oiled Air Fryer cooking basket.

Secure the air-frying lid.

Air fry the salmon fillets at 380 degrees F for about 12 minutes, turning them over halfway through the cooking time.

Chop the salmon fillets using two forks and add them to a salad bowl; add in the remaining ingredients and toss to combine.

Bon appétit!

Per serving: Calories: 243; Fat: 13.3g; Carbs: 5.5g; Protein: 24.4g; Sugars: 2g; Fiber: 1.2g

FISH & SEAFOOD

RICE & GRAINS

361. Shrimp, Couscous, and Feta Salad [PC]

(Ready in about 10 minutes + chilling time | Servings 4)

Ingredients

- 2 cups water
- 1 cup couscous
- 1 pound shrimp, deveined
- Sea salt and cayenne pepper
- 4 tablespoons extra-virgin olive oil
- 2 tablespoons lemon juice, freshly squeezed
- 1 small Persian cucumber, sliced
- 1 Spanish pepper, sliced
- 1 red onion, thinly sliced
- 1/2 cup green olives, pitted and halved
- 2 ounces goat cheese, crumbled
- 1 tablespoon fresh mint, chopped

Directions

Place the water, couscous, and shrimp in the inner pot of your Instant Pot Duo Crisp. Secure the pressure-cooking lid.

Pressure cook for 3 minutes at High pressure. Once cooking is complete, use a quick pressure release; carefully remove the lid.

Allow the shrimp and couscous to cool to room temperature. Toss them with the salt, cayenne pepper, olive oil, lemon juice, cucumber, pepper, and onion; toss to combine well.

Top your salad with the olives, cheese, and fresh mint. Bon appétit!

Per serving: Calories: 455; Fat: 19g; Carbs: 36.5g; Protein: 33.3g; Sugars: 1.7g; Fiber: 2.6g

362. Risotto with Cauliflower and Mozzarella [AF]

(Ready in about 15 minutes | Servings 4)

Ingredients

- 2 cups rice, cooked
- 2 tablespoons olive oil
- 1/2 cup cauliflower, chopped
- 1/2 cup vegetable broth
- 4 tablespoons mozzarella cheese, shredded

Directions

Thoroughly combine all the ingredients in a lightly greased baking pan.

Lower the pan into the Air Fryer cooking basket. Secure the air-frying lid.

Cook at 360 degrees F for about 10 minutes or until cooked through.

Bon appétit!

Per serving: Calories: 218; Fat: 11g; Carbs: 24.6g; Protein: 5g; Sugars: 1.8g; Fiber: 2g

363. Brown Rice Porridge [PC]

(Ready in about 35 minutes | Servings 4)

Ingredients

- 1 ½ cups brown rice
- 1 ½ cups water
- 2 fresh dates, pitted
- 1/2 cup vanilla almond milk
- 1 medium apple, peeled and diced

Directions

Place the brown rice and water in the inner pot of your Instant Pot Duo Crisp.

Pressure cook for 22 minutes at High pressure. Once cooking is complete, use a natural pressure release for 5 minutes; carefully remove the pressure-cooking lid.

Add in the fresh dates, milk, and apple; let it sit in the residual heat for 5 to 6 minutes.

Taste and adjust the seasonings. Enjoy!

Per serving: Calories: 323; Fat: 2.9g; Carbs: 67.5g; Protein: 6.8g; Sugars: 12.4g; Fiber: 3.8g

364. Porridge with Applesauce and Walnut [AF]

(Ready in about 15 minutes | Servings 4)

Ingredients

- 1/2 cup rolled oats
- 1/2 cup rye flakes
- 1 cup milk
- 1 cup applesauce, unsweetened
- 1/2 cup walnuts, chopped
- A pinch of coarse sea salt
- A pinch of freshly grated nutmeg

Directions

Thoroughly combine all the ingredients in a mixing bowl. Spoon the mixture into a lightly greased casserole dish.

Lower the dish into the Air Fryer cooking basket. Secure the air-frying lid.

Choose the "Bake" program and bake your porridge at 380 degrees F for about 12 minutes.

Bon appétit!

Per serving: Calories: 249; Fat: 10.1g; Carbs: 33.6g; Protein: 8.3g; Sugars: 9.2g; Fiber: 4.8g

365. Authentic Asian Congee [PC]

(Ready in about 15 minutes | Servings 4)

Ingredients

- 2 tablespoons sesame oil
- 1 pound chicken fillets, diced
- 1 cup long-grain white rice
- 2 cups water
- 1 tablespoon Chinese rice wine
- 1 teaspoon fresh ginger, peeled and minced
- 2 garlic cloves, minced
- Sea salt and red pepper, to taste
- 2 scallion stalks, sliced

Directions

Select the "Sauté" mode to preheat your Instant Pot Duo Crisp; heat the sesame oil and brown the chicken fillets for about 4 minutes or until no longer pink.

Add in the white rice, water, wine, ginger, garlic, salt, and red pepper; now, secure the pressure-cooking lid.

Pressure cook for 8 minutes at High pressure. Once cooking is complete, use a quick pressure release; carefully remove the lid.

Fluff your rice with a fork, garnish with fresh scallions, and enjoy!

Per serving: Calories: 378; Fat: 10.4g; Carbs: 41.6g; Protein: 28.2g; Sugars: 0.8g; Fiber: 0.9g

366. Brioche Bread Pudding with Almonds [AF]

(Ready in about 35 minutes | Servings 6)

Ingredients

2 cups brioche bread, cubed
1 cup almond milk
2 eggs, whisked
1/4 teaspoon ground cinnamon
1/4 teaspoon ground cardamom
1/2 teaspoon vanilla extract
1/4 cup honey
1/2 cup almonds, chopped

Directions

Place the bread cubes in a lightly greased baking pan.

In a mixing bowl, thoroughly combine the remaining ingredients.

Pour the custard mixture over the bread cubes; set aside for 15 minutes to soak. Lower the baking pan into the Air Fryer cooking basket.

Secure the air-frying lid.

Choose the "Bake" program. Bake the bread pudding at 350 degrees F for about 20 minutes or until the custard is set but still a little wobbly.

Serve at room temperature. Bon appétit!

Per serving: Calories: 196; Fat: 9.2g; Carbs: 22g; Protein: 17.3g; Sugars: 14.8g; Fiber: 2g

367. Wheat Berry and Anasazi Bean Salad [PC]

(Ready in about 35 minutes | Servings 5)

Ingredients

1 ½ cups wheat berries
2 cups Anasazi beans
7 cups water
2 tablespoons olive oil
A pinch of grated nutmeg
1/2 teaspoon kosher salt
1/2 teaspoon cayenne pepper
1 teaspoon dried basil
1/2 teaspoon dried oregano
1/2 teaspoon dried dill weed
1 celery stalk, chopped
1 onion, chopped
1 teaspoon garlic, minced

Directions

Place all the ingredients in the inner pot of your Instant Pot Duo Crisp.

Pressure cook for 25 minutes at High pressure. Once cooking is complete, use a natural pressure release for 10 minutes; carefully remove the pressure-cooking lid.

Ladle the mixture into individual bowls and enjoy!

Per serving: Calories: 440; Fat: 6.7g; Carbs: 78.1g; Protein: 20.8g; Sugars: 1.2g; Fiber: 14.4g

368. Spiced Banana Oatmeal [AF]

(Ready in about 15 minutes | Servings 4)

Ingredients

1 cup old-fashioned oats
1 cup coconut milk
1 cup water
1 banana, mashed
1/2 teaspoon vanilla extract
1/2 teaspoon ground cinnamon
A pinch of grated nutmeg
A pinch of sea salt

Directions

Thoroughly combine all the ingredients in a mixing bowl. Spoon the mixture into lightly greased mugs.

Then, place the mugs in the Air Fryer cooking basket. Secure the air-frying lid.

Air fry the oatmeal at 380 degrees F for about 12 minutes.

Bon appétit!

Per serving: Calories: 217; Fat: 4.7g; Carbs: 35.4g; Protein: 8.8g; Sugars: 6.7g; Fiber: 5.1g

369. Indian Daliya Khichdi [PC]

(Ready in about 25 minutes | Servings 4)

Ingredients

1 cup cracked wheat
3 cups water
A pinch of salt
A pinch of grated nutmeg
4 tablespoons jaggery

Directions

Place all the ingredients in the inner pot of your Instant Pot Duo Crisp.

Pressure cook for 20 minutes at High pressure. Once cooking is complete, use a quick pressure release; carefully remove the pressure-cooking lid.

Bon appétit!

Per serving: Calories: 323; Fat: 2.9g; Carbs: 67.5g; Protein: 6.8g; Sugars: 12.4g; Fiber: 3.8g

370. Multigrain Pilaf with Herbs [AF]

(Ready in about 15 minutes | Servings 4)

Ingredients

1 ½ cups cooked multigrain rice
1 cup vegetable broth
1/2 cup scallions, thinly sliced
1 tablespoon fresh parsley, chopped
1 tablespoon fresh cilantro, chopped
2 tablespoons olive oil
Sea salt and cayenne pepper, to taste
1 teaspoon garlic powder

Directions

Thoroughly combine all the ingredients in a lightly greased baking pan.

Lower the pan into the Air Fryer cooking basket. Secure the air-frying lid.

Air fry at 360 degrees F for about 10 minutes or until cooked through.

Bon appétit!

Per serving: Calories: 168; Fat: 7.1g; Carbs: 19.6g; Protein: 3.7g; Sugars: 1.2g; Fiber: 2g

RICE & GRAINS

371. Jasmine Rice and Pecan Bowl [PC]

(Ready in about 20 minutes | Servings 5)

Ingredients

- 2 cups jasmine rice
- 2 cups water
- Sea salt, to taste
- 1/4 cup extra-virgin olive oil
- 1 tablespoon apple cider vinegar
- 1 tablespoon cilantro, chopped
- 1 English cucumber, sliced
- 1 bell pepper, sliced
- 2 tablespoons pecans, roughly chopped

Directions

Add the jasmine rice, water, and salt to the inner pot of your Instant Pot. Secure the pressure-cooking lid.

Pressure cook for 4 minutes at High pressure. Once cooking is complete, use a natural pressure release for 10 minutes; carefully remove the lid.

Toss the chilled rice with the remaining ingredients; serve at room temperature.

Bon appétit!

Per serving: Calories: 394; Fat: 13.4g; Carbs: 61.2g; Protein: 5.4g; Sugars: 0.6g; Fiber: 2.5g

372. Herb Corn Fritters [AF]

(Ready in about 20 minutes | Servings 5)

Ingredients

- 6 ounces canned corn kernels
- 1/2 small-sized onion, peeled and chopped
- 2 cloves garlic, minced
- 2 tablespoons fresh parsley, chopped
- 2 tablespoons fresh mint, chopped
- 2 tablespoons butter, melted
- 2 eggs, beaten
- 1/2 cup rice flour
- 1 teaspoon baking powder
- Sea salt and ground black pepper, to taste
- 1 teaspoon turmeric powder

Directions

Mix all the ingredients until everything is well combined. Form the mixture into balls.

Secure the air-frying lid.

Air fry the balls at 380 degrees F for about 15 minutes, tossing the basket halfway through the cooking time.

Bon appétit!

Per serving: Calories: 159; Fat: 6.7g; Carbs: 21.3g; Protein: 4.3g; Sugars: 1.8g; Fiber: 1.3g

373. Spanish Oat Groat Stew [PC]

(Ready in about 20 minutes | Servings 4)

Ingredients

- 1 cup oat groats, rinsed
- 2 tablespoons butter
- 1 onion, chopped
- 2 garlic cloves, minced
- 1 Spanish pepper, seeded and sliced
- 1 stalk celery, chopped
- 2 cups vegetable broth
- 1 cup marinara sauce
- 1 teaspoon Italian spice mix
- 2 bay leaves

Directions

Simply throw all the ingredients into the inner pot of your Instant Pot Dupo Crisp; stir to combine.

Secure the pressure-cooking lid.

Pressure cook for 12 minutes at High pressure. Once cooking is complete, use a natural pressure release for 5 minutes; carefully remove the lid.

Taste and adjust the seasonings. Bon appétit!

Per serving: Calories: 259; Fat: 9.3g; Carbs: 34.7g; Protein: 10.7g; Sugars: 4.4g; Fiber: 6.3g

374. Bread Pudding with Prunes [AF]

(Ready in about 40 minutes | Servings 5)

Ingredients

- 8 slices bread, cubed
- 1 cup coconut milk
- 1/4 cup coconut oil
- 1 egg, beaten
- 1/4 cup honey
- 1/2 teaspoon ground cinnamon
- 1/4 teaspoon ground cloves
- A pinch of kosher salt
- 1/2 cup prunes, pitted and chopped

Directions

Place the bread cubes in a lightly greased baking pan.

In a mixing bowl, thoroughly combine the milk, coconut oil, egg, honey, cinnamon, cloves, and salt.

Pour the custard mixture over the bread cubes. Fold in the prunes and set aside for 15 minutes to soak.

Secure the air-frying lid.

Air fry the bread pudding at 350 degrees F for about 20 minutes or until the custard is set but still a little wobbly. Bon appétit!

Per serving: Calories: 317; Fat: 14.3g; Carbs: 44g; Protein: 6.1g; Sugars: 18.2g; Fiber: 1g

375. Brioche Bread Pudding [PC]

(Ready in about 35 minutes | Servings 4)

Ingredients

- 2 tablespoons coconut oil
- 4 eggs, beaten
- 2 cups coconut milk
- 1 cup heavy cream
- 1 cup brown sugar
- 1 teaspoon pure vanilla extract
- A pinch of kosher salt
- A pinch of grated nutmeg
- 1/2 teaspoon ground cinnamon
- 4 cups brioche bread, cubed
- 1/2 cup Sultanas

Directions

In a mixing bowl, thoroughly combine the coconut oil, eggs, coconut milk, heavy cream, sugar, vanilla, salt, nutmeg, and cinnamon.

Fold in the brioche bread and let it soak for about 20 minutes. Spoon the mixture into the inner pot of your Instant Pot Duo Crisp.

Fold in the Sultanas and secure the pressure-cooking lid.

Pressure cook for 15 minutes at High pressure. Once cooking is complete, use a quick pressure release; carefully remove the lid.

Bon appétit!

Per serving: Calories: 548; Fat: 27.3g; Carbs: 63.2g; Protein: 13.6g; Sugars: 44.3g; Fiber: 2g

376. Vanilla and Cinnamon French Toast [AF]

(Ready in about 15 minutes | Servings 3)

Ingredients

2 eggs
1/2 cup milk
2 tablespoons butter, room temperature
1 teaspoon vanilla extract
1/4 teaspoon grated nutmeg
1 teaspoon cinnamon powder
3 slices challah bread

Directions

In a mixing bowl, thoroughly combine the eggs, milk, butter, vanilla, nutmeg, and cinnamon.

Then dip each piece of bread into the egg mixture; place the bread slices in a lightly greased baking pan.

Lower the pan into the Air Fryer basket and secure the air-frying lid.

Air Fryer the bread slices at 330 degrees F for about 4 minutes; turn them over and cook for a further 3 to 4 minutes. Enjoy!

Per serving: Calories: 194; Fat: 12.4g; Carbs: 12.6g; Protein: 6.8g; Sugars: 3.3g; Fiber: 0.8g

377. Spelt Berry and Spinach Bowl [PC]

(Ready in about 35 minutes | Servings 4)

Ingredients

1 ½ cups vegetable broth
1 cup spelt berries
1/4 cup extra-virgin olive oil
1 tablespoon balsamic vinegar
1 tablespoon lemon juice
1 teaspoon honey
1/2 teaspoon cinnamon powder
2 cloves garlic, minced
1 celery rib, sliced
1 cup baby spinach leaves
1 apple, diced

Directions

Simply place the broth and spelt berries in the inner pot of your Instant Pot Duo Crisp. Secure the pressure-cooking lid.

Pressure cook for 30 minutes at High pressure. Once cooking is complete, use a quick pressure release; carefully remove the lid.

Toss the spelt berries with the remaining ingredients and enjoy!

Per serving: Calories: 303; Fat: 14.7g; Carbs: 41g; Protein: 6.8g; Sugars: 10.2g; Fiber: 6.4g

378. Breakfast Muffins with Apples [AF]

(Ready in about 20 minutes | Servings 6)

Ingredients

1/2 cups self-rising flour
1/2 cup rolled oats
1/2 cup agave syrup
1/4 teaspoon grated nutmeg
1/2 teaspoon cinnamon powder
A pinch of coarse salt
1/2 cup milk
1/4 cup coconut oil, room temperature
2 eggs
1 teaspoon coconut extract
1 cup apples, cored and chopped

Directions

Mix all the ingredients in a bowl.

Scrape the batter into silicone baking molds; place the prepared molds in the Air Fryer basket.

Secure the air-frying lid.

Bake your muffins at 320 degrees F for about 15 minutes or until a tester comes out dry and clean. Allow the muffins to cool before unmolding and serving.

Per serving: Calories: 290; Fat: 12g; Carbs: 42.1g; Protein: 5.3g; Sugars: 24.8g; Fiber: 2.1g

379. Millet and Pumpkin Bowl [PC]

(Ready in about 15 minutes | Servings 4)

Ingredients

2 tablespoons butter
1 cup millet
1 carrot, trimmed and chopped
2 tablespoons scallions, chopped
1 pound pumpkin, peeled and diced
Kosher salt and ground black pepper, to taste
2 cups water
1/4 cup pumpkin seeds, lightly toasted

Directions

Place the butter, millet, carrots, scallions, pumpkin, salt, and black pepper in the inner pot of your Instant Pot Du Crisp.

Pour in the water and secure the pressure-cooking lid.

Pressure cook for 12 minutes at High pressure. Once cooking is complete, use a quick pressure release; carefully remove the lid.

Serve the warm millet in the individual bowls, garnished with pumpkin seeds. Bon appétit!

Per serving: Calories: 333; Fat: 11.7g; Carbs: 47.3g; Protein: 9.3g; Sugars: 4.6g; Fiber: 6g

380. Asian Wontons with Chicken [PC+AF]

(Ready in about 20 minutes | Servings 6)

Ingredients

1 tablespoon sesame oil
1 teaspoon garlic, pressed
1 teaspoon fresh ginger, peeled and grated
1/2 pound ground chicken
1 small onion, chopped
1 cup green cabbage, shredded
2 tablespoons soy sauce
2 tablespoons rice wine
6 wonton wrappers

Directions

Heat the oil on the "Sauté" mode and cook the garlic and ginger for about 30 seconds. Then, sauté the chicken, onion, and cabbage for approximately 5 minutes.

Press the "Cancel" button. Add in the soy sauce and rice wine; stir to combine well.

Divide the filling between wonton wrappers and roll them up tightly; seal the wrappers with water.

Lower the wonton wrappers into the Air Fryer cooking basket. Secure the air-frying lid.

Cook the wonton wrappers at 360 degrees F for 6 minutes; turn them over and cook for 5 minutes longer. Bon appétit!

Per serving: Calories: 193; Fat: 6.8g; Carbs: 22.3g; Protein: 10.5g; Sugars: 2.1g; Fiber: 1.2g

381. Wild Rice Salad with Greens [PC]

(Ready in about 25 minutes + chilling time | Servings 4)

Ingredients

1 cup wild rice, rinsed
2 cups water
1/4 cup extra-virgin olive oil
4 ounces baby spinach
4 ounces Romaine lettuce
2 tablespoons fresh basil, roughly chopped
2 tablespoons fresh parsley, roughly chopped
2 tablespoons fresh sage, roughly chopped
4 ounces goat cheese, crumbled
2 tablespoons lemon juice, freshly squeezed
1 teaspoon stone-ground mustard
1 teaspoon honey
Sea salt and freshly ground black pepper, to taste

Directions

Simply stir the rice and water into the inner pot of your Instant Pot Duo Crisp.

Secure the pressure-cooking lid.

Pressure cook for 22 minutes at High pressure. Once cooking is complete, use a quick pressure release and carefully remove the lid.

Let it cool completely. Mix the chilled rice with the other ingredients; gently toss to combine well. Enjoy!

Per serving: Calories: 415; Fat: 24.5g; Carbs: 35.3g; Protein: 16.1g; Sugars: 3.7g; Fiber: 4.3g

382. South Indian Pakoda [AF]

(Ready in about 20 minutes | Servings 4)

Ingredients

1/2 cup rice flour
1/2 cup Ragi
1/2 teaspoon baking powder
1 cup methi, chopped
1 green chilli, finely chopped
1 teaspoon ginger-garlic paste
2 tablespoons sesame oil
Sea salt and ground black pepper, to taste

Directions

Mix all the ingredients until everything is well combined. Form the mixture into patties.

Secure the air-frying lid.

Air fry the patties at 380 degrees F for about 15 minutes or until cooked through. Turn them over halfway through the cooking time.

Bon appétit!

Per serving: Calories: 213; Fat: 7.3g; Carbs: 32.2g; Protein: 2.6g; Sugars: 0.6g; Fiber: 1.2g

383. Bulgur Pilaf with Mushrooms [PC]

(Ready in about 25 minutes | Servings 3)

Ingredients

2 tablespoons butter
1 shallot, chopped
1 teaspoon garlic, minced
8 ounces cremini mushrooms, sliced
1 cup medium-grind bulgur wheat
2 cups vegetable broth
1/2 cup white wine
1 tablespoon Italian spice blend

Directions

Select the "Sauté" mode to preheat your Instant Pot Duo Crisp; melt the butter and sauté the shallot, garlic and mushrooms for about 3 minutes or until they have softened.

Add in the remaining ingredients and secure the pressure-cooking lid.

Pressure cook for 20 minutes at High pressure. Once cooking is complete, use a quick pressure release; carefully remove the lid. Enjoy!

Per serving: Calories: 285; Fat: 9.7g; Carbs: 41.1g; Protein: 11.8g; Sugars: 2.7g; Fiber: 7g

384. The Best Granola Ever [AF]

(Ready in about 20 minutes | Servings 8)

Ingredients

1/2 cup old-fashioned oats
1/4 cup coconut flakes, unsweetened
1/4 cup quinoa flakes
1/4 cup almonds, slivered
1/4 cup hazelnuts, chopped
1/4 cup chia seeds
1 teaspoon ground cinnamon
A pinch of grated nutmeg
A pinch of sea salt
2 tablespoons coconut oil
1/4 cup maple syrup
1 teaspoon vanilla extract
1/2 cup chocolate chips

Directions

Thoroughly combine all the ingredients in a lightly greased baking pan.

Then, place the pan in the Air Fryer cooking basket. Secure the air-frying lid.

Bake your granola at 350 degrees F for about 15 minutes, stirring every 5 minutes.

Store at room temperature in an airtight container for up to three weeks.

Bon appétit!

Per serving: Calories: 334; Fat: 11.4g; Carbs: 49g; Protein: 11.4g; Sugars: 21.1g; Fiber: 6g

385. Barley Porridge with Cinnamon [PC]

(Ready in about 25 minutes | Servings 4)

Ingredients

1 cup whole barley
4 cups water
1/2 teaspoon ground cinnamon
1/2 teaspoon grated nutmeg

Directions

Add all the ingredients to the inner pot of your Instant Pot Duo Crisp; secure the pressure-cooking lid.

Pressure cook for 22 minutes at High pressure. Once cooking is complete, use a quick pressure release; carefully remove the lid.

Ladle your porridge into serving bowls and enjoy!

Per serving: Calories: 178; Fat: 0.6g; Carbs: 39.3g; Protein: 4.9g; Sugars: 0.5g; Fiber: 8g

386. British Buttermilk Scones [AF]

(Ready in about 20 minutes | Servings 6)

Ingredients

1 cup all-purpose flour
1 teaspoon baking powder
1/4 teaspoon salt
1/4 teaspoon grated nutmeg
1/2 cup brown sugar
2 egg, beaten
1/4 cup buttermilk
1/2 teaspoon vanilla extract
6 tablespoons raisins, soaked for 15 minutes

Directions

Mix all the ingredients until everything is well incorporated. Spoon the batter into baking cups; lower the cups into the Air Fryer basket.

Secure the air-frying lid.

Bake your scones at 360 degrees F for about 17 minutes or until a tester comes out dry and clean.

Bon appétit!

Per serving: Calories: 177; Fat: 1.7g; Carbs: 34.5g; Protein: 4.3g; Sugars: 18.7g; Fiber: 0.9g

387. Millet Congee with a Twist [PC]

(Ready in about 15 minutes | Servings 4)

Ingredients

1 cup millet
1 cup water
1 cup dashi
1 teaspoon brown sugar
2 tablespoons soy sauce
1 teaspoon Chinese Five-spice powder

Directions

Place all the ingredients in the inner pot of your Instant Pot Duo Crisp.

Stir to combine and secure the pressure-cooking lid.

Pressure cook for 12 minutes at High pressure. Once cooking is complete, use a quick pressure release; carefully remove the lid.

Bon appétit!

Per serving: Calories: 215; Fat: 3.5g; Carbs: 39.1g; Protein: 6.1g; Sugars: 2.2g; Fiber: 4.4g

388. Vanilla Oatmeal with Almonds [AF]

(Ready in about 15 minutes | Servings 4)

Ingredients

1 cup rolled oats
1 cup water
1 cup milk
1 teaspoon vanilla paste
A pinch of kosher salt
1/2 teaspoon ground cloves
4 tablespoons honey
1/2 cup almonds, slivered

Directions

Thoroughly combine all the ingredients in a mixing bowl. Spoon the mixture into lightly greased ramekins.

Then, place the ramekins in the Air Fryer cooking basket. Secure the air-frying lid.

Bake your oatmeal at 380 degrees F for about 12 minutes. Serve warm or at room temperature.

Bon appétit!

Per serving: Calories: 334; Fat: 11.4g; Carbs: 49g; Protein: 11.4g; Sugars: 21g; Fiber: 6g

389. Wild Rice Porridge [PC]

(Ready in about 25 minutes | Servings 4)

Ingredients

1 cup wild rice
1 ½ cups water
1 cup oat milk
1/2 teaspoon salt
A pinch of grated nutmeg
1/2 cup walnuts, roughly chopped
1/4 cup maple syrup
1/2 cup strawberries, fresh or frozen

Directions

Simply stir the rice, water, milk, salt, and nutmeg into the inner pot of your Instant Pot Duo Crisp. Secure the pressure-cooking lid.

Pressure cook for 22 minutes at High pressure. Once cooking is complete, use a quick pressure release and carefully remove the lid.

Serve in individual bowls, garnished with walnuts, maple syrup, and strawberries.

Enjoy!

Per serving: Calories: 302; Fat: 9.1g; Carbs: 48.4g; Protein: 9.4g; Sugars: 17.1g; Fiber: 3.5g

390. Spicy Macaroni and Cheese [AF]

(Ready in about 20 minutes | Servings 4)

Ingredients

1 cups macaroni
1 cup cream of onion soup
2 tablespoons butter
4 ounces Ricotta cheese
6 ounces mozzarella cheese, crumbled
Kosher salt and ground white pepper, to taste
1/2 teaspoon cumin, ground
1 teaspoon dry mustard
1 teaspoon red chili powder

Directions

Cook the macaroni according to the package directions. Drain the macaroni and place them in the inner pot.

Fold in the remaining ingredients and stir to combine. Secure the air-frying lid.

Bake your macaroni and cheese at 360 degrees F for about 15 minutes. Serve garnished with fresh Italian herbs, if desired.

Bon appétit!

Per serving: Calories: 293; Fat: 11.3g; Carbs: 26.7g; Protein: 21.2g; Sugars: 2g; Fiber: 2.3g

RICE & GRAINS

391. Couscous with Cauliflower and Feta Cheese [PC]

(Ready in about 10 minutes | Servings 5)

Ingredients

- 1 ½ cups couscous
- 3 cups water
- 1 red chili pepper, chopped
- 2 tablespoons olive oil
- 2 tomatoes, pureed
- 2 bouillon cubes
- 1 teaspoon garlic, crushed
- 1 pound cauliflower small florets
- Sea salt and freshly ground black pepper, to taste
- 1/2 cup feta cheese, crumbled

Directions

Add all the ingredients, except for the cheese, to the inner pot of your Instant Pot Duo Crisp.

Secure the pressure-cooking lid.

Pressure cook for 3 minutes at High pressure. Once cooking is complete, use a quick pressure release; carefully remove the lid.

Ladle the couscous mixture into serving bowls; garnish each serving with feta cheese and enjoy!

Per serving: Calories: 317; Fat: 9.3g; Carbs: 48.2g; Protein: 11.6g; Sugars: 4.1g; Fiber: 5.1g

392. Indian Curry with Scallions [PC+AF]

(Ready in about 20 minutes | Servings 4)

Ingredients

- 2 cups jasmine rice
- 1 cup vegetable broth
- 1 teaspoon garlic powder
- 2 tablespoons butter, room temperature
- Kosher salt and red pepper, to taste
- 1/2 cup fresh scallions, chopped

Directions

Add all the ingredients, except for the scallions, to the inner pot of your Instant Pot. Secure the pressure-cooking lid.

Pressure cook for 4 minutes at High pressure. Once cooking is complete, use a natural pressure release for 10 minutes; carefully remove the lid.

Add in fresh scallions and secure the air-frying lid.

Air fry at 360 degrees F for about 5 minutes or until cooked through.

Bon appétit!

Per serving: Calories: 402; Fat: 6.6g; Carbs: 77.1g; Protein: 7.9g; Sugars: 0.4g; Fiber: 3.1g

393. Classic Wild Rice Soup [PC]

(Ready in about 30 minutes | Servings 4)

Ingredients

- 2 tablespoons olive oil
- 1 onion, chopped
- 4 garlic cloves, chopped
- 1 cup wild rice
- 4 cups vegetable broth
- 2 carrots, peeled and sliced
- 1 celery stalk, peeled and sliced
- 2 bay leaves
- 1 whole egg, lightly beaten
- 2 cups baby kale

Directions

Place all the ingredients, except for the egg and kale, in the inner pot of your Instant Pot Duo Crisp.

Secure the pressure-cooking lid.

Pressure cook for 22 minutes at High pressure. Once cooking is complete, use a quick pressure release and carefully remove the lid.

Press the "Sauté" button and fold in the egg and kale; now, let it simmer, stirring continuously, for 5 minutes.

Taste and adjust the seasonings. Ladle your soup into individual bowls and enjoy!

Per serving: Calories: 278; Fat: 9.8g; Carbs: 35.5g; Protein: 13.1g; Sugars: 2.7g; Fiber: 3.5g

394. Orange and Apricot Porridge [AF]

(Ready in about 15 minutes | Servings 4)

Ingredients

- 1/2 cup old fashioned oats
- 1/2 cup quinoa flakes
- 1/4 cup almonds, chopped
- 1/4 cup pecans, chopped
- 2 cups orange juice
- 4 tablespoons honey
- 2 tablespoons coconut oil
- 4 tablespoons dried apricots, chopped

Directions

Thoroughly combine all the ingredients in a mixing bowl. Spoon the mixture into lightly greased mugs.

Then, place the mugs in the Air Fryer cooking basket and secure the air-frying lid.

Bake your porridge at 380 degrees F for about 12 minutes.

Serve immediately. Bon appétit!

Per serving: Calories: 407; Fat: 13.4g; Carbs: 66g; Protein: 7.4g; Sugars: 29.1g; Fiber: 5.1g

395. Provencal Farro Soup [PC]

(Ready in about 25 minutes | Servings 4)

Ingredients

- 2 tablespoons butter, melted
- 1 onion, chopped
- 2 garlic cloves, minced
- 1 cup celery, chopped
- Sea salt and cayenne pepper, to taste
- 1 tablespoon Herbes de Provence
- 1 cup farro
- 4 cups chicken stock

Directions

Melt the butter on the "Sauté" function and sweat the onion for approximately 3 minutes or until just tender.

Add in the garlic and continue sautéing for 30 seconds or so; secure the pressure-cooking lid.

Pressure cook for 12 minutes at High pressure. Once cooking is complete, use a natural pressure release for 5 minutes; carefully remove the lid.

Serve warm with lightly toasted French bread, if desired. Enjoy!

Per serving: Calories: 233; Fat: 8.2g; Carbs: 31.3g; Protein: 10.4g; Sugars: 2.2g; Fiber: 5.4g

396. Old-Fashioned Mocha Muffins [AF]

(Ready in about 20 minutes | Servings 6)

Ingredients

- 1/2 cup coconut flour
- 1/2 cup all-purpose flour
- 1/2 cup cocoa powder
- 1/2 cup brown sugar
- 1/2 teaspoon baking powder
- A pinch of sea salt
- A pinch of grated nutmeg
- 1 tablespoon instant coffee granules
- 1/2 cup milk
- 2 eggs, whisked
- 1/2 teaspoon vanilla extract

Directions

Mix all the ingredients until well-combined; then, divide the batter evenly between silicone baking molds; place them in the Air Fryer cooking basket.

Secure the air-frying lid.

Bake your muffins at 330 degrees F for about 15 minutes or until a tester comes out dry and clean.

Allow the muffins to cool before unmolding and serving. Bon appétit!

Per serving: Calories: 189; Fat: 5.3g; Carbs: 32.6g; Protein: 5.1g; Sugars: 19.4g; Fiber: 3.1g

397. Spicy Spelt Berry Salad [PC]

(Ready in about 35 minutes | Servings 4)

Ingredients

- 1 ½ cups water
- 1 cup spelt berries
- 1 bell pepper, sliced
- 1 jalapeno pepper, chopped
- 1/2 cup canned artichoke hearts, diced
- 1 Persian cucumber, sliced
- 1 red onion, thinly sliced
- 1 cup cherry tomatoes, halved
- 1/4 cup extra-virgin olive oil
- Sea salt and ground black pepper, to taste

Directions

Place the water and spelt berries in the inner pot of your Instant Pot Dup Crisp. Secure the pressure-cooking lid.

Pressure cook for 30 minutes at High pressure. Once cooking is complete, use a quick pressure release; carefully remove the lid.

Toss the spelt berries with the remaining ingredients in a salad bowl. Taste, adjust the seasonings, and enjoy!

Per serving: Calories: 295; Fat: 14.4g; Carbs: 36.7g; Protein: 7.8g; Sugars: 5.5g; Fiber: 6.6g

398. Pakora Fritters with Cheese [AF]

(Ready in about 20 minutes | Servings 4)

Ingredients

- 1 cup rice flour
- 1/2 onion, chopped
- 2 garlic cloves, minced
- 2 tablespoons butter, room temperature
- 1 teaspoon paprika
- 1 teaspoon cumin powder
- 1/2 cup Paneer cheese, crumbled

Directions

Mix all the ingredients until everything is well combined. Form the mixture into patties.

Secure the air-frying lid.

Air fry the patties at 380 degrees F for about 15 minutes or until cooked through. Turn them over halfway through the cooking time.

Bon appétit!

Per serving: Calories: 268; Fat: 11.5g; Carbs: 34.4g; Protein: 6.6g; Sugars: 0.8g; Fiber: 1.5g

399. Sweet Risotto with Almonds and Pears [PC+AF]

(Ready in about 35 minutes | Servings 4)

Ingredients

- 1 cup brown rice
- 1 cup water
- 4 tablespoons brown sugar
- 1 teaspoon ground cinnamon
- 1/4 teaspoon grated nutmeg
- 2 pears, peeled, cored and diced
- 1/2 cup almond milk
- 2 ounces almonds, slivered

Directions

Place the brown rice and water in the inner pot and secure the pressure-cooking lid.

Pressure cook for 22 minutes at High pressure. Once cooking is complete, use a natural pressure release for 5 minutes; carefully remove the lid.

Add in the brown sugar, cinnamon, nutmeg, pears, and almond milk; secure the air-frying lid and cook for 6 minutes.

Spoon your risotto into individual bowls and garnish with the slivered almonds. Enjoy!

Per serving: Calories: 333; Fat: 9.6g; Carbs: 55.3g; Protein: 7.9g; Sugars: 14.7g; Fiber: 6.1g

400. Fried Chinese Rice [PC+AF]

(Ready in about 15 minutes | Servings 4)

Ingredients

- 2 cups multigrain rice
- 1 small onion, finely chopped
- 1 teaspoon garlic, minced
- 2 tablespoons sesame oil
- 1 egg, whisked
- 2 tablespoons soy sauce
- 1 carrot, chopped
- 1 cup green peas
- Sea salt and red chili flakes, to taste

Directions

Place the multigrain rice and 2 cups of water in the inner pot of your Instant Pot Duo Crisp.

Pressure cook for 22 minutes at High pressure. Once cooking is complete, use a natural pressure release for 5 minutes; carefully remove the pressure-cooking lid.

Add in the other ingredients, Secure the air-frying lid.

Air fry at 360 degrees F for about 10 minutes or until cooked through.

Bon appétit!

Per serving: Calories: 253; Fat: 10.5g; Carbs: 32.1g; Protein: 6.8g; Sugars: 4.4g; Fiber: 4.8g

RICE & GRAINS

401. Chicken Legs with Bulgur [PC]

(Ready in about 30 minutes | Servings 4)

Ingredients

1 tablespoon lard, room temperature
1 pound chicken legs, boneless, skinless and diced
Sea salt and ground black pepper, to taste
1 teaspoon hot paprika
1 onion, chopped
2 garlic cloves, minced
1 cup bulgur
3 cups chicken bone broth

Directions

Preheat your Instant Pot Duo Crisp on the "Sauté" mode and brown the chicken legs for about 5 minutes or until no longer pink.

Add in the remaining ingredients, stir, and secure the pressure-cooking lid.

Pressure cook for 20 minutes at High pressure. Once cooking is complete, use a quick pressure release and then, carefully remove the lid.

Bon appétit!

Per serving: Calories: 323; Fat: 8g; Carbs: 31.3g; Protein: 31.7g; Sugars: 2.1g; Fiber: 5.2g

402. Italian Rice Casserole [PC+AF]

(Ready in about 15 minutes | Servings 4)

Ingredients

2 cups brown rice
1 small shallot, minced
2 garlic cloves, minced
2 tablespoons olive oil
1/2 teaspoon paprika
2 eggs, whisked
1 cup half-and-half
1 cup cheddar cheese, shredded
1 tablespoon Italian parsley leaves, chopped
1 cup cream of celery soup
Sea salt and freshly ground black pepper, to taste

Directions

Place the brown rice and 2 ½ cups of water in the inner pot of your Instant Pot Duo Crisp.

Pressure cook for 22 minutes at High pressure. Once cooking is complete, use a natural pressure release for 5 minutes; carefully remove the pressure-cooking lid.

Stir in the remaining ingredients. Secure the air-frying lid.

Air fry at 360 degrees F for about 10 minutes or until cooked through.

Bon appétit!

Per serving: Calories: 332; Fat: 14.1g; Carbs: 38.1g; Protein: 12g; Sugars: 7.4g; Fiber: 2.9g

403. Asian-Style Quinoa Pilaf [PC]

(Ready in about 10 minutes | Servings 4)

Ingredients

2 cups vegetable broth
1 cup quinoa
1 teaspoon garlic, minced
Kosher salt and cayenne pepper, to taste
1 tablespoon gochujang sauce
2 tablespoons soy sauce
2 tablespoons sesame oil
2 scallion stalks, sliced

Directions

Place the vegetable broth, quinoa, garlic, salt, cayenne pepper, gochujang sauce, soy sauce, and sesame oil in the inner pot.

Secure the pressure-cooking lid.

Pressure cook for 5 minutes at High pressure. Once cooking is complete, use a quick pressure release; carefully remove the lid.

Spoon your quinoa into individual bowls and garnish with freshly sliced scallions. Enjoy!

Per serving: Calories: 283; Fat: 11.6g; Carbs: 34.3g; Protein: 11.1g; Sugars: 2.4g; Fiber: 3.4g

404. Crescent Dinner Rolls with Blueberries [AF]

(Ready in about 15 minutes | Servings 6)

Ingredients

1 (8-ounce) can refrigerated crescent dinner rolls
6 ounces cream cheese, room temperature
4 tablespoons granulated sugar
1 teaspoon lemon zest, grated
1 cup fresh blueberries
1 cup powdered sugar
1/4 teaspoon ground cinnamon

Directions

Separate the dough into rectangles. Mix the remaining ingredients until well combined.

Spread each rectangle with the cheese mixture; roll them up tightly.

Place the rolls in the Air Fryer cooking basket. Secure the air-frying lid.

Bake the rolls at 300 degrees F for about 5 minutes; turn them over and bake for a further 5 minutes. Bon appétit!

Per serving: Calories: 343; Fat: 16.3g; Carbs: 44.3g; Protein: 5.6g; Sugars: 29g; Fiber: 1.6g

405. Mac and Cheese with Herbs [PC+AF]

(Ready in about 20 minutes | Servings 4)

Ingredients

8 ounces penne pasta
1 ½ cups water
1 cup vegetable broth
1 teaspoon mustard seeds
1/2 teaspoon fennel seeds
1/2 teaspoon dried oregano
1 teaspoon dried basil
1 teaspoon dried parsley flakes
Sea salt and ground black pepper, to taste
1 teaspoon cayenne pepper
2 ounces cream cheese
4 ounces cheddar cheese

Directions

Place the penne pasta, water, broth, and spices into the inner pot of your Instant Pot Duo Crisp; gently stir to combine and secure the pressure-cooking lid.

Pressure cook for 10 minutes at High pressure. Once cooking is complete, use a quick pressure release; carefully remove the lid.

Stir in the cheese and cover with the air-frying lid; cook for 5 minutes, until the cheese melts. Bon appétit!

Per serving: Calories: 386; Fat: 16.3g; Carbs: 47.9g; Protein: 13.6g; Sugars: 1.3g; Fiber: 6g

406. Creamy Risotto with Parmesan Cheese [PC+AF]

(Ready in about 15 minutes | Servings 4)

Ingredients

- 2 cups Arborio rice, cooked
- 2 tablespoons sesame oil
- 1 shallot, chopped
- 1/2 cup white Italian wine
- 1/2 cup heavy cream
- Coarse sea salt and freshly ground black pepper, to taste
- 4 tablespoons pancetta, chopped
- 1 cup Parmesan cheese, preferably freshly grated
- 1 tablespoon fresh Italian parsley, chopped

Directions

Place the Arborio rice and 2 cups of water in the inner pot of your Instant Pot Duo Crisp.

Pressure cook for 8 minutes at High pressure. Once cooking is complete, use a quick pressure release; carefully remove the lid.

Stir in the remaining ingredients. Secure the air-frying lid.

Air fry at 360 degrees F for about 10 minutes or until cooked through.

Bon appétit!

Per serving: Calories: 430; Fat: 31.2g; Carbs: 27.2g; Protein: 10.1g; Sugars: 1.3g; Fiber: 1.9g

407. Indian Kambu Koozh [PC]

(Ready in about 15 minutes | Servings 4)

Ingredients

- 1 cup millet
- 1 ¾ cup vegetable broth
- 2 tablespoons sesame oil
- 1 green chili, chopped
- 1/2 teaspoon cumin seeds
- 1/4 cup fresh cilantro, roughly chopped
- Kosher salt and ground black pepper, to taste

Directions

Simply throw all the ingredients into the inner pot and secure the pressure-cooking lid.

Pressure cook for 12 minutes at High pressure. Once cooking is complete, use a quick pressure release; carefully remove the lid.

Enjoy!

Per serving: Calories: 263; Fat: 9g; Carbs: 38.5g; Protein: 5.8g; Sugars: 4.4g; Fiber: 1.4g

408. Easy Mediterranean Harcha [AF]

(Ready in about 20 minutes | Servings 6)

Ingredients

- 1 cup all-purpose flour
- 1 teaspoon baking powder
- 4 tablespoons olive oil
- 1/2 cup sour cream
- A pinch of sea salt
- 1 teaspoon Mediterranean seasoning mix

Directions

Mix all the ingredients until well combined. Use a 2-inch biscuit cutter and cut out biscuits. Place the biscuits on a lightly greased baking pan.

Lower the pan into the Air Fryer basket. Secure the air-frying lid.

Bake your biscuits at 360 degrees F for about 15 minutes or until a tester comes out dry and clean.

Bon appétit!

Per serving: Calories: 180; Fat: 9.2g; Carbs: 18.8g; Protein: 2.7g; Sugars: 0.1g; Fiber: 0.6g

409. Autumn Squash and Oat Porridge [PC]

(Ready in about 10 minutes | Servings 4)

Ingredients

- 1 cup steel cut oats
- 3 cups water
- A pinch of sea salt
- A pinch of grated nutmeg
- 1/4 teaspoon ground cinnamon
- 1 teaspoon fresh ginger root, peeled and grated
- 2 cups butternut squash, diced
- 2 tablespoons toasted pumpkin seeds

Directions

Add all the ingredients to the inner pot and secure the pressure-cooking lid.

Pressure cook for 6 minutes at High pressure. Once cooking is complete, use a quick pressure release and carefully remove the lid.

Serve in individual bowls. Bon appétit!

Per serving: Calories: 208; Fat: 4.5g; Carbs: 34.3g; Protein: 8.4g; Sugars: 1.6g; Fiber: 5.8g

410. Herbed Millet Croquettes [AF]

(Ready in about 20 minutes | Servings 4)

Ingredients

- 2 cups millet, cooked
- 2 tablespoons olive oil
- 1 small onion, chopped
- 2 garlic cloves, minced
- 1 tablespoon celery leaves, chopped
- 1 tablespoon parsley leaves, chopped
- Sea salt and ground black pepper, to taste

Directions

Mix all the ingredients until everything is well combined. Form the mixture into patties.

Secure the air-frying lid.

Air fry the patties at 380 degrees F for about 15 minutes or until cooked through; turn them over halfway through the cooking time.

Bon appétit!

Per serving: Calories: 180; Fat: 7.6g; Carbs: 22.5g; Protein: 3.3g; Sugars: 0.8g; Fiber: 1.5g

RICE & GRAINS

411. Indian Sweet Pongal [PC]

(Ready in about 25 minutes | Servings 4)

Ingredients

- 1 ½ cups fine coarse bulgur
- 3 cups water
- 2 tablespoons butter
- 1/2 cup jaggery, powdered
- 1/2 teaspoon ground cinnamon
- 1/4 teaspoon ground cardamom
- 1/4 teaspoon crystallized ginger
- 1/2 cup dried cranberries
- 1 cup coconut milk

Directions

Place the bulgur, water, butter, jaggery, and spices in the inner pot and secure the pressure-cooking lid.

Pressure cook for 20 minutes at High pressure. Once cooking is complete, use a quick pressure release; carefully remove the lid.

Stir in the dried cranberries and coconut milk and continue cooking on the "Sauté" mode for 3 to 4 minutes.

Bon appétit!

Per serving: Calories: 333; Fat: 10g; Carbs: 61.5g; Protein: 10.4g; Sugars: 13.3g; Fiber: 10.7g

412. Mini Cornbread Muffins [AF]

(Ready in about 25 minutes | Servings 6)

Ingredients

- 1/2 cup all-purpose flour
- 1/2 cup yellow cornmeal
- 1 ½ teaspoons baking powder
- 4 tablespoons honey
- A pinch of sea salt
- A pinch of grated nutmeg
- 4 tablespoons coconut oil, room temperature
- 2 eggs, whisked
- 1/2 cup milk

Directions

Mix all the ingredients until everything is well incorporated. Scrape the batter into baking molds and place them in the Air Fryer basket.

Secure the air-frying lid.

Bake your mini cornbread at 360 degrees F for about 22 minutes or until a tester comes out dry and clean.

Allow your mini cornbread to cool before unmolding and serving. Bon appétit!

Per serving: Calories: 243; Fat: 11.4g; Carbs: 31.6g; Protein: 4.5g; Sugars: 12.8g; Fiber: 0.8g

413. Creamed Quinoa Salad [PC]

(Ready in about 10 minutes + chilling time | Servings 4)

Ingredients

- 1 cup quinoa
- 2 cups water
- Sea salt and red pepper, to taste
- 1 Greek cucumber, sliced
- 1 bell pepper, sliced
- 1 red onion, sliced
- 1/2 cup aioli
- 2 tablespoons Greek-style yogurt
- 2 ounces Kalamata olives, pitted and sliced

Directions

Place the water and quinoa in the inner pot and secure the pressure-cooking lid.

Pressure cook for 5 minutes at High pressure. Once cooking is complete, use a quick pressure release; carefully remove the lid.

Toss the chilled quinoa with the remaining ingredients and serve.

Bon appétit!

Per serving: Calories: 377; Fat: 25g; Carbs: 30.5g; Protein: 7.3g; Sugars: 1.8g; Fiber: 3.9g

414. Oregano Polenta Bites [AF]

(Ready in about 20 minutes | Servings 4)

Ingredients

- 1 cup polenta
- Sea salt, to taste
- 1 teaspoon dried oregano
- 2 tablespoons olive oil

Directions

Cook the polenta according to the package directions. Season with the salt and oregano to taste.

Pour the polenta into a large baking sheet. Let it cool and firm up; cut the polenta into rounds. Drizzle the olive oil over them.

Secure the air-frying lid.

Cook the polenta rounds at 350 degrees F for about 15 minutes, turning them halfway through the cooking time.

Bon appétit!

Per serving: Calories: 168; Fat: 7.8g; Carbs: 22.6g; Protein: 2.1g; Sugars: 0.2g; Fiber: 2.2g

415. Kamut and Sausage Medley [PC+AF]

(Ready in about 25 minutes | Servings 4)

Ingredients

- 2 tablespoons butter, room temperature
- 1 pound beef sausage, sliced
- 1 small onion, chopped
- 1 cup kamut
- 2 cups roasted vegetable broth
- Kosher salt and ground black pepper, to taste
- 2 cloves garlic, crushed
- 1 cup Colby cheese, grated

Directions

Melt the butter on the "Sauté" function and cook the sausage until no longer pink; then, sauté the onion for approximately 3 minutes or until they are tender and translucent.

Add in the kamut, broth, salt, pepper, and garlic; secure the pressure-cooking lid.

Pressure cook for 12 minutes at High pressure. Once cooking is complete, use a quick pressure release; carefully remove the lid.

Top your kamut with cheese and secure the air-frying lid; cook for 5 minutes or until the cheese melts.

Bon appétit!

Per serving: Calories: 588; Fat: 36.3g; Carbs: 38.5g; Protein: 31.3g; Sugars: 5.1g; Fiber: 5.6g

416. Bread Pudding with Dried Berries [AF]

(Ready in about 35 minutes | Servings 6)

Ingredients

2 cups sweet raisin bread, cubed
2 eggs, whisked
1 cup milk
1/2 teaspoon vanilla extract
1/4 cup agave syrup
1/4 cup dried cherries
1/4 cup dried cranberries

Directions

Place the bread cubes in a lightly greased inner pot.

In a mixing bowl, thoroughly combine the remaining ingredients.

Pour the egg/milk mixture over the bread cubes; set aside for 15 minutes to soak. Secure the air-frying lid.

Bake your bread pudding at 350 degrees F for about 20 minutes or until the custard is set but still a little wobbly.

Serve at room temperature. Bon appétit!

Per serving: Calories: 152; Fat: 3.3g; Carbs: 26.1g; Protein: 4.3g; Sugars: 18.5g; Fiber: 0.8g

417. Green Rice Porridge [PC]

(Ready in about 20 minutes | Servings 4)

Ingredients

2 tablespoons butter, melted
1/2 cup green onions, chopped
1 cup green peas
1 cup jasmine rice
2 cups vegetable broth
2 cups spinach leaves, torn into pieces

Directions

Melt the butter on the "Sauté" mode and sweat the green onions for 2 to 3 minutes or until just tender.

Add in the green peas, rice, and broth; secure the pressure-cooking lid.

Pressure cook for 4 minutes at High pressure. Once cooking is complete, use a natural pressure release for 10 minutes; carefully remove the lid.

Add in the spinach leaves and secure the pressure-cooking lid one more time. Let it sit in the residual heat until spinach leaves wilt. Enjoy!

Per serving: Calories: 277; Fat: 8g; Carbs: 42.2g; Protein: 8.6g; Sugars: 2.2g; Fiber: 4.3g

418. Traditional Italian Arancini [AF]

(Ready in about 20 minutes | Servings 4)

Ingredients

2 cups quinoa, cooked
2 eggs, whisked
1 small onion, chopped
2 garlic cloves, minced
1 cup broccoli, chopped
1/2 cup breadcrumbs
1/2 cup Parmesan cheese, grated
1 tablespoon fresh Italian herbs, chopped
Sea salt and ground black pepper, to taste

Directions

Start by preheating your Air Fryer to 380 degrees F.

Mix all the ingredients until everything is well combined. Form the mixture into patties.

Secure the air-frying lid.

Air fry the patties for about 15 minutes or until cooked through. Turn them over halfway through the cooking time.

Bon appétit!

Per serving: Calories: 223; Fat: 7.5g; Carbs: 27.2g; Protein: 11.6g; Sugars: 17.8g; Fiber: 2.5g

419. Dijon and Honey Sorghum Salad [PC]

(Ready in about 25 minutes + chilling time | Servings 6)

Ingredients

1 ½ cups sorghum
4 ½ cups water
A pinch of coarse sea salt
1/2 pound cauliflower florets
1 pound asparagus, shaved
4 pickled red onions, sliced
2 teaspoons honey
2 teaspoons Dijon mustard
2 tablespoons champagne vinegar
Sea salt and black pepper

Directions

Throw the sorghum and water into the inner pot of your Instant Pot Duo Crisp. Secure the pressure-cooking lid.

Pressure cook for 20 minutes at High pressure. Once cooking is complete, use a quick pressure release and carefully remove the lid.

Let it cool at room temperature. Mix the chilled sorghum with the remaining ingredients and toss to combine well.

Bon appétit!

Per serving: Calories: 218; Fat: 1.4g; Carbs: 46.4g; Protein: 6.7g; Sugars: 15.7g; Fiber: 6.4g

420. Savory Breakfast Cups [AF]

(Ready in about 20 minutes | Servings 6)

Ingredients

1 cup all-purpose flour
1 teaspoon baking powder
1/2 brown sugar
1 Greek yogurt
1/2 cup prunes, pitted and chopped
1 egg, beaten
1 teaspoon vanilla essence

Directions

Mix all the ingredients until well-combined; then, divide the batter evenly between silicone baking molds; place them in the Air Fryer cooking basket.

Secure the air-frying lid.

Bake your muffins at 330 degrees F for about 15 minutes or until a tester comes out dry and clean.

Allow the muffins to cool before unmolding and serving. Bon appétit!

Per serving: Calories: 172; Fat: 1.2g; Carbs: 35.1g; Protein: 5.1g; Sugars: 15.4g; Fiber: 1.6g

RICE & GRAINS

VEGAN

421. Wild Rice with Spinach and Wine [PC]

(Ready in about 25 minutes | Servings 4)

Ingredients

- 1 cup wild rice
- 2 cups roasted vegetable broth
- 1/4 cup dry white wine
- 1 onion, chopped
- 2 garlic cloves, minced
- 2 tablespoons olive oil, divided
- 4 cups spinach
- Kosher salt and ground black pepper, to taste

Directions

Place the wild rice, broth, wine, onion, garlic, and olive oil in the inner pot of your Instant Pot Do Crisp.

Secure the pressure-cooking lid.

Pressure cook for 22 minutes at High pressure. Once cooking is complete, use a quick pressure release and carefully remove the lid.

Add in the spinach, salt, and black pepper; stir to combine and let it sit in the residual heat for about 6 minutes or until the spinach leaves are wilted.

Serve in individual bowls and enjoy!

Per serving: Calories: 267; Fat: 9.5g; Carbs: 35.5g; Protein: 11.3g; Sugars: 3.5g; Fiber: 3.6g

422. Perfect Crispy Falafel [AF]

(Ready in about 20 minutes | Servings 4)

Ingredients

- 1 (15-ounce) cans chickpeas, rinsed and drained
- 1/4 cup fresh cilantro, chopped
- 2 cloves garlic, minced
- 1 onion, minced
- 2 tablespoons tahini
- 1 teaspoon smoked paprika
- 2 tablespoons fresh lemon juice
- Sea salt and ground black pepper, to taste
- 2 tablespoons olive oil

Directions

Pulse all the ingredients in your food processor until everything is well incorporated.

Shape the mixture into balls and place them in a lightly greased Air Fryer cooking basket.

Secure the air-frying lid.

Air fry the falafel at 380 degrees F for about 15 minutes, shaking the basket occasionally to ensure even cooking.

Serve in pita bread with toppings of your choice. Enjoy!

Per serving: Calories: 214; Fat: 12.5g; Carbs: 20.8g; Protein: 4.5g; Sugars: 18.3g; Fiber: 5.7g

423. Vegetable Millet Porridge [PC]

(Ready in about 15 minutes | Servings 4)

Ingredients

- 1 cup millet
- 2 cups vegetable broth
- 1 tomato, pureed
- 1 onion, chopped
- 1 zucchini, diced
- 1 carrot, chopped
- 2 tablespoons olive oil
- Sea salt and ground black pepper, to season
- 1 bay leaf

Directions

Place all the ingredients in the inner pot of your Instant Pot Duo Crisp. Secure the pressure-cooking lid.

Pressure cook for 12 minutes at High pressure. Once cooking is complete, use a quick pressure release; carefully remove the lid.

Enjoy!

Per serving: Calories: 293; Fat: 9.6g; Carbs: 42.1g; Protein: 8.6g; Sugars: 2.7g; Fiber: 5.3g

424. Eggplant with Red Lentils [AF]

(Ready in about 15 minutes | Servings 2)

Ingredients

- 1 medium eggplants, halved
- 2 tablespoons olive oil
- 1 onion, minced
- 2 garlic cloves, minced
- 2 tablespoons tomato paste
- 6 ounces red lentils, canned and drained
- Sea salt and ground black pepper, to taste

Directions

Toss the eggplants with the oil; place them in the Air Fryer cooking basket.

Secure the air-frying lid.

Mix the remaining ingredients to make the filling. Spoon the filling into the eggplant halves.

Cook the stuffed eggplants at 400 degrees F for about 15 minutes.

Serve warm and enjoy!

Per serving: Calories: 336; Fat: 14.5g; Carbs: 44.5g; Protein: 16g; Sugars: 16g; Fiber: 16.7g

425. Cremini Mushroom and Barley Stew [PC]

(Ready in about 25 minutes | Servings 4)

Ingredients

- 2 tablespoons olive oil
- 1 onion, chopped
- 2 garlic cloves, minced
- 1 pound Cremini mushrooms, sliced
- 1 celery stalk, diced
- 2 tomatoes, chopped
- 1/2 cup pearl barley
- 4 cups vegetable broth
- 1 teaspoon dried thyme, chopped
- 1 teaspoon dried parsley, chopped

Directions

Press the "Sauté" button and heat the olive oil. Sauté the onion, garlic, and mushrooms for about 3 minutes or until tender and fragrant.

Next, add in the remaining ingredients. Secure the pressure-cooking lid.

Pressure cook for 20 minutes at High pressure. Once cooking is complete, use a quick pressure release; carefully remove the lid.

Bon appétit!

Per serving: Calories: 233; Fat: 9.2g; Carbs: 30.4g; Protein: 10.9g; Sugars: 6.1g; Fiber: 6.7g

426. Fried Cucumber Bites [AF]

(Ready in about 20 minutes | Servings 4)

Ingredients

2 cucumbers, sliced
2 tablespoons olive oil
1/2 cup cornmeal
Sea salt and ground black pepper, to taste

Directions

Toss the cucumbers with the remaining ingredients; place them in the Air Fryer cooking basket.

Secure the air-frying lid.

Air fry the cucumbers at 400 degrees F for about 15 minutes, shaking the basket occasionally to ensure even cooking.

Serve warm and enjoy!

Per serving: Calories: 144; Fat: 7.2g; Carbs: 17.4g; Protein: 1.9g; Sugars: 1.2g; Fiber: 1.5g

427. Greek Sweet Potato Stew [PC]

(Ready in about 15 minutes | Servings 4)

Ingredients

2 tablespoons olive oil
1 large red onion, chopped
2 garlic cloves, minced
1 pound sweet potatoes, peeled and diced
1 teaspoon dried Greek oregano
1 teaspoon dried sage, crushed
2 carrots, diced
2 celery stalks, diced
3 cups vegetable stock
1 cup tomato sauce
1 bay laurel

Directions

Stir all the ingredients into the inner pot of your Instant Po Duo Crisp. Secure the pressure-cooking lid.

Pressure cook for 10 minutes at High pressure. Once cooking is complete, use a quick pressure release; carefully remove the lid.

Serve hot and enjoy!

Per serving: Calories: 277; Fat: 8.7g; Carbs: 40.5g; Protein: 8.6g; Sugars: 11.2g; Fiber: 8.4g

428. Aromatic Roasted Peppers [AF]

(Ready in about 20 minutes | Servings 2)

Ingredients

4 bell peppers, seeded and halved lengthwise
2 tablespoons olive oil
1 tablespoon fresh parsley, chopped
2 cloves garlic, minced
Sea salt and ground black pepper, to taste

Directions

Toss the peppers with the remaining ingredients; place them in the Air Fryer cooking basket.

Secure the air-frying lid.

Air fry the peppers at 400 degrees F for about 15 minutes, shaking the basket halfway through the cooking time.

Taste, adjust the seasonings and serve at room temperature. Bon appétit!

Per serving: Calories: 220; Fat: 14.3g; Carbs: 24.4g; Protein: 3.7g; Sugars: 0.5g; Fiber: 3.6g

429. One-Pot Vegan Minestrone [PC]

(Ready in about 25 minutes | Servings 4)

Ingredients

2 tablespoons olive oil
1 onion, chopped
2 cloves garlic, crushed
1 stalk celery, chopped
2 carrots, chopped
2 tomatoes, pureed
1 teaspoon dried basil
1 teaspoon dried oregano
1 cup white cannellini beans, soaked overnight
4 cups vegetable broth
1 cup elbow pasta

Directions

Choose the "Sauté" button to preheat your Instant Pot Duo Crisp. Now, heat the olive oil and sauté the onion for about 3 minutes or until tender and translucent.

Stir the remaining ingredients into the inner pot and secure the pressure-cooking lid.

Pressure cook for 10 minutes at High pressure. Once cooking is complete, use a natural pressure release for 10 minutes; carefully remove the lid.

Bon appétit!

Per serving: Calories: 299; Fat: 7.6g; Carbs: 46.5g; Protein: 14g; Sugars: 3.7g; Fiber: 10.4g

430. Moroccan-Spiced Carrot [AF]

(Ready in about 20 minutes | Servings 3)

Ingredients

3/4 pound carrots, peeled and sliced
2 tablespoons coconut oil
1 tablespoon Moroccan spice mix
Sea salt and ground black pepper, to taste

Directions

Toss the carrots with the remaining ingredients; then, arrange the carrots in the Air Fryer cooking basket.

Secure the air-frying lid.

Air fry the carrots at 380 degrees F for 15 minutes, shaking the basket halfway through the cooking time.

Bon appétit!

Per serving: Calories: 125; Fat: 9.3g; Carbs: 10.4g; Protein: 1.1g; Sugars: 5.3g; Fiber: 3.2g

431. Sorghum, Spinach, and Avocado Bowl [PC]

(Ready in about 25 minutes | Servings 4)

Ingredients

1 cup sorghum
3 cups water
2 tablespoons appeal cider vinegar
4 tablespoons extra-virgin olive oil
3 cups baby spinach
2 garlic cloves, minced
1 cup cherry tomatoes, halved
1 Greek cucumber, peeled and sliced
1 avocado, peeled, pitted and diced
2 ounces Kalamata olives, pitted and sliced
Kosher salt and ground black pepper, to taste
1/4 cup pumpkin seeds, lightly toasted

Directions

Put the sorghum and water into the inner pot of your Instant Pot Duo Crisp.

Pressure cook for 20 minutes at High pressure. Once cooking is complete, use a quick pressure release and carefully remove the lid.

Toss the chilled sorghum with the other ingredients and serve at room temperature or well-chilled!

Per serving: Calories: 323; Fat: 20.5g; Carbs: 33g; Protein: 7.4g; Sugars: 2.8g; Fiber: 7.5g

432. Easy Garlic Cabbage [AF]

(Ready in about 10 minutes | Servings 4)

Ingredients

1 pound cabbage, cut into wedges
1 teaspoon garlic, minced
2 tablespoons olive oil
1 teaspoon red pepper flakes
Sea salt and ground black pepper, to taste

Directions

Toss the cabbage wedges with the remaining ingredients. Secure the air-frying lid.

Air fry the cabbage wedges at 350 degrees F for 7 minutes, shaking the basket halfway through the cooking time.

Taste and adjust the seasonings. Bon appétit!

Per serving: Calories: 96; Fat: 6.9g; Carbs: 8.5g; Protein: 1.7g; Sugars: 4.3g; Fiber: 2.4g

433. Rich and Easy Vegan Biryani [PC]

(Ready in about 10 minutes | Servings 4)

Ingredients

2 tablespoons sesame oil
1 onion, chopped
2 cloves garlic, chopped
1 (1-inch) piece ginger, grated
1/2 teaspoon ground cumin
1 teaspoon chili powder
1/2 teaspoon cardamom
1/2 teaspoon turmeric
4 cups vegetable broth
1 ½ cups basmati rice, rinsed
1/4 cup cashews, chopped
1/4 cup fresh cilantro, chopped

Directions

Press the "Sauté" button to preheat your Instant Pot Duo Crisp; then, heat the sesame oil and sauté the onion for 2 to 3 minutes or until tender.

Add in the garlic and ginger and continue sautéing for 30 seconds or so. Add in the spices, broth, and rice.

Secure the pressure-cooking lid.

Pressure cook for 5 minutes at High pressure. Once cooking is complete, use a quick pressure release; carefully remove the lid.

Garnish the hot Biryani with cashews and cilantro, and enjoy!

Per serving: Calories: 367; Fat: 9.5g; Carbs: 62.5g; Protein: 6.6g; Sugars: 1.6g; Fiber: 3.2g

434. The Best Chickpea Fritters Ever [AF]

(Ready in about 20 minutes | Servings 4)

Ingredients

16 ounces canned chickpeas, drained and rinsed
1/4 cup flaxseeds, ground
2 garlic cloves, minced
1 medium-sized onion, chopped
2 tablespoons fresh lemon juice
2 tablespoons olive oil
1/2 teaspoon ground cumin
1/4 teaspoon ground allspice
Sea salt and ground black pepper, to taste

Directions

Pulse all the ingredients in your food processor until everything is well incorporated. Shape the mixture into patties.

Place them in the Air Fryer cooking basket. Secure the air-frying lid.

Cook the burgers at 380 degrees F for about 15 minutes, turning them over halfway through the cooking time. Bon appétit!

Per serving: Calories: 295; Fat: 14g; Carbs: 33.4g; Protein: 10.6g; Sugars: 6.6g; Fiber: 10g

435. Herb Vegetable Soup [PC]

(Ready in about 20 minutes | Servings 4)

Ingredients

2 tablespoons olive oil
1 onion, chopped
2 carrots, chopped
1 celery stalk, chopped
2 cloves garlic, minced
1 zucchini, diced
2 tomatoes, crushed
1 cup sweet potato, peeled and sliced
2 tablespoons fresh parsley, roughly chopped
1 tablespoon fresh mint, roughly chopped
2 bay leaves

Directions

Choose the "Sauté" button to preheat your Instant Pot Duo Crisp. Now, heat the olive oil and sauté the onion, carrot, and celery for about 3 minutes or until they are crisp-tender.

Stir the remaining ingredients into the inner pot and secure the pressure-cooking lid.

Pressure cook for 10 minutes at High pressure. Once cooking is complete, use a natural pressure release for 5 minutes; carefully remove the lid. Bon appétit!

Per serving: Calories: 137; Fat: 7g; Carbs: 15.3g; Protein: 1.9g; Sugars: 5.5g; Fiber: 3.4g

436. Parsnip Fries with Mayonnaise [AF]

(Ready in about 20 minutes | Servings 4)

Ingredients

1 pound parsnip, trimmed and sliced
2 tablespoons vegan mayonnaise
1/2 teaspoon cayenne pepper
1/2 teaspoon dried oregano
Kosher salt and ground black pepper, to taste

Directions

Toss the parsnip with the remaining ingredients; place them in the Air Fryer cooking basket.

Secure the air-frying lid.

Air fry the parsnip slices at 400 degrees F for about 15 minutes, shaking the basket occasionally to ensure even cooking.

Serve warm and enjoy!

Per serving: Calories: 138; Fat: 5.5g; Carbs: 21.5g; Protein: 1.6g; Sugars: 6g; Fiber: 5.2g

437. Thai-Style Butternut Squash Curry [PC]

(Ready in about 15 minutes | Servings 4)

Ingredients

2 tablespoons olive oil
1 small onion, chopped
2 cloves garlic, minced
1 teaspoon ginger, peeled and minced
1 chili pepper, chopped
1 teaspoon curry powder
1/2 teaspoon red pepper flakes
1 pound butternut squash, peeled and diced
1 cup vegetable broth
1 tomato, crushed
3 cups kale leaves
1 cup full-fat coconut milk

Directions

Press the "Sauté" button and heat the olive oil. Once hot, cook the onion, garlic and ginger for 3 to 4 minutes or until tender and aromatic.

Next, add in the curry powder, red pepper, squash, broth, and tomato. Secure the pressure-cooking lid.

Pressure cook for 6 minutes at High pressure. Once cooking is complete, use a quick pressure release; carefully remove the lid.

Add in the kale and coconut milk. Cover with the lid and let it sit in the residual heat for about 6 minutes or until the kale leaves are wilted. Bon appétit!

Per serving: Calories: 270; Fat: 21.5g; Carbs: 20.5g; Protein: 3.6g; Sugars: 4.5g; Fiber: 4.6g

438. Beets with Tofu Cheese [AF]

(Ready in about 35 minutes | Servings 2)

Ingredients

1/2 pound red beets, peeled and sliced
2 tablespoons mayonnaise
Sea salt and ground black pepper, to taste
1/2 teaspoon cumin powder
1 tablespoon Dijon mustard
2 ounces tofu cheese, crumbled

Directions

Toss the red beets with the mayo, salt, black pepper, cumin powder, and Dijon mustard until well coated on all sides.

Secure the air-frying lid.

Air fry the red beets at 390 degrees F for about 30 minutes, tossing the basket every 10 minutes to ensure even cooking.

Top the roasted beets with tofu cheese and enjoy!

Per serving: Calories: 135; Fat: 6.7g; Carbs: 14.5g; Protein: 5.7g; Sugars: 9g; Fiber: 4.2g

439. Barley Pilaf with Herbs [PC]

(Ready in about 25 minutes | Servings 4)

Ingredients

1 medium onion, chopped
2 garlic cloves, minced
2 bell peppers, cored and diced
1 cup dry pearl barley
2 ½ cups vegetable broth
Sea salt and ground black pepper, to taste
4 tablespoons olive oil
2 tablespoons fresh cilantro, chopped
2 tablespoons fresh parsley, chopped

Directions

Press the "Sauté" button and heat the olive oil. Sauté the onion, garlic, and peppers for about 3 minutes or until tender and aromatic.

Next, add in the remaining ingredients. Secure the pressure-cooking lid.

Pressure cook for 22 minutes at High pressure. Once cooking is complete, use a quick pressure release; carefully remove the lid.

Bon appétit!

Per serving: Calories: 322; Fat: 14.2g; Carbs: 45g; Protein: 6g; Sugars: 3.3g; Fiber: 8.5g

440. Polenta Bites with Peppers [AF]

(Ready in about 20 minutes | Servings 4)

Ingredients

1 pound prepared polenta
2 tablespoons olive oil
1 bell peppers, seeded and sliced

Directions

Cut the polenta into pieces. Drizzle the olive oil over them and top each piece with the peppers.

Secure the air-frying lid.

Air fry the polenta bites at 350 degrees F for about 15 minutes.

Bon appétit!

Per serving: Calories: 242; Fat: 10.9g; Carbs: 32.5g; Protein: 3.1g; Sugars: 1.2g; Fiber: 1.8g

VEGAN

441. Green Pea and Farro Stew [PC]

(Ready in about 15 minutes | Servings 4)

Ingredients

2 tablespoons olive oil
1 onion, chopped
1 carrot, chopped
1 celery stalk, chopped
4 cups vegetable broth
1 tomato, pureed
1 cup farro, rinsed
1 bay leaf
1 cup green peas

Directions

Press the "Sauté" button. Then, heat the olive oil and sauté the onion, carrot, and celery for about 3 minutes or until tender and aromatic.

Next, add in the remaining ingredients. Secure the pressure-cooking lid.

Pressure cook for 12 minutes at High pressure. Once cooking is complete, use a quick pressure release; carefully remove the lid.

Bon appétit!

Per serving: Calories: 251; Fat: 7.8g; Carbs: 41.1g; Protein: 7.7g; Sugars: 6.4g; Fiber: 8.6g

442. Japanese Broccoli Tempura [AF]

(Ready in about 10 minutes | Servings 4)

Ingredients

1 cup all-purpose flour
1/2 cup beer
2 tablespoons sesame oil
1/2 teaspoon cayenne pepper
1 teaspoon chili powder
Sea salt and ground black pepper, to taste
1 pound broccoli florets

Directions

In a mixing bowl, thoroughly combine the flour, beer, oil, and spices.

Dip the broccoli florets in tempura mixture and place them in a lightly oiled Air Fryer cooking basket.

Secure the air-frying lid.

Air fry the broccoli florets at 395 degrees F for 6 minutes, shaking the basket halfway through the cooking time.

Bon appétit!

Per serving: Calories: 232; Fat: 7.6g; Carbs: 33.8g; Protein: 6.9g; Sugars: 2.6g; Fiber: 4.3g

443. Easy Yellow Lentil Curry [PC]

(Ready in about 15 minutes | Servings 4)

Ingredients

1 ½ tablespoons olive oil
1 onion, chopped
2 garlic cloves, minced
1 red chili pepper, seeded and minced
1/2 teaspoon coriander seeds
1 teaspoon cayenne pepper
1 cup yellow lentils
3 cups vegetable broth
1 cup coconut cream

Directions

Select the "Sauté" mode and heat the oil; now, sauté the onion, garlic, and chili pepper for about 4 minutes or until they are tender.

Add in the coriander seeds, cayenne pepper, lentils, and vegetable broth; secure the pressure-cooking lid.

Pressure cook for 6 minutes at High pressure. Once cooking is complete, use a quick pressure release; carefully remove the lid.

Add in the coconut cream and let it simmer on the "Sauté" mode for about 5 minutes or until the liquid has thickened slightly; serve hot and enjoy!

Per serving: Calories: 286; Fat: 26.2g; Carbs: 12.5g; Protein: 4.6g; Sugars: 1.8g; Fiber: 2.5g

444. Vegan Smoked Sausage [PC+AF]

(Ready in about 50 minutes | Servings 4)

Ingredients

1 onion, chopped
2 cloves garlic, minced
2 tablespoons olive oil
1/4 cup tomato paste
2 tablespoons sun-dried tomatoes, chopped
Kosher salt and ground black pepper, to taste
1/2 teaspoon liquid smoke
1 cup vital wheat gluten

Directions

Pulse all the ingredients in your food processor until everything is well incorporated.

Shape the mixture into three sausages and roll them in a piece of aluminum foil; twist the ends closed.

Secure the pressure-cooking lid. Choose the "Steam" mode and cook the sausages for about 40 minutes.

Secure the air-frying lid.

Air fry the sausage at 390 degrees F for about 15 minutes, shaking the basket halfway through the cooking time. Bon appétit!

Per serving: Calories: 211; Fat: 7.5g; Carbs: 12.5g; Protein: 25.5g; Sugars: 4.4g; Fiber: 1.7g

445. Country-Style Vegetable Soup [PC]

(Ready in about 15 minutes | Servings 4)

Ingredients

2 tablespoons olive oil
1 white onion, chopped
2 carrots, peeled and chopped
1 celery stalks, chopped
1 cup sweet potatoes, diced
1 cup butternut squash, diced
1 teaspoon garlic powder
1/2 teaspoon cumin powder
1 teaspoon curry powder
2 vegan bouillon cubes
4 cups water
2 bay leaves
2 cups collard greens, torn into pieces

Directions

Add all the ingredients, except for the collard greens, to the inner pot of your Instant Pot Duo Crisp.

Secure the pressure-cooking lid.

Pressure cook for 10 minutes at High pressure. Once cooking is complete, use a quick pressure release and then, carefully remove the lid.

Afterwards, fold in the collard greens, cover with the lid, and let it simmer on the "Sauté" mode until they are wilted. Serve hot and enjoy!

Per serving: Calories: 128; Fat: 7.4g; Carbs: 13.4g; Protein: 2.4g; Sugars: 3.8g; Fiber: 3.6g

446. Italian-Style Zucchini [AF]

(Ready in about 15 minutes | Servings 4)

Ingredients

1 pound zucchini, sliced
1 teaspoon granulated garlic
2 tablespoons olive oil
Sea salt and ground black pepper, to taste
1 teaspoon Italian seasoning
2 tablespoons white balsamic vinegar

Directions

Toss the zucchini slices with the remaining ingredients and place them in the Air Fryer cooking basket.

Secure the air-frying lid.

Air fry the zucchini slices at 390 degrees F for about 10 minutes, shaking the basket halfway through the cooking time. Work in batches.

Bon appétit!

Per serving: Calories: 99; Fat: 7.5g; Carbs: 6.6g; Protein: 3.4g; Sugars: 1.8g; Fiber: 1.7g

447. Spicy Kale Pilaf [PC]

(Ready in about 10 minutes | Servings 5)

Ingredients

2 tablespoons olive oil
1 onion, chopped
2 cloves garlic, chopped
1 ½ cups white rice
2 cups vegetable broth
2 tablespoons cilantro, chopped
2 cups kale leaves
2 green chili peppers, chopped
Sea salt and cayenne pepper, to taste

Directions

Press the "Sauté" button and heat the olive oil. Sauté the onion and garlic for about 3 minutes or until tender and aromatic.

Next, add in the remaining ingredients. Secure the pressure-cooking lid.

Pressure cook for 4 minutes at High pressure. Once cooking is complete, use a quick pressure release; carefully remove the lid.

Bon appétit!

Per serving: Calories: 278; Fat: 5.8g; Carbs: 50.1g; Protein: 4.9g; Sugars: 2.5g; Fiber: 2.6g

448. Stuffed Peppers with Tofu and Corn [AF]

(Ready in about 20 minutes | Servings 2)

Ingredients

2 bell peppers, seeded and halved
4 ounces firm tofu, crumbled
4 tablespoons canned sweetcorn
1 tomato, crushed
Sea salt and ground black pepper, to taste
1 teaspoon garlic, minced
1 teaspoon smoked paprika

Directions

Arrange the peppers in the Air Fryer cooking basket.

Mix the remaining ingredients until well combined. Divide the filling between the peppers.

Secure the air-frying lid. Air fry the peppers at 400 degrees F for about 15 minutes.

Bon appétit!

Per serving: Calories: 184; Fat: 5.7g; Carbs: 25.7g; Protein: 12.4g; Sugars: 3.9g; Fiber: 4.9g

449. Classic Vegan Stroganoff [PC]

(Ready in about 20 minutes | Servings 4)

Ingredients

2 tablespoons olive oil
1 pound brown mushrooms, thinly sliced
1 large onion, diced
1 celery stalk, chopped
1 large carrot, sliced
4 garlic cloves, minced
4 cups vegetable broth
1 pound red potatoes, peeled and diced
1 tablespoon fresh rosemary leaves, chopped
1/2 cup red wine
2 tablespoons tomato paste
Sea salt and ground black pepper, to taste

Directions

Heat the olive oil on the "Sauté" mode. Now, cook the mushrooms and onion for 3 to 4 minutes or until they are tender and aromatic.

Add in the remaining ingredient; gently stir to combine and secure the pressure-cooking lid.

Pressure cook for 10 minutes at High pressure. Once cooking is complete, use a natural pressure release for 5 minutes; carefully remove the lid.

Bon appétit!

Per serving: Calories: 197; Fat: 7g; Carbs: 30.5g; Protein: 6.4g; Sugars: 6.9g; Fiber: 4.3g

450. Baby Potatoes with Mediterranean Herbs [AF]

(Ready in about 25 minutes | Servings 3)

Ingredients

1 pound baby potatoes
2 tablespoons olive oil
1 teaspoon dried thyme
1 teaspoon dried rosemary
1 teaspoon dried basil
1 teaspoon dried oregano
1 teaspoon dried parsley flakes
1 teaspoon garlic, minced
Sea salt and ground black pepper, to taste
1 teaspoon cayenne pepper

Directions

Toss the potatoes with the remaining ingredients until well coated on all sides.

Arrange the potatoes in the Air Fryer basket. Secure the air-frying lid.

Air fry the potatoes at 400 degrees F for about 20 minutes, shaking the basket halfway through the cooking time. Bon appétit!

Per serving: Calories: 202; Fat: 9g; Carbs: 27.5g; Protein: 3.4g; Sugars: 1.2g; Fiber: 3.8g

451. Easy French Lentil Salad [PC]

(Ready in about 15 minutes + chilling time | Servings 4)

Ingredients

1 cup French lentils
1 Greek cucumber, sliced
1 cup cherry tomatoes, halved
1 red onion, thinly sliced
1/4 cup fresh parsley, roughly chopped
1/2 cup Kalamata olives, pitted and halved
1/4 cup olive oil
2 tablespoons red wine vinegar
1 tablespoon lemon juice
1 teaspoon dried oregano

Directions

Add the lentils to the inner pot of your Instant Pot Duo Crisp; pour in 3 cups of water and secure the pressure-cooking lid.

Pressure cook for 10 minutes at High pressure. Once cooking is complete, use a quick pressure release; carefully remove the lid.

Drain the lentils and transfer them to a salad bowl; add in the remaining ingredients and gently toss to combine well. Enjoy!

Per serving: Calories: 326; Fat: 16.1g; Carbs: 34.5g; Protein: 12.6g; Sugars: 2.8g; Fiber: 6.8g

452. Asian Spicy Tofu [AF]

(Ready in about 25 minutes + marinating time | Servings 3)

Ingredients

12 ounces extra-firm tofu, cubed
1 tablespoon soy sauce
1 tablespoon sesame oil
1 teaspoon sriracha
1 teaspoon shallot powder
1 teaspoon garlic, minced

Directions

Toss the tofu with the remaining ingredients. Let it marinate for 30 minutes.

Place the tofu cubes in the Air Fryer cooking basket, discarding the marinade. Secure the air-frying lid.

Air fry the tofu cubes at 360 degrees F for 10 minutes; shake the basket and continue to cook for 12 minutes more. Bon appétit!

Per serving: Calories: 164; Fat: 12.2g; Carbs: 3.9g; Protein: 11.7g; Sugars: 1.6g; Fiber: 0.9g

453. Two Bean Peppery Salad [PC]

(Ready in about 35 minutes | Servings 5)

Ingredients

1 cup red kidney beans, soaked
1 cup pinto beans, soaked
2 bell peppers, diced
1 jalapeno pepper, chopped
1 red onion, chopped
1 Persian cucumber, sliced
1/2 cup apple cider vinegar
1/4 cup extra-virgin olive oil
1 tablespoon Dijon mustard
Sea salt and ground black pepper, to taste
2 tablespoons fresh cilantro, roughly chopped

Directions

Place the soaked beans in the inner pot of your Instant Pot Duo Crisp; pour in 6 cups of water.

Secure the pressure-cooking lid.

Pressure cook for 30 minutes at High pressure. Once cooking is complete, use a natural pressure release; carefully remove the lid.

Drain your beans and toss them with the remaining ingredients. Serve well-chilled and enjoy!

Per serving: Calories: 373; Fat: 11.8g; Carbs: 50.3g; Protein: 17.4g; Sugars: 4.1g; Fiber: 12.2g

454. Homemade Lebanese Falafel [AF]

(Ready in about 20 minutes | Servings 4)

Ingredients

12 ounces canned chickpeas, rinsed and drained
1 bell pepper, seeded and minced
1 small onion, quartered
2 cloves garlic, roughly chopped
1/4 cup fresh parsley, roughly chopped
1/4 cup fresh scallions, chopped
1/2 teaspoon cumin, ground
Kosher salt and ground black pepper, to taste
1 teaspoon paprika
1 teaspoon coriander
2 tablespoons plain flour
2 tablespoons olive oil

Directions

Pulse all the ingredients in your food processor until everything is well incorporated.

Shape the mixture into balls and place them in a lightly greased Air Fryer cooking basket.

Secure the air-frying lid.

Cook the falafel at 380 degrees F for about 15 minutes, shaking the basket occasionally to ensure even cooking.

Serve in pita bread with toppings of your choice. Enjoy!

Per serving: Calories: 216; Fat: 9.4g; Carbs: 27.3g; Protein: 7.4.5g; Sugars: 5.5g; Fiber: 6.7g

455. Vegan Irish Stew with Guinness [PC]

(Ready in about 15 minutes | Servings 4)

Ingredients

1 tablespoon sesame oil
1 rib celery, chopped
1 onion, chopped
3 cloves garlic, minced
4 cups vegetable broth
1/2 cup Guinness beer
1 parsnip, trimmed and chopped
1/2 cup tomato puree
2 bay leaves
1 teaspoon cayenne pepper
Sea salt and freshly ground black pepper, to taste

Directions

Stir all the ingredients into the inner pot of your Instant Pot Duo Crisp.

Secure the pressure-cooking lid.

Pressure cook for 10 minutes at High pressure. Once cooking is complete, use a quick pressure release; carefully remove the lid.

Bon appétit!

Per serving: Calories: 188; Fat: 9.7g; Carbs: 14.5g; Protein: 8.4g; Sugars: 4.7g; Fiber: 3g

456. Fingerling Potatoes with Tofu and Herbs [AF]

(Ready in about 25 minutes | Servings 3)

Ingredients

1 pound French fingerling potatoes, halved lengthwise
2 tablespoons olive oil
2 cloves garlic, pressed
1 tablespoon fresh parsley, chopped
1 tablespoon fresh coriander, chopped
1 tablespoon fresh chives, chopped
Sea salt and ground black pepper, to taste
2 ounces tofu cheese, crumbled

Directions

Toss the potatoes with the remaining ingredients, except for the tofu cheese, until well coated on all sides.

Arrange the potatoes in the Air Fryer basket. Secure the air-frying lid.

Air fry the potatoes at 400 degrees F for about 15 minutes, shaking the basket halfway through the cooking time.

Top with the tofu cheese and continue cooking an additional 5 minutes.

Bon appétit!

Per serving: Calories: 344; Fat: 18.7g; Carbs: 40.3g; Protein: 5.7g; Sugars: 1.3g; Fiber: 3.9g

457. Classic Tabbouleh Salad [PC]

(Ready in about 15 minutes + chilling time | Servings 4)

Ingredients

1 cup whole kamut
2 cups water
1 small shallot, chopped
2 garlic cloves, minced
1 bell pepper, chopped
1 red chili pepper, chopped
4 tablespoons olive oil
1 tablespoon fresh lemon juice
1 tablespoon apple cider vinegar
1/4 cup fresh mint leaves, roughly chopped
1 Persian cucumber, sliced

Directions

Add the kamut and water to the inner pot and secure the pressure-cooking lid.

Pressure cook for 12 minutes at High pressure. Once cooking is complete, use a quick pressure release and then, carefully remove the lid.

Toss the chilled kamut with the remaining ingredients in a salad bowl.

Bon appétit!

Per serving: Calories: 292; Fat: 14.5g; Carbs: 36.3g; Protein: 7.5g; Sugars: 5.4g; Fiber: 5.7g

458. Chinese Broccoli Florets [AF]

(Ready in about 10 minutes | Servings 4)

Ingredients

1/2 pound broccoli florets
2 tablespoons sesame oil
2 scallions, chopped
1 teaspoon Five-spice powder
Sea salt and ground black pepper, to taste

Directions

Toss the broccoli florets with the remaining ingredients until well coated.

Arrange the broccoli florets in the Air Fryer basket.

Secure the air-frying lid.

Air fry the broccoli florets at 395 degrees F for 6 minutes, shaking the basket halfway through the cooking time.

Bon appétit!

Per serving: Calories: 88; Fat: 7g; Carbs: 5.7g; Protein: 2.6g; Sugars: 1.7g; Fiber: 1.9g

459. Creamed Mushroom and Shallot Soup [PC]

(Ready in about 15 minutes | Servings 4)

Ingredients

2 tablespoons olive oil
1 ½ pounds white mushrooms, sliced
1 shallot, diced
Sea salt and ground black pepper, to taste
2 garlic cloves, chopped
4 cups vegetable broth

Directions

Press the "Sauté" button and heat the olive oil. Then, cook the mushrooms and shallot for about 3 minutes or until they've softened.

Add the remaining ingredients to the inner pot.

Then, secure the pressure-cooking lid.

Pressure cook for 10 minutes at High pressure. Once cooking is complete, use a quick pressure release; carefully remove the lid.

Lastly, puree the soup until creamy and uniform and serve hot. Bon appétit!

Per serving: Calories: 143; Fat: 8.8g; Carbs: 8g; Protein: 10.4g; Sugars: 4.1g; Fiber: 1.7g

460. Sticky Red Beets [AF]

(Ready in about 35 minutes | Servings 4)

Ingredients

1 pound red beets, peeled and diced
2 teaspoons olive oil
Coarse sea salt and ground black pepper, to taste
2 tablespoons agave syrup
2 tablespoons balsamic vinegar

Directions

Toss the red beets with the remaining ingredients until well coated on all sides.

Secure the air-frying lid.

Air fry the red beets at 390 degrees F for about 30 minutes, tossing the basket every 10 minutes to ensure even cooking. Bon appétit!

Per serving: Calories: 114; Fat: 2.4g; Carbs: 21.7g; Protein: 2.2g; Sugars: 17g; Fiber: 3.3g

461. Squash and Spinach Medley [PC]

(Ready in about 15 minutes | Servings 4)

Ingredients

1 pound acorn squash, peeled, seeds removed and diced
2 tablespoons olive oil
1 cup vegetable broth
1 tablespoon pure maple syrup
2 cup baby spinach
1 shallot, chopped
1 tablespoon Dijon mustard

Directions

Add the acorn squash, olive oil, and vegetable broth to the inner pot of your Instant Pot Duo Crisp.

Secure the pressure-cooking lid.

Pressure cook for 6 minutes at High pressure. Once cooking is complete, use a quick pressure release; carefully remove the lid.

Add in the baby spinach, shallot, and mustard. Toss to combine and serve at room temperature. Bon appétit!

Per serving: Calories: 137; Fat: 7.5g; Carbs: 16.5g; Protein: 2.7g; Sugars: 3.5g; Fiber: 2.4g

462. Paprika Green Beans [AF]

(Ready in about 10 minutes | Servings 3)

Ingredients

3/4 pound green beans, trimmed and halved
1/2 cup vegan mayonnaise
1 teaspoon granulated garlic
1 teaspoon paprika
Kosher salt and ground black pepper, to taste

Directions

Toss the green beans with the remaining ingredients until well coated on all sides.

Secure the air-frying lid.

Air fry the green beans at 390 degrees F for about 6 minutes, tossing the basket halfway through the cooking time. Enjoy!

Per serving: Calories: 174; Fat: 13.1g; Carbs: 12.2g; Protein: 4.9g; Sugars: 4.8g; Fiber: 4g

463. Za'atar and White Wine Cauliflower [PC]

(Ready in about 20 minutes | Servings 4)

Ingredients

1 ½ pounds whole head of cauliflower
1 cup cream of celery soup
1/2 cup white wine
2 tablespoons olive oil
Coarse sea salt and ground black pepper, to taste
1 tablespoon zaatar spice

Directions

Toss the whole head of cauliflower with the remaining ingredients in the inner pot of your Instant Pot Duo Crisp.

Secure the pressure-cooking lid.

Pressure cook for 10 minutes at High pressure. Once cooking is complete, use a quick pressure release; carefully remove the lid.

Lastly, secure the air-frying lid; broil your cauliflower for about 6 minutes, if desired. Enjoy!

Per serving: Calories: 136; Fat: 8.8g; Carbs: 13g; Protein: 4.3g; Sugars: 4.3g; Fiber: 4.4g

464. Asian Fried Tempeh [AF]

(Ready in about 25 minutes | Servings 3)

Ingredients

10 ounces tempeh
2 tablespoons soy sauce
1 tablespoon rice vinegar
1 teaspoon cayenne pepper
Sea salt and ground black pepper, to taste

Directions

Toss the tempeh with the remaining ingredients. Let it marinate for 30 minutes.

Place the tempeh in the Air Fryer cooking basket, discarding the marinade. Secure the air-frying lid.

Air fry the tempeh at 360 degrees F for 10 minutes; turning it over and continue to cook for 12 minutes more. Bon appétit!

Per serving: Calories: 214; Fat: 12.2g; Carbs: 11.6g; Protein: 18g; Sugars: 2.2g; Fiber: 0.7g

465. Old-Fashioned Cabbage Soup [PC]

(Ready in about 15 minutes | Servings 4)

Ingredients

2 tablespoons olive oil
1 onion, chopped
3 cloves garlic, minced
2 tomatoes, pureed
4 cups vegetable broth
Kosher salt and ground black pepper, to taste
1 teaspoon cayenne pepper
2 bay leaves
1 pound cabbage, shredded
2 carrots, trimmed and chopped

Directions

Choose the "Sauté" button to preheat your Instant Pot Duo Crisp. Then, heat the olive oil and cook the onion and garlic for about 3 minutes or until they've softened.

Stir the remaining ingredients into the inner pot. Secure the pressure-cooking lid.

Pressure cook for 10 minutes at High pressure. Once cooking is complete, use a quick pressure release; carefully remove the lid.

Bon appétit!

Per serving: Calories: 133; Fat: 7g; Carbs: 15.8g; Protein: 2.6g; Sugars: 7.6g; Fiber: 4g

466. Crispy Baby Bellas [AF]

(Ready in about 15 minutes | Servings 4)

Ingredients

1 pound baby bella mushrooms, cleaned
4 garlic cloves, peeled and minced
1/2 panko crumbs
2 tablespoons sesame oil
Sea salt and ground black pepper, to taste
1/2 teaspoon onion powder
1/2 teaspoon smoked paprika

Directions

Toss your mushrooms with the remaining ingredients. Arrange them in a lightly greased Air Fryer basket.

Secure the air-frying lid.

Air fry the mushrooms at 375 degrees F for about 10 minutes, shaking the basket halfway through the cooking time. Enjoy!

Per serving: Calories: 151; Fat: 7.9g; Carbs: 16g; Protein: 5.6g; Sugars: 3.6g; Fiber: 2g

467. Mexican Kidney Bean Chili [PC]

(Ready in about 30 minutes | Servings 5)

Ingredients

2 tablespoons olive oil
1 onion, chopped
2 garlic cloves, minced
1 red chili pepper, chopped
1 bell pepper, chopped
1 (14-ounce) can tomatoes
1 pound red kidney beans, rinsed
3 cups vegetable broth
1 teaspoon Mexican oregano
1 lime, cut into wedges

Directions

Press the "Sauté" button to preheat your Instant Pot Duo Crisp; now, heat the olive oil and cook the onion for approximately 3 minutes or until tender and translucent.

After that, add in the garlic, peppers, tomatoes, beans, broth, and oregano. Secure the pressure-cooking lid.

Pressure cook for 20 minutes at High pressure. Once cooking is complete, use a natural pressure release for 5 minutes; carefully remove the lid.

Spoon your chili into individual bowls, garnish with lime wedges, and serve hot. Enjoy!

Per serving: Calories: 383; Fat: 5.6g; Carbs: 62.1g; Protein: 23.6g; Sugars: 4.2g; Fiber: 23g

468. Vegan Moroccan Kefta [AF]

(Ready in about 20 minutes | Servings 4)

Ingredients

- 16 ounces canned chickpeas, rinsed and drained
- 1 medium onion, chopped
- 3 cloves garlic, roughly chopped
- 1 large carrot, peeled and roughly chopped
- 1/4 cup fresh parsley, roughly chopped
- 1/4 cup fresh coriander, roughly chopped
- 1/2 teaspoon ginger, peeled and grated
- 1/2 teaspoon cinnamon, ground
- 2 tablespoons olive oil
- Sea salt and ground black pepper, to taste

Directions

Pulse all the ingredients in your food processor until everything is well incorporated.

Form the mixture into balls and place them in a lightly greased Air Fryer cooking basket.

Secure the air-frying lid.

Air fry the meatballs at 380 degrees F for about 15 minutes, shaking the basket occasionally to ensure even cooking.

Serve in pita bread with toppings of your choice. Enjoy!

Per serving: Calories: 246; Fat: 10g; Carbs: 32.1g; Protein: 9g; Sugars: 7.2g; Fiber: 8.8g

469. Chickpea and Avocado Salad [PC]

(Ready in about 45 minutes + chilling time | Servings 5)

Ingredients

- 1 cup chickpeas, rinsed
- 1 cup French lentils
- 2 garlic cloves, halved lengthwise
- 4 tablespoons olive oil
- 1/4 cup fresh lime juice
- 1 teaspoon stone-ground mustard
- 1 teaspoon agave syrup
- Sea salt and ground black pepper, to taste
- 1 tablespoon fresh mint, roughly chopped
- 1 tablespoon fresh dill, roughly chopped
- 1 avocado, peeled, pitted, and diced

Directions

Add the rinsed chickpeas and 3 cups of water to the inner pot of your Instant Pot Duo Crisp. Secure the pressure-cooking lid.

Pressure cook for 30 minutes at High pressure. Once cooking is complete, use a natural pressure release; carefully remove the lid.

Then, add in the French lentils and secure the lid again.

Pressure cook for 10 minutes at High pressure. Once cooking is complete, use a quick pressure release; carefully remove the lid.

Allow your chickpeas and lentils to cool completely; then, toss them with the remaining ingredients and serve well-chilled. Enjoy!

Per serving: Calories: 463; Fat: 19.6g; Carbs: 57.1g; Protein: 19.6g; Sugars: 7.2g; Fiber: 12.3g

470. Tangy Roasted Cabbage [AF]

(Ready in about 10 minutes | Servings 4)

Ingredients

- 1 pound cabbage, cut into wedges
- 2 tablespoons olive oil
- 1 teaspoon garlic, minced
- Kosher salt and freshly ground black pepper, to taste
- 1/4 teaspoon cumin powder
- 1/2 teaspoon bay leaf, crushed
- 2 tablespoons fresh lemon juice
- 1 teaspoon red pepper flakes, crushed

Directions

Toss the cabbage wedges with the remaining ingredients. Secure the air-frying lid.

Cook the cabbage wedges at 350 degrees F for 7 minutes, shaking the basket halfway through the cooking time.

Taste and adjust the seasonings. Bon appétit!

Per serving: Calories: 99; Fat: 7g; Carbs: 7.4g; Protein: 1.6g; Sugars: 3.8g; Fiber: 3g

471. Creamed Corn and Split Pea Chowder [PC]

(Ready in about 20 minutes | Servings 4)

Ingredients

- 2 teaspoons sesame oil
- 1 onion, chopped
- 2 garlic cloves, minced
- 1 celery stalk, chopped
- 1 ½ cups green split peas
- 4 cups vegetable stock
- 1 cup coconut milk, unsweetened
- 1 cup sweet corn kernels, frozen

Directions

Select the "Sauté" mode to preheat your Instant Pot Duo Crisp. Now, heat the oil and sauté the onion for about 3 minutes or until tender and translucent.

Stir the garlic, celery, peas, and vegetable stock into the inner pot of your Instant Pot Duo Crisp.

Secure the pressure-cooking lid.

Pressure cook for 10 minutes at High pressure. Once cooking is complete, use a quick pressure release; carefully remove the lid.

Add in the coconut milk and sweet corn and allow it to simmer for about 5 minutes longer or until cooked through. Bon appétit!

Per serving: Calories: 199; Fat: 5g; Carbs: 28.5g; Protein: 9.4g; Sugars: 7.6g; Fiber: 7.6g

472. Spicy Potato Wedges [AF]

(Ready in about 25 minutes | Servings 4)

Ingredients

1 pound potatoes, peeled and cut into wedges
2 tablespoons olive oil
1 teaspoon red chili powder
1 teaspoon garlic powder
Kosher salt and ground black pepper, to taste

Directions

Toss the potatoes with the remaining ingredients until well coated on all sides. Arrange the potatoes in the Air Fryer basket.

Secure the air-frying lid.

Air fry the potatoes at 400 degrees F for about 20 minutes, shaking the basket halfway through the cooking time. Bon appétit!

Per serving: Calories: 147; Fat: 6.8g; Carbs: 19.8g; Protein: 2.2g; Sugars: 0.8g; Fiber: 2.5g

473. Vegetable and Lentil Mélange [PC]

(Ready in about 15 minutes | Servings 4)

Ingredients

2 tablespoons olive oil
1 onion, chopped
2 cloves garlic, chopped
2 carrots, chopped
1 stalk celery, chopped
1 ½ cups red lentils
1/2 teaspoon dried rosemary
1/2 teaspoon mustard seeds
4 cups vegetable broth

Directions

Select the "Sauté" mode and heat the olive oil; once hot, sauté the onion and garlic for about 3 minutes or until tender.

Stir in the remaining ingredients and secure the pressure-cooking lid.

Pressure cook for 10 minutes at High pressure. Once cooking is complete, use a quick pressure release; carefully remove the lid.

Bon appétit!

Per serving: Calories: 245; Fat: 8.5g; Carbs: 51.5g; Protein: 17.6g; Sugars: 2.7g; Fiber: 9g

474. Breakfast Red Bean Sausage [AF]

(Ready in about 20 minutes | Servings 4)

Ingredients

1 cup canned red beans, drained and rinsed
1/2 cup oats
1/4 cup walnuts
1 small onion, peeled and quartered
2 garlic cloves
1 red bell pepper, chopped
2 chia eggs (2 tablespoons ground chia seeds + 4 tablespoons water
1 tablespoon marinara sauce
1/2 teaspoon ground cumin
1/2 teaspoon mustard seeds
1 tablespoon olive oil
Sea salt and ground black pepper, to taste

Directions

Pulse all the ingredients in your food processor until everything is well incorporated.

Shape the mixture into four sausages and place them in a lightly greased Air Fryer basket.

Secure the air-frying lid.

Cook the sausage at 390 degrees F for about 15 minutes, shaking the basket halfway through the cooking time.

Bon appétit!

Per serving: Calories: 218; Fat: 8.4g; Carbs: 8.5g; Protein: 2.4g; Sugars: 2.4g; Fiber: 6.5g

475. Vanilla Oatmeal with Almonds [PC]

(Ready in about 10 minutes | Servings 4)

Ingredients

1 cup steel cut oats
2 cups almond milk
1/2 cup almonds, slivered
4 teaspoons agave syrup
1 teaspoon vanilla extract
1/4 teaspoon ground cardamom
1/2 teaspoon ground cinnamon

Directions

Add all the ingredients to the inner pot of your Instant Pot Duo Crisp. Stir to combine and secure the pressure-cooking lid.

Pressure cook for 6 minutes at High pressure. Once cooking is complete, use a quick pressure release and carefully remove the lid.

Serve in individual bowls. Bon appétit!

Per serving: Calories: 253; Fat: 7g; Carbs: 37.6g; Protein: 10.5g; Sugars: 11.7g; Fiber: 4.4g

476. Fried Bok Choy [AF]

(Ready in about 10 minutes | Servings 4)

Ingredients

1 pound baby Bok choy, separate leaves
2 tablespoons sesame oil
2 garlic cloves, minced
1 teaspoon Five-spice powder

Directions

Toss the Bok choy with the remaining ingredients until well coated on all sides.

Secure the air-frying lid.

Cook the Bok choy at 350 degrees F for 6 minutes, shaking the basket halfway through the cooking time. Bon appétit!

Per serving: Calories: 78; Fat: 7g; Carbs: 2.9g; Protein: 1.9g; Sugars: 1g; Fiber: 1.3g

477. Quinoa with Butternut Squash and Leeks [PC]

(Ready in about 15 minutes | Servings 4)

Ingredients

1 pound butternut squash, peeled and diced
2 tablespoons sesame oil
1 cup quinoa
2 cup water
2 vegetable bouillon cubes
1 small leek, diced
2 tablespoons parsley, chopped
1 teaspoon paprika

Directions

Add all the ingredients to the inner pot of your Instant Pot Duo Crisp.

Secure the pressure-cooking lid.

Pressure cook for 6 minutes at High pressure. Once cooking is complete, use a quick pressure release; carefully remove the lid.

Spoon the mixture into individual bowls. Bon appétit!

Per serving: Calories: 287; Fat: 9.9g; Carbs: 43.5g; Protein: 7.7g; Sugars: 1.2g; Fiber: 5.3g

478. Potato Wedges with Italian Herbs [AF]

(Ready in about 25 minutes | Servings 4)

Ingredients

1 pound potatoes, peeled and cut into wedges
2 tablespoons olive oil
1 teaspoon granulated garlic
1 tablespoon Italian herb mix
1 teaspoon cayenne pepper
Kosher salt and freshly ground black pepper, to taste

Directions

Toss the potatoes with the remaining ingredients until well coated on all sides. Arrange the potatoes in the Air Fryer basket.

Secure the air-frying lid.

Air fry the potatoes at 400 degrees F for about 20 minutes, shaking the basket halfway through the cooking time.

Bon appétit!

Per serving: Calories: 149; Fat: 6.8g; Carbs: 20.3g; Protein: 2.3g; Sugars: 0.9g; Fiber: 2.6.3g

479. Chili with White Wine and Spinach [PC]

(Ready in about 20 minutes | Servings 4)

Ingredients

2 tablespoons olive oil
1 onion, chopped
2 cloves garlic, chopped
2 bell peppers, chopped
1 small red chili pepper, chopped
1/2 cup dry white wine
1/2 teaspoon ground cumin
1/2 teaspoon mustard seeds
1 teaspoon smoked paprika
Sea salt and ground black pepper
2 tomatoes, crushed
1 tablespoon brown sugar
4 ½ cups vegetable broth
1 ½ cups Great Northern beans
2 cups baby spinach

Directions

Choose the "Sauté" function to preheat your Instant Pot. Heat the olive oil and sauté the onion, garlic, and peppers for about 3 minutes or until the vegetables have softened.

Add in the wine, spices, tomatoes, sugar, broth, and beans.

Secure the pressure-cooking lid.

Pressure cook for 10 minutes at High pressure. Once cooking is complete, use a quick pressure release; carefully remove the lid.

Fold in the baby spinach and cover with the lid again; allow it so sit for about 5 minutes until thoroughly cooked.

Bon appétit!

Per serving: Calories: 402; Fat: 11.4g; Carbs: 59g; Protein: 20.4g; Sugars: 11g; Fiber: 16.4g

480. Dijon Fried Tofu Cubes

(Ready in about 25 minutes + marinating time | Servings 4)

Ingredients

14 ounces extra-firm tofu, pressed and cubed
2 tablespoons soy sauce
1 tablespoon Dijon mustard
1/4 cup red wine
2 teaspoons sesame oil
1 teaspoon garlic, minced
1 chili pepper, seeded and minced
4 tablespoons corn flour
Sea salt and ground black pepper, to taste

Directions

Toss the tofu with the soy sauce, mustard, red wine, sesame oil, garlic, and chili pepper. Let it marinate for 30 minutes.

Toss the tofu cubes with the corn flour, salt, and black pepper; place them in the Air Fryer cooking basket, discarding the marinade.

Secure the air-frying lid.

Air fry the tofu cubes at 360 degrees F for 10 minutes; shake the basket and continue to cook for 12 minutes more. Bon appétit!

Per serving: Calories: 137; Fat: 9.9g; Carbs: 12.3g; Protein: 11.6g; Sugars: 3.4g; Fiber: 1.6g

SNACKS & APPETIZERS

481. Restaurant-Style Buffalo Chicken Wings [PC+AF]

(Ready in about 20 minutes | Servings 5)

Ingredients

- 2 pounds chicken wings
- Sea salt and cayenne pepper, to taste
- 1 teaspoon garlic powder
- 1 teaspoon onion powder
- 1/4 cup butter, melted
- 1/2 cup hot sauce
- 1 cup chicken bone broth
- 1 cup blue cheese, crumbled

Directions

Press the "Sauté" button to preheat your Instant Pot Duo Crisp; now, sear the chicken wings for about 4 minutes; turn them on the other side and cook an additional 3 minutes.

Stir the spices, butter, hot sauce, and broth into the inner pot. Secure the pressure-cooking lid.

Pressure cook for 15 minutes at High pressure. Once cooking is complete, use a quick pressure release; carefully remove the lid.

Toss the chicken wings with the crumbled cheese; secure the air-frying lid and let it cook until the cheese melts. Bon appétit!

Per serving: Calories: 415; Fat: 23.6g; Carbs: 0.8g; Protein: 46.6g; Sugars: 0.1g; Fiber: 0.1g

482. Restaurant-Style Onion Rings [AF]

(Ready in about 10 minutes | Servings 4)

Ingredients

- 1 cup all-purpose flour
- Sea salt and black pepper, to taste
- 1 teaspoon red pepper flakes, crushed
- 1/2 teaspoon cumin powder
- 1 egg
- 1 cup breadcrumbs
- 1 medium yellow onion, sliced

Directions

In a shallow bowl, mix the flour, salt, black pepper, red pepper flakes, and cumin powder.

Whisk the egg in another shallow bowl. Place the breadcrumbs in a separate bowl.

Dip the onion rings in the flour, then in the eggs, then in the breadcrumbs. Place the onion rings in the Air Fryer basket.

Secure the air-frying lid.

Air fry the onion rings at 380 degrees F for about 8 minutes or until golden brown and cooked through.

Bon appétit!

Per serving: Calories: 243; Fat: 2.8g; Carbs: 44.7g; Protein: 8.6g; Sugars: 2.5g; Fiber: 2.3g

483. Sticky Little Smokies [PC]

(Ready in about 15 minutes | Servings 4)

Ingredients

- 1 pound mini smoked sausage links
- 1/2 cup chicken bone broth
- 1/2 cup strawberry jelly
- 1/2 cup barbeque sauce
- 1 teaspoon black whole peppercorns

Directions

Add all the ingredients to the inner pot of your Instant Pot Duo Crisp. Secure the pressure-cooking lid.

Pressure cook for 5 minutes at High pressure. Once cooking is complete, use a natural pressure release for 5 minutes; carefully remove the lid.

Turn your Instant Pot Duo Crisp to "Keep Warm" until ready to serve. Enjoy!

Per serving: Calories: 232; Fat: 11.8g; Carbs: 6.2g; Protein: 25.5g; Sugars: 2.2g; Fiber: 0.9g

484. Crispy Chicken Wings [AF]

(Ready in about 20 minutes | Servings 3)

Ingredients

- 3/4 pound chicken wings
- 1 tablespoon olive oil
- 1 teaspoon mustard seeds
- 1 teaspoon cayenne pepper
- 1 teaspoon garlic powder
- Sea salt and ground black pepper, to taste

Directions

Toss the chicken wings with the remaining ingredients. Secure the air-frying lid.

Air fry the chicken wings at 380 degrees F for 18 minutes, turning them over halfway through the cooking time. Bon appétit!

Per serving: Calories: 284; Fat: 21.4g; Carbs: 0.3g; Protein: 21.1g; Sugars: 0.3g; Fiber: 0.3g

485. Spiced Butternut Squash [PC]

(Ready in about 10 minutes | Servings 4)

Ingredients

- 2 pounds butternut squash, peeled, seeded, and diced
- 2 tablespoons coconut oil
- 2 tablespoons maple syrup
- A pinch of grated nutmeg
- 1/2 teaspoon ground cinnamon
- 1/2 teaspoon ground cardamom

Directions

Place all the ingredients in the inner pot of your Instant Pot Duo Crisp.

Secure the pressure-cooking lid.

Pressure cook for 6 minutes at High pressure. Once cooking is complete, use a quick pressure release.

Serve at room temperature and enjoy!

Per serving: Calories: 178; Fat: 7.1g; Carbs: 30.3g; Protein: 1.8g; Sugars: 6g; Fiber: 3.6g

486. Honey and Wine Baby Carrots [AF]

(Ready in about 20 minutes | Servings 3)

Ingredients

3/4 pound baby carrots, halved lengthwise
2 tablespoons coconut oil
1/2 teaspoon cumin powder
2 tablespoons honey
2 tablespoons white wine

Directions

Toss the carrots with the remaining ingredients; then, arrange the carrots in the Air Fryer cooking basket.

Secure the air-frying lid.

Cook the carrots at 380 degrees F for 15 minutes, shaking the basket halfway through the cooking time. Bon appétit!

Per serving: Calories: 162; Fat: 9.3g; Carbs: 21.1g; Protein: 0.9g; Sugars: 17g; Fiber: 3.4g

487. Corn on the Cob with Herb Butter [PC]

(Ready in about 10 minutes | Servings 3)

Ingredients

3 ears corn, husks removed
1 cup water
2 tablespoons butter, softened
2 tablespoons parsley, chopped
1 tablespoon rosemary, chopped
1 tablespoon cilantro, chopped

Directions

Add a metal trivet and 1 cup of water to the bottom of your Instant Pot Duo Crisp.

Place the ears of corn on top of the trivet and secure the pressure-cooking lid.

Pressure cook for 2 minutes. Once cooking is complete, use a quick pressure release; carefully remove the lid. Bon appétit!

Per serving: Calories: 202; Fat: 9.5g; Carbs: 29g; Protein: 5.1g; Sugars: 5g; Fiber: 4.2g

488. Homemade Apple Chips [AF]

(Ready in about 15 minutes | Servings 4)

Ingredients

2 large sweet, crisp apples, cored and sliced
1 teaspoon ground cinnamon
1/2 teaspoon grated nutmeg
A pinch of salt

Directions

Toss the apple slices with the remaining ingredients and arrange them in a single layer in the Air Fryer cooking basket.

Secure the air-frying lid.

Air fry the apple chips for about 9 minutes at 390 degrees F, shaking the basket halfway through the cooking time. Work in batches. Bon appétit!

Per serving: Calories: 47; Fat: 0.1g; Carbs: 12.3g; Protein: 0.2g; Sugars: 9.5g; Fiber: 2.2g

489. Hot 'n' Spicy Spareribs [PC]

(Ready in about 45 minutes | Servings 5)

Ingredients

2 ½ pounds spare ribs
1 tablespoon Dijon mustard
1 tablespoon smoked paprika
2 tablespoons brown sugar
2 garlic cloves, minced
Sea salt and ground black pepper, to taste
1/2 cup hot sauce
1 cup cranberry juice, unsweetened
1 thyme sprig
2 rosemary sprigs
2 bay leaves

Directions

Place all the ingredients in the inner pot of your Instant Pot Duo Crisp; secure the pressure-cooking lid.

Pressure cook for 40 minutes at High pressure. Once cooking is complete, use a quick pressure release; carefully remove the lid. Bon appétit!

Per serving: Calories: 476; Fat: 27g; Carbs: 11.3g; Protein: 46g; Sugars: 8.9g; Fiber: 1.6g

490. Spicy Chicken Drumettes [AF]

(Ready in about 20 minutes | Servings 5)

Ingredients

2 pounds chicken drumettes
1 teaspoon ancho chile pepper
1 teaspoon smoked paprika
1 teaspoon onion powder
1 teaspoon garlic powder
Kosher salt and ground black pepper, to taste
1/4 teaspoon black pepper
2 tablespoons olive oil

Directions

Toss the chicken drumettes with the remaining ingredients.

Secure the air-frying lid.

Air fry the chicken drumettes at 380 degrees F for 18 minutes, turning them over halfway through the cooking time. Bon appétit!

Per serving: Calories: 404; Fat: 25.8g; Carbs: 3.7g; Protein: 37.5g; Sugars: 0.5g; Fiber: 1.3g

491. Sweet and Spicy Chicken Drumettes [PC]

(Ready in about 20 minutes | Servings 5)

Ingredients

2 pounds chicken drumettes
Coarse sea salt, to taste
1 cup Thai chicken stock
1/2 cup Thai sweet chili sauce
2 tablespoons soy sauce
2 tablespoons rice wine vinegar
1 tablespoon garlic, minced
2 tablespoons peanut oil

Directions

Press the "Sauté" button and brown the chicken drumettes for about 5 minutes.

Stir the other ingredients into the inner pot. Secure the pressure-cooking lid.

Pressure cook for 15 minutes at High pressure. Once cooking is complete, use a quick pressure release; carefully remove the lid. Bon appétit!

Per serving: Calories: 283; Fat: 10.6g; Carbs: 6.4g; Protein: 37.6g; Sugars: 3.1g; Fiber: 1.8g

492. Mediterranean-Style Eggplant Chips [AF]

(Ready in about 20 minutes | Servings 4)

Ingredients

1 pound eggplant, sliced
2 tablespoons olive oil
1 teaspoon garlic, minced
Sea salt and ground black pepper, to taste
2 tablespoons lemon juice, freshly squeezed

Directions

Toss the eggplant pieces with the remaining ingredients until they are well coated on all sides.

Arrange the eggplant in the Air Fryer basket. Secure the air-frying lid.

Air fry the eggplant at 400 degrees F for about 15 minutes, shaking the basket halfway through the cooking time.

Bon appétit!

Per serving: Calories: 95; Fat: 7g; Carbs: 8.4g; Protein: 1.6g; Sugars: 4.7g; Fiber: 3.6g

493. Crab Legs with Herbs [PC]

(Ready in about 10 minutes | Servings 4)

Ingredients

1 ½ pounds crab legs
1 cup fish broth
1/4 cup butter
2 cloves garlic, minced
1 tablespoon Cajun seasoning mix
1 tablespoon fresh parsley, chopped
1 tablespoon fresh cilantro, chopped
2 tablespoons whiskey

Directions

Add all the ingredients to the inner pot of your Instant Pot Duo Crisp.

Secure the pressure-cooking lid. Pressure cook for 3 minutes at High pressure. Once cooking is complete, use a quick pressure release; carefully remove the lid.

Bon appétit!

Per serving: Calories: 275; Fat: 13.5g; Carbs: 5.2g; Protein: 31.2g; Sugars: 2g; Fiber: 0.4g

494. Parmesan Green Bean Chips [AF]

(Ready in about 10 minutes | Servings 4)

Ingredients

1 pound green beans
4 tablespoons all-purpose flour
2 eggs, whisked
1/2 cup breadcrumbs
1/2 cup grated parmesan cheese
1 teaspoon cayenne pepper
1/2 teaspoon mustard seeds
1 teaspoon garlic powder
Sea salt and ground black pepper, to taste

Directions

In a shallow bowl, thoroughly combine the flour and eggs; mix to combine well.

Then, in another bowl, mix the remaining ingredients. Dip the green beans in the egg mixture, then, in the breadcrumb mixture.

Secure the air-frying lid.

Air fry the green beans at 390 degrees F for about 6 minutes, tossing the basket halfway through the cooking time.

Enjoy!

Per serving: Calories: 181; Fat: 8.8g; Carbs: 17g; Protein: 11.1g; Sugars: 4.1g; Fiber: 3.5g

495. Moroccan Spiced Sweet Potatoes [PC]

(Ready in about 10 minutes | Servings 4)

Ingredients

1 pound sweet potatoes, peeled and cubed
2 tablespoons butter, at room temperature
1 cup water
1/4 cup brown sugar
1 teaspoon Moroccan spice blend
2 ounces pecan halves

Directions

Place all the ingredients in the inner pot of your Instant Pot Duo Crisp.

Secure the pressure-cooking lid.

Pressure cook for 4 minutes at High pressure. Once cooking is complete, use a quick pressure release.

Enjoy!

Per serving: Calories: 262; Fat: 16.1g; Carbs: 28.3g; Protein: 3.6g; Sugars: 7.6g; Fiber: 3.9g

496. Cheese Zucchini Fries [AF]

(Ready in about 15 minutes | Servings 4)

Ingredients

1 pound zucchini, sliced
1 cup Pecorino Romano cheese, grated
Sea salt and cayenne pepper, to taste

Directions

Toss the zucchini slices with the remaining ingredients and arrange them in a single layer in the Air Fryer cooking basket.

Secure the air-frying lid.

Air fry the zucchini slices for about 10 minutes at 390 degrees F, shaking the basket halfway through the cooking time. Work in batches.

Bon appétit!

Per serving: Calories: 133; Fat: 7g; Carbs: 8.1g; Protein: 10.6g; Sugars: 0.5g; Fiber: 1.4g

497. Italian-Style Pepperoni Dip [PC+AF]

(Ready in about 25 minutes | Servings 4)

Ingredients

6 ounces cream cheese
5 ounces pepperoni, diced
1 teaspoon Italian seasoning mix
1 pound shrimp, deveined
1/4 cup green onions, sliced
6 ounces cheddar cheese, grated
1/2 cup hot sauce
1/2 cup chicken bone broth

Directions

Add 1 cup of water and metal trivet to the inner pot. Spritz a baking dish with a nonstick cooking spray.

Place the cream cheese on the bottom of the prepared baking dish. Add the pepperoni, Italian seasoning mix, shrimp, green onions, cheese, hot sauce, and chicken broth. Scatter sliced olives over the top.

Lower the dish onto the prepared trivet.

Secure the pressure-cooking lid. Pressure cook for 18 minutes at High pressure. Once cooking is complete, use a quick pressure release; carefully remove the lid.

Secure the air-frying lid and let it cook for 5 minutes more or until cooked through. Bon appétit!

Per serving: Calories: 275; Fat: 13.5g; Carbs: 5.2g; Protein: 31.2g; Sugars: 2g; Fiber: 0.4g

498. Tomato Chips with Herbs [AF]

(Ready in about 20 minutes | Servings 2)

Ingredients

1 beefsteak tomato, thinly sliced
2 tablespoons extra-virgin olive oil
Coarse sea salt and fresh ground pepper, to taste
1 teaspoon dried basil
1 teaspoon dried thyme
1 teaspoon dried rosemary

Directions

Toss the tomato slices with the remaining ingredients until they are well coated on all sides.

Arrange the tomato slices in the Air Fryer cooking basket.

Secure the air-frying lid.

Cook the tomato slices at 360 degrees F for about 10 minutes. Turn the temperature to 330 degrees F and continue to cook for a further 5 minutes. Bon appétit!

Per serving: Calories: 145; Fat: 13.7g; Carbs: 6g; Protein: 1.3g; Sugars: 3.5g; Fiber: 1.7g

499. BBQ Spicy Broccoli Bites [PC]

(Ready in about 10 minutes | Servings 4)

Ingredients

1 ½ pounds broccoli florets
1/2 cup vegetable broth
1/2 cup BBQ sauce
2 tablespoons avocado oil
2 cloves garlic, chopped
1 chili pepper, chopped
Cayenne pepper, to taste

Directions

Place all the remaining ingredients in the inner pot of your Instant Pot Duo Crisp.

Secure the pressure-cooking lid. Pressure cook for 3 minutes at High pressure. Once cooking is complete, use a quick pressure release.

Serve at room temperature and enjoy!

Per serving: Calories: 135; Fat: 7.6g; Carbs: 15.1g; Protein: 5.6g; Sugars: 4.7g; Fiber: 5.2g

500. Chinese Potato Chips [AF]

(Ready in about 20 minutes | Servings 3)

Ingredients

2 large-sized potatoes, peeled and thinly sliced
2 tablespoons olive oil
1 teaspoon Sichuan peppercorns
1 teaspoon garlic powder
1/2 teaspoon Chinese five-spice powder
Sea salt, to taste

Directions

Toss the potatoes with the remaining ingredients and place them in the Air Fryer cooking basket.

Secure the air-frying lid.

Air fry the potato chips at 360 degrees F for 16 minutes, shaking the basket halfway through the cooking time and working in batches. Enjoy!

Per serving: Calories: 281; Fat: 10.1g; Carbs: 43.5g; Protein: 1.5g; Sugars: 1.9g; Fiber: 5.1g

501. Street-Style Corn on the Cob [PC]

(Ready in about 10 minutes | Servings 4)

Ingredients

4 ears corn on the cob, husked and halved
1 cup water
4 ounces cream cheese
2 tablespoons fresh parsley, chopped
1 teaspoon smoked paprika
Sea salt and ground black pepper, to taste

Directions

Add a metal trivet and 1 cup of water to the bottom of your Instant Pot. Place the ears of corn on top of the trivet and secure the pressure-cooking lid.

Mix the cheese, parsley, smoked paprika, salt, and black pepper; set aside.

Pressure cook the corn on the cob for 3 minutes. Once cooking is complete, use a quick pressure release; carefully remove the lid.

Spread the cheese mixture over each corn on the cob. Bon appétit!

Per serving: Calories: 160; Fat: 17.2g; Carbs: 14.8g; Protein: 4.1g; Sugars: 2.3g; Fiber: 1.8g

SNACKS & APPETIZERS

502. Spicy Mixed Nuts [AF]

(Ready in about 10 minutes | Servings 4)

Ingredients

1 egg white lightly beaten
1/2 cup pecan halves
1/2 cup almonds
1/2 cup walnuts
Sea salt and cayenne pepper, to taste
1 teaspoon chili powder
1/2 teaspoon ground cinnamon
1/2 teaspoon ground allspice

Directions

Place all the ingredients in the Air Fryer cooking basket.

Secure the air-frying lid.

Air fry the nuts at 330 degrees F for 6 minutes, shaking the basket halfway through the cooking time and work in batches. Enjoy!

Per serving: Calories: 264; Fat: 24.2g; Carbs: 8.8g; Protein: 7.6g; Sugars: 2.2g; Fiber: 4.7g

503. Hot Paprika Potato Bites with Bacon [PC]

(Ready in about 20 minutes | Servings 4)

Ingredients

2 ounces bacon, diced
1 ½ pounds potatoes, peeled and cut into wedges
1 cup chicken bone broth
1 garlic clove, minced
1 teaspoon hot paprika
Kosher salt and ground black pepper, to taste
1 bay laurel
1 thyme sprig

Directions

Press the "Sauté" button to preheat your Instant Pot Duo Crisp; once hot, cook the bacon until crisp; reserve.

Add the remaining ingredients to the inner pot and gently stir to combine. Secure the pressure-cooking lid.

Pressure cook for 15 minutes at High pressure. Once cooking is complete, use a quick pressure release; carefully remove the lid.

Garnish your potatoes with the reserved bacon and enjoy!

Per serving: Calories: 206; Fat: 6.1g; Carbs: 31.9g; Protein: 6.9g; Sugars: 2.1g; Fiber: 4.2g

504. Homemade Yam Chips [AF]

(Ready in about 20 minutes | Servings 2)

Ingredients

1 large-sized yam, peeled and cut into 1/4-inch sticks
1 tablespoon olive oil
Kosher salt and red pepper, to taste

Directions

Toss the yam with the remaining ingredients and place them in the Air Fryer cooking basket.

Secure the air-frying lid.

Air fry the yam sticks at 360 degrees F for 15 minutes, tossing halfway through the cooking time and working in batches. Enjoy!

Per serving: Calories: 141; Fat: 6.6g; Carbs: 20.5g; Protein: 1.5g; Sugars: 0.3g; Fiber: 3.1g

505. Beet, Arugula, and Orange Salad [PC]

(Ready in about 20 minutes | Servings 4)

Ingredients

1 pound mixed beets
2 cups arugula
1 blood oranges, peeled and sliced
1/4 cup hazelnuts, toasted and chopped
4 tablespoons olive oil
2 tablespoons balsamic vinegar
1/2 teaspoon garlic powder
1 teaspoon cumin seeds
1 teaspoon mustard seeds

Directions

Place 1 cup of water and a steamer basket in your Instant Pot Duo Crisp. Place the beets in the steamer basket.

Secure the pressure-cooking lid.

Pressure cook for 15 minutes at High pressure. Once cooking is complete, use a quick pressure release; carefully remove the lid.

Peel the beets and slice them into bite-sized pieces. Afterwards, toss the chilled beets with the remaining ingredients.

Bon appétit!

Per serving: Calories: 246; Fat: 19.2g; Carbs: 14.6g; Protein: 3.9g; Sugars: 9.3g; Fiber: 4.3g

506. Golden Beet Fries [AF]

(Ready in about 35 minutes | Servings 2)

Ingredients

1/2 pound golden beets, peeled and thinly sliced
Kosher salt and ground black pepper, to taste
1 teaspoon paprika
2 tablespoons olive oil
1/2 teaspoon garlic powder
1 teaspoon ground turmeric

Directions

Toss the beets with the remaining ingredients and place them in the Air Fryer cooking basket.

Secure the air-frying lid.

Air fry your chips at 330 degrees F for 30 minutes, shaking the basket occasionally and working in batches. Enjoy!

Per serving: Calories: 188; Fat: 13.6g; Carbs: 15.1g; Protein: 2.7g; Sugars: 9g; Fiber: 4.2g

507. Buttery Mashed Cauliflower [PC]

(Ready in about 10 minutes | Servings 4)

Ingredients

1 ½ pounds cauliflower florets
1 cup water
Sea salt and ground black pepper, to taste
1 teaspoon garlic powder
1 tablespoon butter
1/4 cup full-fat milk

SNACKS & APPETIZERS

Directions

Place the cauliflower and water in the inner pot of your Instant Pot Duo Crisp.

Secure the pressure-cooking lid.

Pressure cook for 3 minutes at High pressure. Once cooking is complete, use a quick pressure release.

Mash the cauliflower with the remaining ingredients.

Bon appétit!

Per serving: Calories: 85; Fat: 3.6g; Carbs: 10g; Protein: 3.9g; Sugars: 3.9g; Fiber: 3.5g

508. Gochugaru Chicken Drumettes [AF]

(Ready in about 20 minutes | Servings 4)

Ingredients

1 pound chicken drumettes
4 tablespoons soy sauce
1/4 cup rice vinegar
4 tablespoons honey
2 tablespoons sesame oil
1 teaspoon Gochugaru, Korean chili powder
2 tablespoons scallions, chopped
2 garlic cloves, minced

Directions

Toss the chicken drumettes with the remaining ingredients.

Secure the air-frying lid.

Cook the chicken drumettes at 380 degrees F for 18 minutes, turning them over halfway through the cooking time.

Bon appétit!

Per serving: Calories: 304; Fat: 12.8g; Carbs: 22.4g; Protein: 24.5g; Sugars: 20.5g; Fiber: 0.7g

509. Autumn Acorn Squash [PC]

(Ready in about 10 minutes | Servings 4)

Ingredients

2 pounds acorn squash, peeled, seeded, and cubed
2 tablespoons peanut oil
A pinch of kosher salt
A pinch of grated nutmeg
1/2 teaspoon ground cinnamon
1/4 teaspoon ground cardamom

Directions

Place all the ingredients in the inner pot of your Instant Pot Duo Crisp.

Secure the pressure-cooking lid.

Pressure cook for 6 minutes at High pressure. Once cooking is complete, use a quick pressure release.

Serve at room temperature and enjoy!

Per serving: Calories: 155; Fat: 6.9g; Carbs: 23.9g; Protein: 1.9g; Sugars: 0.1g; Fiber: 3.6g

510. Herbed Carrot Bites [AF]

(Ready in about 20 minutes | Servings 4)

Ingredients

1 pound carrots, cut into slices
2 tablespoons coconut oil
1 teaspoon paprika
1/2 teaspoon garlic powder
1/2 teaspoon dried oregano
1/2 teaspoon dried parsley flakes
Sea salt and ground black pepper, to taste

Directions

Toss the carrots with the remaining ingredients; then, arrange the carrots in the Air Fryer cooking basket.

Secure the air-frying lid.

Air fry the carrots at 380 degrees F for 15 minutes, shaking the basket halfway through the cooking time.

Bon appétit!

Per serving: Calories: 113; Fat: 7.2g; Carbs: 12.4g; Protein: 1.2g; Sugars: 6.1g; Fiber: 3.6g

511. Asparagus Bites with Parmesan Cheese [PC]

(Ready in about 10 minutes | Servings 4)

Ingredients

1 ½ pounds asparagus spears, trimmed
1 cup vegetable broth
2 tablespoons butter, melted
2 garlic cloves, minced
Kosher salt and ground black pepper, to taste
2 ounces parmesan cheese, grated

Directions

Place the asparagus, vegetable broth, butter, garlic, salt, and black pepper in the inner pot and secure the pressure-cooking lid.

Pressure cook for 3 minutes at High pressure. Once cooking is complete, use a quick pressure release; carefully remove the lid.

Toss the asparagus with parmesan cheese and enjoy!

Per serving: Calories: 165; Fat: 10.2g; Carbs: 10.2g; Protein: 9.3g; Sugars: 4g; Fiber: 3.8g

512. Homemade Tortilla Chips [AF]

(Ready in about 10 minutes | Servings 4)

Ingredients

4 corn tortillas, cut into wedges
1 tablespoon olive oil
1 tablespoon Mexican oregano
2 tablespoons lime juice
1 teaspoon chili powder
1 teaspoon ground cumin
Sea salt, to taste

Directions

Toss the tortilla wedges with the remaining ingredients.

Secure the air-frying lid.

Cook your tortilla chips at 360 degrees F for about 5 minutes or until crispy, working in batches. Enjoy!

Per serving: Calories: 88; Fat: 4.2g; Carbs: 11.7g; Protein: 1.5g; Sugars: 0.4g; Fiber: 1.8g

513. Sticky Baby Carrots [PC]

(Ready in about 10 minutes | Servings 4)

Ingredients

2 pounds baby carrots
1 cup water
Sea salt and cayenne pepper, to taste
2 tablespoons whiskey
2 tablespoons ghee, melted
1/4 cup honey
1/2 teaspoon ground cardamom
1/2 teaspoon ground cinnamon

Directions

Place 1 cup of water and a steamer basket in the inner pot. Place the carrots in the steamer basket.

Secure the pressure-cooking lid.

Pressure cook for 3 minutes at High pressure. Once cooking is complete, use a quick pressure release; carefully remove the lid.

Toss the carrots with the remaining ingredients and enjoy!

Per serving: Calories: 208; Fat: 6.1g; Carbs: 39.2g; Protein: 2.2g; Sugars: 27.5g; Fiber: 7.2g

514. Parmesan Zucchini Chips [AF]

(Ready in about 15 minutes | Servings 4)

Ingredients

1 pound zucchini, cut into sticks
1/2 cup Parmesan cheese
1/2 cup almond flour
1 egg, whisked
2 tablespoons olive oil
1 teaspoon hot paprika
Sea salt and ground black pepper, to taste

Directions

Toss the zucchini sticks with the remaining ingredients and arrange them in a single layer in the Air Fryer cooking basket.

Secure the air-frying lid.

Air fry the zucchini sticks for about 10 minutes at 390 degrees F, shaking the basket halfway through the cooking time. Work in batches.

Bon appétit!

Per serving: Calories: 227; Fat: 17.6g; Carbs: 9.2g; Protein: 10.8g; Sugars: 1.2g; Fiber: 3.1g

515. Dijon Sticky Cocktail Meatballs [PC]

(Ready in about 15 minutes | Servings 5)

Ingredients

1 pound cooked meatballs, frozen
1/3 cup brown sugar
1 tablespoon Dijon mustard
1/2 cup ketchup
1 teaspoon garlic powder
1/2 teaspoon onion powder
1 teaspoon dried oregano

Directions

Place the cooked meatballs in the inner pot of your Instant Pot Duo Crisp. Now, in a mixing bowl, thoroughly combine the remaining ingredients.

Stir the sauce into the inner pot of your Instant Pot Duo Crisp. Secure the pressure-cooking lid.

Pressure cook for 5 minutes at High pressure. Once cooking is complete, use a natural pressure release for 5 minutes; carefully remove the lid.

Serve the warm meatballs with cocktail sticks and enjoy!

Per serving: Calories: 315; Fat: 20.2g; Carbs: 21.3g; Protein: 13.5g; Sugars: 14.2g; Fiber: 2.2g

516. Asian-Style Ribs [AF]

(Ready in about 40 minutes | Servings 4)

Ingredients

2 pounds spare ribs
1/4 cup soy sauce
1/4 cup rice vinegar
1/4 cup sesame oil
2 garlic cloves, minced

Directions

Toss all the ingredients in a lightly greased Air Fryer cooking basket.

Secure the air-frying lid.

Air fry the ribs at 350 degrees F for 35 minutes, turning them over halfway through the cooking time. Bon appétit!

Per serving: Calories: 153; Fat: 7g; Carbs: 21.2g; Protein: 2.6g; Sugars: 1.5g; Fiber: 2.8g

517. Artichokes with Herbs and Cheese [PC]

(Ready in about 15 minutes | Servings 2)

Ingredients

1/2 cup breadcrumbs
1/2 cup Pecorino cheese, grated
2 tablespoons olive oil
1 teaspoon garlic powder
1/2 teaspoon onion powder
Sea salt and ground black pepper, to taste
2 tablespoons fresh parsley, chopped
2 tablespoons fresh chives, chopped
1 tablespoon fresh basil, chopped
2 medium artichokes

Directions

Thoroughly combine the breadcrumbs, cheese, olive oil, garlic, spices, and herbs.

Separate the leaves to open up the artichokes and stuff them with the prepared filling.

Add 1 cup of water and metal trivet to the inner pot. Lower your artichokes onto the trivet and secure pressure-cooking lid.

Pressure cook for 11 minutes at High pressure. Once cooking is complete, use a quick pressure release; carefully remove the lid.

Bon appétit!

Per serving: Calories: 368; Fat: 24.1g; Carbs: 25.7g; Protein: 15.1g; Sugars: 3.5g; Fiber: 9.6g

518. Cheddar Cauliflower Balls [AF]

(Ready in about 15 minutes | Servings 4)

Ingredients

1 pound cauliflower, grated
1/2 cup cheddar cheese, shredded
1 ounce butter, room temperature
Sea salt and ground black pepper, to taste
1/2 cup tortilla chips, crushed
2 eggs whisked

Directions

Thoroughly combine all the ingredients in a mixing bowl. Shape the mixture into bite-sized balls.

Secure the air-frying lid.

Air fry the cauliflower balls at 350 degrees F for about 13 minutes, turning them over halfway through the cooking time.

Bon appétit!

Per serving: Calories: 208; Fat: 12.2g; Carbs: 17.2g; Protein: 7.9g; Sugars: 4g; Fiber: 3.1g

519. Sweet Vanilla Popcorn [PC]

(Ready in about 15 minutes | Servings 4)

Ingredients

1/4 cup coconut oil
1 cup popcorn kernels
1/2 cup brown sugar
1 ½ teaspoons ground cinnamon
A pinch of sea salt
A pinch of grated nutmeg
1 teaspoon vanilla essence

Directions

Press the "Sauté" button to preheat your Instant Pot Duo Crisp; once hot, melt the coconut oil and stir until it begins to simmer.

Add in the popcorn kernels and secure the pressure-cooking lid. When the popping slows down, press the "Cancel" button.

Toss your popcorn with the sugar, cinnamon, salt, nutmeg, and vanilla. Enjoy!

Per serving: Calories: 279; Fat: 16.3g; Carbs: 31.3g; Protein: 3.1g; Sugars: 12.4g; Fiber: 4g

520. Cheese and Garlic Broccoli Florets [AF]

(Ready in about 15 minutes | Servings 4)

Ingredients

1 pound broccoli florets
1 teaspoon granulated garlic
1 tablespoon onion flakes, dried
1 teaspoon red pepper flakes, crushed
2 tablespoons olive oil
1/2 cup Pecorino Romano cheese, grated

Directions

Toss all the ingredients in a lightly oiled Air Fryer basket.

Secure the air-frying lid.

Air fry the broccoli florets at 370 degrees F for about 10 minutes, shaking the basket halfway through the cooking time.

Enjoy!

Per serving: Calories: 156; Fat: 10.6g; Carbs: 10.5g; Protein: 6.g; Sugars: 2.4g; Fiber: 3.1g

521. Grape Jelly Party Kielbasa [PC]

(Ready in about 15 minutes | Servings 7)

Ingredients

1 ½ pounds kielbasa, sliced into ½-inch rounds
1/2 teaspoon mustard seeds
1/2 cup bottled chili sauce
1 cup grape jelly
1 bay laurel

Directions

Place all the ingredients in the inner pot of your Instant Pot Duo Crisp.

Secure the pressure-cooking lid.

Pressure cook for 5 minutes at High pressure. Once cooking is complete, use a natural pressure release for 5 minutes; carefully remove the lid.

Serve with toothpicks and enjoy!

Per serving: Calories: 262; Fat: 17.2g; Carbs: 13g; Protein: 13.5g; Sugars: 7.2g; Fiber: 1.2g

522. Green Tomato Crisps [AF]

(Ready in about 20 minutes | Servings 4)

Ingredients

1/2 cup all-purpose flour
Sea salt and ground black pepper, to taste
1 teaspoon garlic powder
1 teaspoon cayenne pepper
2 eggs
1/2 cup milk
2 tablespoons olive oil
1 cup breadcrumbs
1 pound green tomatoes, sliced

Directions

In a shallow bowl, mix the flour, salt, black pepper, garlic powder, and cayenne pepper.

Whisk the egg and milk in another shallow bowl. Mix the olive oil and breadcrumbs in a separate bowl.

Dip the green tomatoes in the flour, then in the eggs, then in the breadcrumbs. Place the green tomatoes in the Air Fryer basket.

Secure the air-frying lid.

Cook the green tomatoes at 390 degrees F for about 15 minutes or until golden brown and cooked through.

Serve with toothpicks. Bon appétit!

Per serving: Calories: 215; Fat: 10.4g; Carbs: 23.2g; Protein: 7.6g; Sugars: 2.8g; Fiber: 1.8g

SNACKS & APPETIZERS

523. Vegetarian Cauliflower Wings [PC]

(Ready in about 15 minutes | Servings 4)

Ingredients

1 pound cauliflower florets
1/2 cup vegetable broth
1/2 cup marinara sauce
1/2 teaspoon smoked paprika
Sea salt and ground black pepper, to taste
2 tablespoons olive oil
1 tablespoon Italian seasoning mix
2 ounces parmesan cheese, grated

Directions

Add the cauliflower, broth, marinara sauce, paprika, salt, black pepper, and olive oil to the inner pot of your Instant Pot Duo Crisp.

Secure the pressure-cooking lid.

Pressure cook for 3 minutes at High pressure. Once cooking is complete, use a quick pressure release.

Toss the cauliflower florets with the Italian seasoning mix and parmesan cheese. Cover with the lid and allow them to sit for 5 minutes in the residual heat. Bon appétit!

Per serving: Calories: 169; Fat: 11.3g; Carbs: 12.2g; Protein: 7.1g; Sugars: 4.2g; Fiber: 3.4g

524. Double Cheese Jalapeno Poppers [AF]

(Ready in about 10 minutes | Servings 4)

Ingredients

4 ounces Cottage cheese, crumbled
4 ounces cheddar cheese, shredded
1 teaspoon mustard seeds
8 jalapenos, seeded and sliced in half lengthwise
8 slices bacon, sliced in half lengthwise

Directions

Thoroughly combine the cheese and mustard seeds. Spoon the mixture into jalapeno halves.

Wrap each jalapeno with half a slice of bacon and secure with toothpicks.

Secure the air-frying lid.

Air fry the jalapeno poppers at 370 degrees for about 7 minutes or until golden brown. Bon appétit!

Per serving: Calories: 300; Fat: 24.4g; Carbs: 6.2g; Protein: 13.3g; Sugars: 4.3g; Fiber: 0.8g

525. Potato Wedges with Tomato Sauce [PC]

(Ready in about 20 minutes | Servings 4)

Ingredients

1 ½ pounds potatoes, peeled and cut into wedges
2 cloves garlic, crushed
1 thyme sprig, chopped
2 rosemary sprigs, chopped
Sea salt and ground black pepper, to taste
4 tablespoons butter, melted
1/2 cup tomato sauce
1/2 cup vegetable stock

Directions

Place all the ingredients in the inner pot of your Instant Pot Duo Crisp; secure the pressure-cooking lid.

Pressure cook for 15 minutes at High pressure. Once cooking is complete, use a quick pressure release; carefully remove the lid.

Bon appétit!

Per serving: Calories: 278; Fat: 11.8g; Carbs: 38.1g; Protein: 4.7g; Sugars: 5.5g; Fiber: 6g

526. Crispy Cauliflower Bites [AF]

(Ready in about 20 minutes | Servings 4)

Ingredients

2 eggs, whisked
1 cup breadcrumbs
Sea salt and ground black pepper, to taste
1 teaspoon cayenne pepper
1 teaspoon chili powder
1/2 teaspoon onion powder
1/2 teaspoon cumin powder
1/2 teaspoon garlic powder
1 pound cauliflower florets

Directions

Mix the eggs, breadcrumbs, and spices until well combined. Dip the cauliflower florets in the batter.

Secure the air-frying lid.

Air fry the cauliflower florets at 350 degrees F for about 15 minutes, turning them over halfway through the cooking time.

Bon appétit!

Per serving: Calories: 178; Fat: 4.1g; Carbs: 27.2g; Protein: 9.1g; Sugars: 4.6g; Fiber: 4.1g

527. Vanilla Ginger Yam Bites [PC]

(Ready in about 10 minutes | Servings 4)

Ingredients

3 tablespoons coconut oil
2 pounds yams
1/4 teaspoon ground nutmeg
1 teaspoon ground cinnamon
1/4 teaspoon ginger
1/4 cup honey
1 teaspoon pure vanilla extract

Directions

Melt the coconut oil on the "Sauté" function; sauté the yams for about 2 minutes or until just tender.

Stir the remaining ingredients into the inner pot of your Instant Pot Duo Crisp.

Secure the pressure-cooking lid.

Pressure cook for 6 minutes at High pressure. Once cooking is complete, use a quick pressure release; carefully remove the lid.

Bon appétit!

Per serving: Calories: 426; Fat: 10.6g; Carbs: 80.9g; Protein: 3.5g; Sugars: 18.3g; Fiber: 9.6g

SNACKS & APPETIZERS

528. Grandma's Pumpkin Chips [AF]

(Ready in about 20 minutes | Servings 4)

Ingredients

1 pound pumpkin, peeled and sliced
2 tablespoons coconut oil
1 teaspoon ground allspice
1/2 teaspoon chili powder
1/2 teaspoon garlic powder
1/2 teaspoon ground cumin
Sea salt and ground black pepper, to taste

Directions

Toss the pumpkin slices with the remaining ingredients until well coated on all sides.

Secure the air-frying lid.

Air fry the chips for about 13 minutes, tossing the basket once or twice.

Bon appétit!

Per serving: Calories: 97; Fat: 7g; Carbs: 9.2g; Protein: 1.6g; Sugars: 3.7g; Fiber: 1g

529. Easy Mashed Pumpkin [PC]

(Ready in about 10 minutes | Servings 5)

Ingredients

2 pounds pumpkin, peeled, seeded, and diced
2 tablespoons coconut oil
1 cup water
A pinch of sea salt
A pinch of grated nutmeg
1/4 teaspoon ground cinnamon

Directions

Place all the ingredients in the inner pot of your Instant Pot Duo Crisp; secure the pressure-cooking lid.

Pressure cook for 5 minutes at High pressure. Once cooking is complete, use a quick pressure release; carefully remove the lid.

Bon appétit!

Per serving: Calories: 98; Fat: 5.6g; Carbs: 11.9g; Protein: 1.8g; Sugars: 5.1g; Fiber: 1g

530. Mediterranean Sweet Potato Bites [AF]

(Ready in about 20 minutes | Servings 3)

Ingredients

2 large-sized sweet potatoes, peeled and cut into 1/4-inch sticks
2 teaspoons olive oil
1 teaspoon garlic powder
1 tablespoon Mediterranean herb mix
Kosher salt and freshly ground black pepper, to taste

Directions

Toss the sweet potato with the remaining ingredients and place them in the Air Fryer cooking basket.

Secure the air-frying lid.

Air fry the sweet potato sticks at 360 degrees F for 15 minutes, tossing halfway through the cooking time and working in batches.

Enjoy!

Per serving: Calories: 79; Fat: 3.6g; Carbs: 18.5g; Protein: 1.6g; Sugars: 3.7g; Fiber: 2.6g

531. Herbed Brussels Sprouts [PC]

(Ready in about 10 minutes | Servings 4)

Ingredients

1 ½ pounds Brussels sprouts, trimmed
1 cup vegetable broth
1 apple, cored and diced
2 tablespoons peanut oil
Sea salt and ground black pepper
1 teaspoon dried thyme
1 teaspoon dried rosemary

Directions

Place the Brussels sprouts, vegetable broth, and apple in the inner pot of your Instant Pot. Secure the pressure-cooking lid.

Pressure cook for 3 minutes at High pressure. Once cooking is complete, use a quick pressure release; carefully remove the lid.

Toss the Brussels sprouts with the remaining ingredients and serve warm or at room temperature!

Per serving: Calories: 171; Fat: 7.7g; Carbs: 22.9g; Protein: 7.2g; Sugars: 9.1g; Fiber: 7.8g

532. Dijon and Pancetta Shrimp [AF]

(Ready in about 10 minutes | Servings 4)

Ingredients

12 shrimp, peeled and deveined
3 slices pancetta, cut into strips
2 tablespoons maple syrup
1 tablespoon Dijon mustard

Directions

Wrap the shrimp in pancetta strips and toss them with maple syrup and mustard.

Place the shrimp in a lightly greased Air Fryer cooking basket.

Secure the air-frying lid.

Air fry the shrimp at 400 degrees F for 6 minutes, tossing the basket halfway through the cooking time.

Bon appétit!

Per serving: Calories: 118; Fat: 7.9g; Carbs: 7.2g; Protein: 4.3g; Sugars: 6.2g; Fiber: 0.2g

533. Seafood and Bacon Dip [PC+AF]

(Ready in about 20 minutes | Servings 9)

Ingredients

- 9 ounces cream cheese, softened
- 1 ½ pounds prawns, deveined
- 2 ounces bacon, diced
- 2 tablespoons butter
- 1 jalapeno pepper, chopped
- 2 garlic cloves, minced
- 1 teaspoon Cajun seasoning
- Sea salt and ground black pepper, to taste
- 1/2 cup mayonnaise
- 2 tablespoons dry white wine
- 1 teaspoon lemon juice
- 1 cup chicken broth
- 1 cup mozzarella cheese, shredded

Directions

Add 1 cup of water and a metal trivet to the inner pot. Spritz a baking dish with cooking spray.

Place the cream cheese on the bottom of the baking dish. Add in the prawns, bacon, butter, jalapeno pepper, garlic, spices, mayonnaise, wine, lemon juice, and broth.

Lower the dish onto the prepared trivet. Secure the pressure-cooking lid.

Pressure cook for 18 minutes at High pressure. Once cooking is complete, use a quick pressure release; carefully remove the lid.

Scatter mozzarella cheese over the top. Secure the air-frying lid and choose the "Broil" function. Let it cook for about 5 minutes or until the cheese melts. Bon appétit!

Per serving: Calories: 269; Fat: 18g; Carbs: 4.7g; Protein: 22.5g; Sugars: 1.5g; Fiber: 0.4g

534. Greek Potato Bites [AF]

(Ready in about 40 minutes | Servings 4)

Ingredients

- 1 pound potatoes, cut into wedges
- 2 tablespoons olive oil
- Sea salt and ground black pepper, to taste
- 1 teaspoon paprika
- 1 teaspoon dried parsley flakes
- 1 teaspoon Greek seasoning mix

Directions

Toss the potatoes with the remaining ingredients and place them in the Air Fryer cooking basket.

Secure the air-frying lid.

Air fry the potato wedges at 400 degrees F for 35 minutes, shaking the basket halfway through the cooking time.

Enjoy!

Per serving: Calories: 153; Fat: 7g; Carbs: 21.2g; Protein: 2.6g; Sugars: 1.5g; Fiber: 2.6g

535. Ricotta and Chicken Dipping Sauce [PC]

(Ready in about 20 minutes | Servings 10)

Ingredients

- 1 pound chicken breasts, boneless, skinless, chopped
- 1 cup chicken stock
- 1/2 cup hot sauce
- 6 ounces Ricotta cheese, crumbled
- 1 tablespoon Ranch seasoning mix
- 4 ounces cheddar cheese, grated

Directions

Add 1 cup of water and metal trivet to the inner pot of your Instant Pot Duo Crisp. Now, brush a souffle dish with a nonstick cooking oil.

Place the chicken breast, stock, hot sauce, Ricotta cheese, and Ranch seasoning mix on the bottom of the prepared dish.

Lower the dish onto the metal trivet and secure the pressure-cooking lid.

Pressure cook for 18 minutes at High pressure. Once cooking is complete, use a quick pressure release; carefully remove the lid.

Scatter grated cheddar cheese over the top. Secure the air-frying lid and choose the "Broil" function for about 5 minutes or until the cheese melts. Bon appétit!

Serve with dippers of choice and enjoy!

Per serving: Calories: 142; Fat: 7.6g; Carbs: 3.2g; Protein: 13.8g; Sugars: 1.4g; Fiber: 0.3g

536. Cheese and Bacon-Stuffed Poblanos [AF]

(Ready in about 10 minutes | Servings 4)

Ingredients

- 8 poblano peppers, seeded and halved
- 4 ounces Gruyere cheese
- 4 ounces bacon, chopped

Directions

Stuff the peppers with the cheese and bacon; transfer them to a lightly oiled Air Fryer basket.

Secure the air-frying lid.

Air fry the peppers at 370 degrees for about 7 minutes or until golden brown.

Bon appétit!

Per serving: Calories: 242; Fat: 17.2g; Carbs: 10.4g; Protein: 13.3g; Sugars: 4.6g; Fiber: 2.1g

537. Creamed Stuffed Eggs [PC]

(Ready in about 10 minutes | Servings 6)

Ingredients

6 eggs
3 tablespoons mayonnaise
3 tablespoons cream cheese
1/2 teaspoon turmeric powder
1 teaspoon balsamic vinegar
1 teaspoon fresh dill, chopped
Coarse sea salt and ground black pepper, to taste

Directions

Place 1 cup of water and a steamer rack in the inner pot of your Instant Pot Duo Crisp. Arrange the eggs on the rack.

Secure the pressure-cooking lid. Pressure cook for 5 minutes at High pressure. Once cooking is complete, use a quick pressure release; carefully remove the lid.

Peel the eggs and slice them into halves; separate the egg yolks from egg whites.

In a mixing bowl, thoroughly combine the egg yolks along with the remaining ingredients.

Use a piping bag to fill the egg white halves. Enjoy!

Per serving: Calories: 136; Fat: 11.5g; Carbs: 1.8g; Protein: 6.8g; Sugars: 1g; Fiber: 0.2g

538. Beer Battered Sweet Onion Rings [AF]

(Ready in about 10 minutes | Servings 4)

Ingredients

1/2 cup beer
1 cup plain flour
1 teaspoon baking powder
1 teaspoon cayenne pepper
Sea salt and ground black pepper, to taste
2 eggs, whisked
1 cup tortilla chips, crushed
2 sweet onions

Directions

In a shallow bowl, mix the beer, flour, baking powder, cayenne pepper, salt, and black pepper.

Whisk the egg in another shallow bowl. Place the crushed tortilla chips in a separate bowl.

Dip the onion rings in the flour mixture, then in the eggs, then in the tortilla chips. Place the onion rings in the Air Fryer basket.

Secure the air-frying lid.

Cook the onion rings at 380 degrees F for about 8 minutes or until golden brown and cooked through.

Bon appétit!

Per serving: Calories: 365; Fat: 9.2g; Carbs: 59g; Protein: 9.7g; Sugars: 9.3g; Fiber: 4g

539. Pizza Dipping Sauce [PC]

(Ready in about 20 minutes | Servings 8)

Ingredients

7 ounces cream cheese, softened
2 ounces pancetta, diced
1/2 teaspoon dried oregano
1/2 teaspoon dried basil
1 cup mozzarella cheese, shredded
1 cup pizza sauce
1/2 cup green olives, pitted and sliced

Directions

Add 1 cup of water and a metal trivet to the inner pot. Spritz a souffle dish with cooking spray.

Place the cream cheese on the bottom of the souffle dish. Add the pancetta, spices, mozzarella cheese, and pizza sauce. Scatter sliced olives over the top.

Lower the dish onto the prepared trivet.

Secure the pressure-cooking lid. Pressure cook for 18 minutes at High pressure. Once cooking is complete, use a quick pressure release; carefully remove the lid.

Serve the pizza dipping sauce with chips or breadsticks, if desired. Bon appétit!

Per serving: Calories: 151; Fat: 11.6g; Carbs: 4.3g; Protein: 7.5g; Sugars: 2.2g; Fiber: 0.9g

540. Mom's Famous Kale Chips [AF]

(Ready in about 10 minutes | Servings 4)

Ingredients

4 cups kale, torn into pieces
1 tablespoon sesame oil
1 teaspoon garlic powder
Sea salt and ground black pepper, to taste

Directions

Toss the kale leaves with the remaining ingredients and place them in the Air Fryer cooking basket.

Secure the air-frying lid.

Air fry your chips at 360 degrees F for 8 minutes, shaking the basket occasionally and working in batches.

Enjoy!

Per serving: Calories: 45; Fat: 3.5g; Carbs: 3g; Protein: 1.1g; Sugars: 0.9g; Fiber: 0.8g

DESSERTS

541. Crumble Cake with Blueberries [PC]

(Ready in about 25 minutes | Servings 7)

Ingredients

- 1 ½ cups fresh blueberries
- 1/4 teaspoon ground star anise
- 1/4 teaspoon ground cinnamon
- A pinch of grated nutmeg
- 1/2 cup butter, softened
- 1 cup brown sugar
- 1 cup rolled oats
- 1/2 cup pecans, chopped
- 1 teaspoon baking powder
- 1 teaspoon baking soda
- A pinch of sea salt
- 2 large eggs
- 6 tablespoons maple syrup

Directions

Arrange the fresh blueberries on the bottom of the inner pot. Sprinkle the fresh blueberries with star anise, cinnamon, nutmeg, butter, and sugar.

In a mixing bowl, thoroughly combine the rolled oats, pecans, baking powder, baking soda, salt, eggs, and maple syrup. Drop the topping mixture by the spoonful on top of the blueberry layer.

Secure the pressure-cooking lid. Pressure cook for 10 minutes at High pressure. Once cooking is complete, use a natural pressure release for 10 minutes; carefully remove the lid.

Allow your crumble to cool on a wire rack before serving and enjoy!

Per serving: Calories: 460; Fat: 21.6g; Carbs: 62.3g; Protein: 6.7g; Sugars: 44.3g; Fiber: 3.3g

542. Nutty Chocolate Cake [AF]

(Ready in about 25 minutes | Servings 5)

Ingredients

- 1/2 cup butter, melted
- 1 cup turbinado sugar
- 3 eggs
- 1 teaspoon vanilla extract
- 1/4 teaspoon salt
- 1/4 teaspoon ground cloves
- 1/2 teaspoon ground cinnamon
- 1/2 cup all-purpose flour
- 1/4 cup almond flour
- 5 ounces chocolate chips

Directions

Brush the sides and bottom of a baking pan with a nonstick cooking spray.

In a mixing bowl, beat the butter and sugar until fluffy. Next, fold in the eggs and beat again until well combined.

After that, add in the remaining ingredients. Mix until everything is well combined.

Secure the air-frying lid.

Bake your cake at 340 degrees F for 20 minutes. Enjoy!

Per serving: Calories: 431; Fat: 23.8g; Carbs: 49.5g; Protein: 6.6g; Sugars: 34.1g; Fiber: 1.8g

543. Classic Mini Cheesecakes [PC]

(Ready in about 40 minutes | Servings 4)

Ingredients

- 1 cup cracker crumbs
- 1 tablespoon maple syrup
- 4 tablespoons peanut butter
- 12 ounces cream cheese, room temperature
- 1/2 cup granulated sugar
- 2 eggs, room temperature
- 1 tablespoon all-purpose flour
- 1/4 cup sour cream
- 1 teaspoon vanilla extract

Directions

Spritz four ramekins with a nonstick cooking spray.

Mix the cracker crumbs, maple syrup, and peanut butter. Press the crust mixture into the prepared ramekins.

Thoroughly combine the remaining ingredients. Pour this mixture into ramekins and cover them with a piece of foil.

Place a metal trivet and 1 cup of water in the inner pot. Lower the ramekins onto the trivet.

Secure the pressure-cooking lid. Pressure cook for 25 minutes at High pressure. Once cooking is complete, use a natural pressure release for 10 minutes; carefully remove the lid.

Bon appétit!

Per serving: Calories: 463; Fat: 35.3g; Carbs: 26.5g; Protein: 9.7g; Sugars: 21.3g; Fiber: 0.4g

544. Chocolate and Coconut Brownies [AF]

(Ready in about 25 minutes | Servings 6)

Ingredients

- 1 stick butter, melted
- 1 cup brown sugar
- 2 eggs
- 3/4 cup all-purpose flour
- 1/2 teaspoon baking powder
- 1/4 cup cocoa powder
- 2 tablespoons coconut oil
- 1 teaspoon coconut extract
- A pinch of sea salt

Directions

In a mixing bowl, beat the melted butter and sugar until fluffy. Next, fold in the eggs and beat again until well combined.

After that, add in the remaining ingredients. Mix until everything is well incorporated.

Spritz the sides and bottom of a baking pan with a nonstick cooking spray. Scrape the batter into the pan. Secure the air-frying lid.

Bake in the preheated Air Fryer at 340 degrees F for 20 minutes. Enjoy!

Per serving: Calories: 325; Fat: 21.8g; Carbs: 30.8g; Protein: 4.2g; Sugars: 16.2g; Fiber: 1.5g

545. Pear Crisp with a Twist [PC]

(Ready in about 20 minutes | Servings 5)

Ingredients

1 pound pears, peeled, cored, and chopped
1 teaspoon fresh lemon juice
1/2 cup brown sugar
1/4 teaspoon ground cardamom
1/2 teaspoon ground cinnamon
1 cup rolled oats
4 tablespoons coconut oil
1/2 teaspoon vanilla extract
1/4 cup honey

Directions

Place the pears on the bottom of the inner pot. Sprinkle the pears with lemon juice, brown sugar, cardamom, and cinnamon.

In a mixing bowl, thoroughly combine the rolled oats, coconut oil, vanilla, and honey. Drop the mixture by the spoonful on top of the pears.

Secure the pressure-cooking lid. Pressure cook for 8 minutes at High pressure. Once cooking is complete, use a natural pressure release for 10 minutes; carefully remove the lid.

Bon appétit!

Per serving: Calories: 383; Fat: 13.3g; Carbs: 64.3g; Protein: 5.8g; Sugars: 40.1g; Fiber: 6.8g

546. Old-Fashioned Brownie Muffins [AF]

(Ready in about 20 minutes | Servings 6)

Ingredients

3/4 cup all-purpose flour
1 teaspoon baking powder
1/4 teaspoon ground cinnamon
1/4 teaspoon ground cardamom
3/4 cup granulated sugar
1/4 cups unsweetened cocoa powder
A pinch of sea salt
1 stick butter, at room temperature
3/4 cup milk
2 eggs, beaten

Directions

Mix all the ingredients in a bowl. Scrape the batter into silicone baking molds; place them in the Air Fryer basket.

Secure the air-frying lid.

Bake your cupcakes at 330 degrees F for about 15 minutes or until a tester comes out dry and clean.

Allow the cupcakes to cool before unmolding and serving. Bon appétit!

Per serving: Calories: 337; Fat: 18g; Carbs: 40.6g; Protein: 5.5g; Sugars: 26.2.9g; Fiber: 1.8g

547. Greek Blueberry Cheesecake [PC]

(Ready in about 35 minutes + chilling time | Servings 8)

Ingredients

1 cup graham cracker crumbs
2 teaspoons honey
4 tablespoons almond butter
14 ounces cream cheese, room temperature
1/2 cup granulated sugar
4 tablespoons Greek-style yogurt
2 eggs, room temperature
4 tablespoons all-purpose flour
1 cup blueberry pie filling

Directions

Spritz a baking pan with a nonstick cooking spray.

Mix the cracker crumbs, honey, and almond butter. Press the crust mixture into the prepared ramekins.

Beat the cream cheese with sugar; add in the yogurt, eggs, and flour and continue to beat until well combined. Pour this mixture into the prepared baking pan and cover them with a piece of foil.

Place a metal trivet and 1 cup of water in the inner pot. Lower the baking pan onto the trivet.

Secure the pressure-cooking lid. Pressure cook for 25 minutes at High pressure. Once cooking is complete, use a natural pressure release for 10 minutes; carefully remove the lid.

Spread the blueberry pie filling over the top of your cake and serve well-chilled. Enjoy!

Per serving: Calories: 386; Fat: 25.3g; Carbs: 35.4g; Protein: 5.6g; Sugars: 24.1g; Fiber: 1.5g

548. Grandma's Caramelized Plums [AF]

(Ready in about 20 minutes | Servings 4)

Ingredients

1 pound plums, halved and pitted
2 tablespoons coconut oil
4 tablespoons brown sugar
4 whole cloves
1 cinnamon stick
4 whole star anise

Directions

Toss the plums with the remaining ingredients.

Throw the plums and 1/4 cup of water into the inner pot. Secure the air-frying lid.

Air fry the plums at 340 degrees F for 17 minutes. Serve at room temperature.

Bon appétit!

Per serving: Calories: 145; Fat: 7.2g; Carbs: 20.9g; Protein: 0.7g; Sugars: 19g; Fiber: 1.6g

DESSERTS

549. White Chocolate Chip Fudge [PC]

(Ready in about 25 minutes | Servings 7)

Ingredients

1 ¼ cups granulated sugar
1/2 cup heavy whipping cream
5 ounces white chocolate chips
1/4 cup coconut oil
1 tablespoon lemon zest
1 tablespoon fresh lemon juice
1 teaspoon crystallized ginger
1 teaspoon vanilla extract

Directions

In a mixing bowl, beat all the ingredients until well combined. Pour the mixture into a lightly greased baking pan.

Add a metal rack and 1 cup of water to the inner pot. Place the baking pan onto the rack.

Secure the pressure-cooking lid. Pressure cook for 10 minutes at High pressure. Once cooking is complete, use a natural pressure release for 10 minutes; carefully remove the lid.

Enjoy!

Per serving: Calories: 278; Fat: 15.6g; Carbs: 32.3g; Protein: 1.6g; Sugars: 24.1g; Fiber: 0.8g

550. Fried Plantain with Raisins [AF]

(Ready in about 10 minutes | Servings 2)

Ingredients

2 plantains, peeled
1/2 cup coconut, shredded
1 tablespoon coconut oil
4 tablespoons brown sugar
1/2 teaspoon cinnamon powder
1/2 teaspoon cardamom powder
4 tablespoons raisins

Directions

In the peel, slice your plantains lengthwise; make sure not to slice all the way through the plantains.

Divide the remaining ingredients between the plantain pockets. Place the plantain boats in the Air Fryer basket.

Secure the air-frying lid. Cook the plantain at 395 degrees F for 7 minutes.

Eat with a spoon and enjoy!

Per serving: Calories: 354; Fat: 7.5g; Carbs: 74.5g; Protein: 2.8g; Sugars: 44.1g; Fiber: 5.3g

551. Pumpkin Pie with Pecans [PC]

(Ready in about 50 minutes | Servings 8)

Ingredients

1 cup vanilla cookie crumbs
1/2 cup pecans, lightly toasted and chopped
2 tablespoons peanut butter
1/2 cup brown sugar
A pinch of salt
1 teaspoon pumpkin pie spice
1 egg, beaten
2 cups pumpkin puree
1/2 cup almond milk

Directions

Place a metal trivet and 1 cup of water in the inner pot. Brush a springform pan with a nonstick cooking spray.

Then, mix the cookie crumbs, pecans, and peanut butter. Press the crust mixture evenly into the bottom of your pan; let it freeze for approximately 15 minutes.

In another bowl, thoroughly combine the remaining ingredients. Pour the filling mixture into the pie crust; cover the top of the pie with aluminum foil.

Lower the pan onto the trivet. Secure the pressure-cooking lid.

Pressure cook for 35 minutes at High pressure. Once cooking is complete, use a natural pressure release; carefully remove the lid.

Bon appétit!

Per serving: Calories: 339; Fat: 23.5g; Carbs: 23.6g; Protein: 12.2g; Sugars: 13.2g; Fiber: 3.1g

552. Souffle Apple Pancakes [AF]

(Ready in about 20 minutes | Servings 3)

Ingredients

1 small apple, peeled, cored, and sliced
1 tablespoon coconut oil, melted
1 egg, whisked
1/4 cup plain flour
1/4 teaspoon baking powder
1/4 cup full-fat coconut milk
A pinch of granulated sugar
A pinch of kosher salt
1/2 teaspoon vanilla paste

Directions

Drizzle the apple slices with the melted coconut oil; arrange the apple slices in a baking pan.

Mix the remaining ingredients to make the batter. Pour the batter over the apples. Transfer the baking pan to the Air Fryer cooking basket.

Secure the air-frying lid.

Bake your pancake at 350 degrees F for about 13 minutes or until it is golden brown around the edges.

Bon appétit!

Per serving: Calories: 174; Fat: 10.8g; Carbs: 16.1g; Protein: 3.5g; Sugars: 6g; Fiber: 1.8g

553. Fudgy Mocha Cake [PC]

(Ready in about 35 minutes | Servings 8)

Ingredients

1 cup all-purpose flour
1/2 teaspoon baking soda
1/2 cup coconut milk
1 teaspoon fresh lemon juice
1/4 cup cocoa powder
1 teaspoon espresso powder
A pinch of sea salt
1/4 cup coconut oil, melted
1/4 cup honey
1 teaspoon pure vanilla extract

DESSERTS

Directions

Add 1 cup of water and a metal trivet to the inner pot of your Instant Pot. Lightly grease a baking pan with a nonstick spray.

In a mixing bowl, combine all ingredients to make a thick batter.

Spoon the batter into the prepared pan. Lower the baking pan onto the trivet.

Secure the pressure-cooking lid. Pressure cook for 20 minutes at High pressure. Once cooking is complete, use a natural pressure release for 10 minutes; carefully remove the lid.

Transfer the cake to a cooling rack before slicing and serving. Bon appétit!

Per serving: Calories: 168; Fat: 7.6g; Carbs: 23.3g; Protein: 2.7g; Sugars: 9.6g; Fiber: 1.3g

554. French Toast Bake [AF]

(Ready in about 10 minutes | Servings 2)

Ingredients

- 2 eggs
- 2 tablespoons coconut oil, melted
- 1/4 cup milk
- 1/2 teaspoon vanilla extract
- 1/4 teaspoon ground cinnamon
- 1/8 teaspoon ground nutmeg
- 4 thick slices baguette

Directions

In a mixing bowl, thoroughly combine the eggs, coconut oil, milk, vanilla, cinnamon, and nutmeg.

Then, dip each piece of bread into the egg mixture; place the bread slices in a lightly greased baking pan.

Secure the air-frying lid.

Air Fryer the bread slices at 330 degrees F for about 4 minutes; turn them over and cook for a further 3 to 4 minutes. Enjoy!

Per serving: Calories: 310; Fat: 20.5g; Carbs: 22.3g; Protein: 9g; Sugars: 4.1g; Fiber: 1.3g

555. Chocolate Banana Cake [PC]

(Ready in about 35 minutes | Servings 7)

Ingredients

- 1 cup cake flour
- 1/4 cup almond flour
- 1/4 cup butter, softened
- 1/2 cup bittersweet chocolate chunks
- 4 tablespoons cocoa powder
- A pinch of coarse sea salt
- A pinch of grated nutmeg
- 1/2 teaspoon ground cinnamon
- 1 cup light brown sugar
- 1 teaspoon pure vanilla extract
- 1 banana, mashed
- 1 large egg, whisked

Directions

Thoroughly combine all the ingredients in a mixing bowl. Pour the mixture into a lightly greased baking pan.

Place a metal trivet and 1 cup of water in the inner pot. Lower the baking pan onto the metal trivet.

Secure the pressure-cooking lid.

Pressure cook for 20 minutes at High pressure. Once cooking is complete, use a natural pressure release for 10 minutes; carefully remove the lid. Enjoy!

Per serving: Calories: 368; Fat: 9.9g; Carbs: 66.1g; Protein: 4.6g; Sugars: 43.1g; Fiber: 2.8g

556. French-Style Cronuts [AF]

(Ready in about 20 minutes | Servings 4)

Ingredients

- 3/4 cup all-purpose flour
- 1/4 cup butter
- 1/4 cup water
- 1/2 cup full-fat milk
- 1/4 teaspoon kosher salt
- A pinch of grated nutmeg
- 3 eggs, beaten

Directions

In a mixing bowl, thoroughly combine all the ingredients. Place the batter in a piping bag fitted with a large open star tip.

Pipe your cronuts into circles and lower them onto the greased Air Fryer pan.

Secure the air-frying lid.

Cook your cronuts in the preheated Air Fryer at 360 degrees F for 10 minutes, flipping them halfway through the cooking time.

Repeat with the remaining batter and serve immediately. Enjoy!

Per serving: Calories: 250; Fat: 15.5g; Carbs: 19.3g; Protein: 7.9g; Sugars: 1.7g; Fiber: 0.6g

557. Peach Cake with Pecans [PC]

(Ready in about 25 minutes | Servings 7)

Ingredients

- 2 cups peaches, pitted and sliced
- 2 tablespoons sugar
- 1 teaspoon lemon zest
- 2 tablespoons cornstarch
- 1/2 teaspoon ground cinnamon
- 1 cup all-purpose flour
- 1 teaspoon baking powder
- 1 cup sugar
- 1/2 cup pecans, coarsely chopped
- 1/2 cup coconut oil
- 1 egg, beaten

Directions

Arrange the peaches on the bottom of the inner pot. Sprinkle them with sugar, lemon zest, cornstarch, and cinnamon.

In a mixing bowl, thoroughly combine the remaining ingredients to make the streusel topping. Place the streusel topping on top of the peach layer.

Secure the pressure-cooking lid. Pressure cook for 10 minutes at High pressure. Once cooking is complete, use a natural pressure release for 10 minutes; carefully remove the lid.

Bon appétit!

Per serving: Calories: 346; Fat: 21.6g; Carbs: 37g; Protein: 3.7g; Sugars: 19.7g; Fiber: 1.9g

558. Almond Chocolate Cake [AF]

(Ready in about 25 minutes | Servings 6)

Ingredients

- 1 stick butter, melted
- 1/2 cups brown sugar
- 2 eggs, at room temperature
- 5 ounces chocolate chips
- 1/2 teaspoon pure vanilla extract
- 1/2 teaspoon pure almond extract
- 1/4 cup cocoa powder
- 1/4 cup all-purpose flour
- 1/2 cup almond flour
- 1/2 teaspoon baking powder
- 2 ounces almonds, slivered
- 4 tablespoons coconut milk

Directions

In a mixing bowl, beat the butter and sugar until fluffy. Next, fold in the eggs and beat again until well combined.

Brush the sides and bottom of a baking pan with a nonstick cooking spray. After that, add in the remaining ingredients. Mix until everything is well combined.

Secure the air-frying lid.

Bake in the preheated Air Fryer at 340 degrees F for 20 minutes. Enjoy!

Per serving: Calories: 345; Fat: 22.8g; Carbs: 32.5g; Protein: 6g; Sugars: 21g; Fiber: 3.1g

559. Greek Dried Fruit Compote (Hosafi) [PC]

(Ready in about 15 minutes | Servings 9)

Ingredients

- 1 cup prunes, pitted
- 1 cup dried apricots
- 1 cup dried apples
- 3 cups water
- 1 cup brown sugar
- 1 vanilla bean, split
- 1 teaspoon whole cloves
- 1 cinnamon stick
- 1 teaspoon lemon zest, grated

Directions

Place the ingredients in the inner pot of your Instant Pot Duo Crisp.

Secure the pressure-cooking lid.

Pressure cook for 2 minutes at High pressure. Once cooking is complete, use a natural pressure release for 10 minutes; carefully remove the lid.

Serve with Greek yogurt, if desired. Enjoy!

Per serving: Calories: 133; Fat: 0.2g; Carbs: 34.3g; Protein: 1.5g; Sugars: 19.6g; Fiber: 1.4g

560. Classic Cranberry Scones [AF]

(Ready in about 20 minutes | Servings 4)

Ingredients

- 1 cup all-purpose flour
- 1 teaspoon baking powder
- 1/4 cup caster sugar
- A pinch of sea salt
- 1/4 teaspoon ground cinnamon
- 4 tablespoons butter
- 1 egg, beaten
- 1/4 cup milk
- 2 ounces dried cranberries

Directions

Mix all the ingredients until everything is well incorporated. Spoon the batter into baking cups; lower the cups into the Air Fryer basket.

Secure the air-frying lid.

Bake your scones at 360 degrees F for about 17 minutes or until a tester comes out dry and clean.

Bon appétit!

Per serving: Calories: 325; Fat: 14.8g; Carbs: 42.5g; Protein: 6g; Sugars: 16.1g; Fiber: 1.7g

561. Classic Apple Crumble [PC]

(Ready in about 25 minutes | Servings 4)

Ingredients

- 1 pound apples, peeled, cored, and chopped
- 1 tablespoon fresh lemon juice
- 4 tablespoons brown sugar
- 1/2 teaspoon cinnamon
- 1/2 cup almond flour
- 1 cup oats
- 1/4 cup honey
- 1/2 cup butter, softened

Directions

Place the apples on the bottom of the inner pot. Sprinkle the apples with lemon juice, brown sugar, and cinnamon.

In a mixing bowl, thoroughly combine the remaining ingredients to make the streusel topping. Place the streusel topping on top of the apple layer.

Secure the pressure-cooking lid.

Pressure cook for 10 minutes at High pressure. Once cooking is complete, use a natural pressure release for 10 minutes; carefully remove the lid.

Bon appétit!

Per serving: Calories: 418; Fat: 24.9g; Carbs: 57.2g; Protein: 4.7g; Sugars: 37.1g; Fiber: 6.6g

562. Cinnamon Baked Donuts [AF]

(Ready in about 20 minutes | Servings 4)

Ingredients

- 12 ounces flaky large biscuits
- 1/4 cup granulated sugar
- 1 teaspoon ground cinnamon
- 1/4 teaspoon grated nutmeg
- 2 tablespoons coconut oil

Directions

Separate the dough into biscuits and place them in a lightly oiled Air Fryer cooking basket.

Mix the sugar, cinnamon, nutmeg, and coconut oil until well combined.

Drizzle your donuts with the cinnamon mixture. Secure the air-frying lid.

Bake your donuts in the preheated Air Fryer at 340 degrees F for approximately 10 minutes or until golden. Repeat with the remaining donuts.

Bon appétit!

Per serving: Calories: 347; Fat: 16.2g; Carbs: 52.1g; Protein: 5.5g; Sugars: 9g; Fiber: 1.5g

563. Cinnamon Rolls with Apples and Walnuts [PC]

(Ready in about 45 minutes | Servings 10)

Ingredients

12 frozen egg dinner rolls, thawed
1 cup powdered sugar
1 stick butter, melted
2 tablespoons full-fat milk
1/4 cup walnuts, ground
1 cup granulated sugar
1 teaspoon ground cinnamon

Directions

Add 1 cup of water and a metal trivet to the inner pot of your Instant Pot. Brush a Bundt pan with a nonstick cooking spray; set aside.

Cut the dinner rolls into quarters. Thoroughly combine the powdered sugar, butter, milk, and walnuts in a mixing bowl.

In another bowl, mix the sugar and cinnamon. Dip the rolls in the sugar/butter mixture and roll them in the cinnamon sugar.

Arrange the rolls in the prepared Bundt pan. Cover the pan with a piece of aluminum foil; allow it to sit overnight at room temperature.

On an actual day, lower the pan onto the trivet.

Secure the pressure-cooking lid. Pressure cook for 25 minutes at High pressure. Once cooking is complete, use a natural pressure release for 10 minutes; carefully remove the lid. Bon appétit!

Per serving: Calories: 348; Fat: 13.2g; Carbs: 54g; Protein: 4.5g; Sugars: 33.1g; Fiber: 1.8g

564. Cinnamon Baked Peaches [AF]

(Ready in about 20 minutes | Servings 3)

Ingredients

3 peaches, halved
1 tablespoon fresh lime juice
1 teaspoon ground cinnamon
1/2 teaspoon grated nutmeg
1/2 cup brown sugar
4 tablespoons coconut oil

Directions

Toss the peaches with the remaining ingredients.

Place peaches and 1/4 cup of water in the inner pot of your Instant Pot Duo Crisp. Secure the air-frying lid.

Cook the peaches at 340 degrees F for 15 minutes. Serve at room temperature. Bon appétit!

Per serving: Calories: 280; Fat: 18.8g; Carbs: 31.8g; Protein: 1.4g; Sugars: 26.9g; Fiber: 2.8g

565. Stuffed Pears with Pistachios and Sultanas [PC]

(Ready in about 10 minutes | Servings 4)

Ingredients

4 large pears, cored (leave the bottom 1/2 inch of the apples intact)
1/4 cup pistachios, roughly chopped
1/4 cup Sultana raisins, soaked for 15 minutes
2 tablespoons coconut oil
2 tablespoons honey
1 tablespoon fresh orange juice
1/2 teaspoon ground cardamom
1/2 teaspoon ground cinnamon

Directions

Add a metal rack and 1 cup of water to the inner pot. Prepare your pears.

Mix the remaining ingredients to make a stuffing. Stuff the prepared pears with the filling mixture and lower them onto the metal rack.

Secure the pressure-cooking lid.

Pressure cook for 3 minutes at High pressure. Once cooking is complete, use a quick pressure release; carefully remove the lid. Bon appétit!

Per serving: Calories: 253; Fat: 10.9g; Carbs: 40.6g; Protein: 3.3g; Sugars: 29g; Fiber: 11.4g

566. Pumpkin Pie with Walnuts [AF]

(Ready in about 40 minutes | Servings 4)

Ingredients

12 ounces refrigerated pie crusts
1/2 cup pumpkin puree, canned
1 ounce walnuts, coarsely chopped
1/2 cup granulated sugar
1 teaspoon pumpkin pie spice mix
1 teaspoon fresh ginger, peeled and grated

Directions

Place the first pie crust in a lightly greased pie plate.

In a mixing bowl, thoroughly combine the remaining ingredients to make the filling. Spoon the filling into the prepared pie crust.

Unroll the second pie crust and place it on top of the filling.

Secure the air-frying lid.

Bake the pie at 350 degrees F for 35 minutes or until the top is golden brown. Bon appétit!

Per serving: Calories: 534; Fat: 26.5g; Carbs: 72.3g; Protein: 3.9g; Sugars: 26g; Fiber: 3g

567. Greek Risogalo (Rice Pudding) [PC]

(Ready in about 10 minutes | Servings 4)

Ingredients

1 cup white rice
1/2 cup full-fat milk
1 cup water
1 tablespoon butter
1/3 cup white sugar
A pinch of sea salt
1 teaspoon lemon rind
2 eggs, beaten

Directions

Place all the ingredients in the inner pot of your Instant Pot Duo Crisp.

Secure the pressure-cooking lid.

Pressure cook for 4 minutes at High pressure. Once cooking is complete, use a quick pressure release; carefully remove the lid.

Dust with a sprinkle of ground cinnamon, if desired, and serve warm.

Per serving: Calories: 276; Fat: 5.8g; Carbs: 47.7g; Protein: 6.9g; Sugars: 9.7g; Fiber: 1.3g

568. Moist Raisin and Chocolate Cupcakes [AF]

(Ready in about 20 minutes | Servings 4)

Ingredients

- 3/4 cup all-purpose flour
- 1/2 teaspoon baking powder
- 1/2 cup unsweetened cocoa powder
- A pinch of kosher salt
- 1/4 teaspoon grated nutmeg
- 1/2 teaspoon ground cinnamon
- 4 tablespoons coconut oil
- 3/4 cup brown sugar
- 2 eggs, whisked
- 1/2 teaspoon vanilla extract
- 3/4 cup yogurt
- 2 tablespoons raisins

Directions

Mix all the ingredients in a bowl. Scrape the batter into silicone baking molds; place them in the Air Fryer basket.

Secure the air-frying lid.

Bake your cupcakes at 330 degrees F for about 15 minutes or until a tester comes out dry and clean.

Allow the cupcakes to cool before unmolding and serving. Bon appétit!

Per serving: Calories: 360; Fat: 18g; Carbs: 45.6g; Protein: 8.7g; Sugars: 22g; Fiber: 4g

569. Indian Chai Hot Chocolate [PC]

(Ready in about 10 minutes | Servings 4)

Ingredients

- 3 tablespoons cocoa powder
- 2 cups full-fat milk
- 4 tablespoons brown sugar
- 1/4 cup bittersweet chocolate chunks
- 1/4 teaspoon pure vanilla extract
- 2 tablespoons masala chai syrup

Directions

Add all the ingredients to the inner to of your Instant Pot Duo Crisp.

Secure the pressure-cooking lid.

Pressure cook for 6 minutes at Low pressure. Once cooking is complete, use a quick pressure release; carefully remove the lid. Enjoy!

Per serving: Calories: 185; Fat: 3.1g; Carbs: 36.7g; Protein: 5.4g; Sugars: 31.6g; Fiber: 1.6g

570. Vegan Chocolate Chip Cake [AF]

(Ready in about 25 minutes | Servings 6)

Ingredients

- 1/2 cup coconut oil, room temperature
- 1 cup brown sugar
- 2 chia eggs (2 tablespoons ground chia seeds + 4 tablespoons water)
- 1/4 cup all-purpose flour
- 1/4 cup coconut flour
- 1/2 cup cocoa powder
- 1/2 cup dark chocolate chips
- A pinch of grated nutmeg
- A pinch of sea salt
- 2 tablespoons coconut milk

Directions

Now, spritz the sides and bottom of a baking pan with a nonstick cooking spray.

In a mixing bowl, beat the coconut oil and brown sugar until fluffy. Next, fold in the chia eggs and beat again until well combined.

Secure the air-frying lid.

After that, add in the remaining ingredients. Mix until everything is well incorporated.

Bake your cake at 340 degrees F for 20 minutes. Enjoy!

Per serving: Calories: 279; Fat: 208g; Carbs: 25.8g; Protein: 2.9g; Sugars: 16.9g; Fiber: 2.5g

571. Chocolate Chip Bread Pudding [PC]

(Ready in about 40 minutes | Servings 8)

Ingredients

- 1 cup double cream
- 3 eggs
- 1/2 cup brown sugar
- 2 tablespoons cocoa powder
- 1/2 teaspoon ground cinnamon
- 1/2 teaspoon ground cloves
- 1 teaspoon vanilla essence
- 8 cups challah bread, torn into pieces
- 4 ounces dark chocolate chips

Directions

In a mixing bowl, thoroughly combine the double cream, eggs, brown sugar, cocoa powder, cinnamon, ground cloves, and vanilla.

Fold in the bread pieces and let it soak for about 20 minutes. Spoon the mixture into a lightly greased inner pot.

Fold in the chocolate chips and secure the pressure-cooking lid.

Pressure cook for 15 minutes at High pressure. Once cooking is complete, use a quick pressure release; carefully remove the lid. Bon appétit!

Per serving: Calories: 312; Fat: 14.8g; Carbs: 38.8g; Protein: 6.7g; Sugars: 19.1g; Fiber: 3.4g

572. Baked Apples with Sultanas and Pecans [PC+AF]

(Ready in about 15 minutes | Servings 2)

Ingredients

- 2 medium apples
- 4 tablespoons pecans, chopped
- 4 tablespoons Sultanas
- 2 tablespoons butter, at room temperature
- 1/2 teaspoon cinnamon
- 1/4 teaspoon grated nutmeg

Directions

Cut the apples in half and spoon out some of the flesh.

Add a metal rack and 1 cup of water to the inner pot. Secure the pressure-cooking lid.

Pressure cook for 3 minutes at High pressure. Once cooking is complete, use a quick pressure release; carefully remove the lid.

In a mixing bowl, thoroughly combine the remaining ingredients. Stuff the apple halves and transfer them to the inner pot.

Secure the air-frying lid.

Bake the apples at 340 degrees F for 7 minutes. Serve at room temperature and enjoy!

Per serving: Calories: 295; Fat: 22.2g; Carbs: 27.8g; Protein: 1.9g; Sugars: 19.2g; Fiber: 6.1g

573. Kid-Friendly Mini Cheesecakes [PC]

(Ready in about 40 minutes | Servings 4)

Ingredients

3/4 cup digestive biscuits, ground into fine crumbs
2 tablespoons maple syrup
4 tablespoons butter, at room temperature
15 ounces cream cheese, softened
1/4 cup granulated sugar
4 tablespoons sour cream
3 tablespoons all-purpose flour
1 teaspoon pure vanilla extract
1 egg, beaten
1/4 cup colorful sprinkles (funfetti)

Directions

Brush four ramekins with a nonstick cooking spray.

Mix the biscuits, maple syrup, and butter. Press the crust mixture into the prepared ramekins.

Thoroughly combine the cream cheese, granulated sugar, sour cream, flour, vanilla, and egg. Pour the filling mixture into ramekins; cover your ramekins with foil.

Place a metal trivet and 1 cup of water in the inner pot. Lower the ramekins onto the trivet.

Secure the pressure-cooking lid.

Pressure cook for 25 minutes at High pressure. Once cooking is complete, use a natural pressure release for 10 minutes; carefully remove the lid.

Sprinkle your cheesecakes with funfetti and place it in your refrigerator until ready to serve. Enjoy!

Per serving: Calories: 593; Fat: 51g; Carbs: 25.3g; Protein: 9.2g; Sugars: 16g; Fiber: 0.2g

574. Plum Mini Tarts [AF]

(Ready in about 25 minutes | Servings 6)

Ingredients

1 cup purple plums, pitted and coarsely chopped
1/2 cup brown sugar
1/2 teaspoon ground cinnamon
12 ounces refrigerated flaky cinnamon rolls

Directions

Toss the plums with the sugar and cinnamon.

Spray muffin cups with a nonstick cooking spray. Separate the dough into 6 rolls and press them into the prepared muffin cups.

Spoon the filling into each dough-lined cup.

Secure the air-frying lid.

Bake the mini plum tarts at 350 degrees F for 20 minutes or until the top is golden brown. Bon appétit!

Per serving: Calories: 257; Fat: 9g; Carbs: 40.4g; Protein: 3.7g; Sugars: 28.7g; Fiber: 2g

575. Honey Vanilla Pudding [PC]

(Ready in about 15 minutes | Servings 4)

Ingredients

1 cup millet, rinsed
1 cup water
3/4 cup coconut milk
1/4 cup honey, chopped
1/2 teaspoon ground cinnamon
1/2 teaspoon ground cardamom
A pinch of sea salt
A pinch of grated nutmeg
1 teaspoon vanilla paste

Directions

Place all the ingredients in the inner pot of your Instant Pot Duo Crisp.

Stir to combine and secure the pressure-cooking lid.

Pressure cook for 12 minutes at High pressure. Once cooking is complete, use a quick pressure release; carefully remove the lid.

Bon appétit!

Per serving: Calories: 359; Fat: 3.5g; Carbs: 74.1g; Protein: 7.2g; Sugars: 37.2g; Fiber: 4.6g

576. Vanilla Chocolate Cupcakes [AF]

(Ready in about 20 minutes | Servings 6)

Ingredients

3/4 cup plain flour
1/2 teaspoon baking powder
1/4 cup cocoa powder
3/4 cup caster sugar
1 egg, whisked
2 ounces butter, at room temperature
3/4 cup whole milk
2 ounces chocolate chips
1/2 teaspoon vanilla extract

Directions

Mix all the ingredients in a bowl. Scrape the batter into silicone baking molds; place them in the Air Fryer basket.

Secure the air-frying lid.

Bake your cupcakes at 330 degrees F for about 15 minutes or until a tester comes out dry and clean.

Allow the cupcakes to cool before unmolding and serving. Bon appétit!

Per serving: Calories: 247; Fat: 10g; Carbs: 36.6g; Protein: 4.7g; Sugars: 21g; Fiber: 1.8g

577. Berry Cobbler Pie [PC]

(Ready in about 20 minutes | Servings 8)

Ingredients

- 1 pound mixed berries
- 1/2 cup brown sugar
- 2 tablespoons cornstarch
- 1/4 teaspoon ground cinnamon
- 1 teaspoon crystallized ginger
- 1/2 cup all-purpose flour
- 1/2 cup rolled oats
- 1 teaspoon baking powder
- 1/4 teaspoon kosher salt
- 1/2 cup honey
- 1/2 cup butter

Directions

Arrange the mixed berries on the bottom of the inner pot of your Instant Pot Duo Crisp. Sprinkle the mixed berries with brown sugar, cornstarch, cinnamon, and ginger.

In a mixing bowl, thoroughly combine the flour, rolled oats, baking powder, salt, eggs, honey, and butter. Drop the topping mixture by spoonfuls on top of the mixed berry layer.

Secure the pressure-cooking lid. Pressure cook for 8 minutes at High pressure. Once cooking is complete, use a natural pressure release for 10 minutes; carefully remove the lid.

Allow your cobbler to cool on a wire rack before serving. Serve with vanilla ice cream, if desired, and enjoy!

Per serving: Calories: 298; Fat: 12.4g; Carbs: 46.1g; Protein: 3g; Sugars: 29.2g; Fiber: 2.7g

578. Grilled Fruit Skewers [AF]

(Ready in about 15 minutes | Servings 4)

Ingredients

- 1 cup melon, cut into 1-inch chunks
- 1 cup pineapple, cut into 1-inch chunks
- 1 banana, cut into 1-inch chunks
- 1 peach, cut into 1-inch chunks
- 2 tablespoons coconut oil, melted
- 2 tablespoons honey

Directions

Toss your fruits with the coconut oil and honey.

Thread the fruits onto skewers and place them in the Air Fryer cooking basket.

Secure the air-frying lid.

Then, cook the skewers at 400 degrees F for approximately 10 minutes, turning them over halfway through the cooking time.

Bon appétit!

Per serving: Calories: 167; Fat: 7g; Carbs: 27.6g; Protein: 1.3g; Sugars: 22.1g; Fiber: 2.3g

579. Middle Eastern Pudding (Sahlab) [PC]

(Ready in about 10 minutes | Servings 4)

Ingredients

- 1 cup couscous
- 1 cup water
- 1 cup canned coconut milk
- 1 teaspoon vanilla paste
- 1 cardamon pod green, seeded and crushed
- 1/2 teaspoon cardamom
- 1/2 teaspoon cinnamon
- 1/2 cup brown sugar
- 4 tablespoons walnuts, chopped
- 4 tablespoons raisins

Directions

Place all the ingredients in the inner pot of your Instant Pot Duo Crisp. Gently stir to combine and secure the pressure-cooking lid.

Pressure cook for 3 minutes at High pressure. Once cooking is complete, use a quick pressure release; carefully remove the lid.

Bon appétit!

Per serving: Calories: 387; Fat: 7.2g; Carbs: 72.4g; Protein: 10.3g; Sugars: 32.1g; Fiber: 4.1g

580. Coconut and Blueberry Fritters [AF]

(Ready in about 15 minutes | Servings 4)

Ingredients

- 3/4 cup all-purpose flour
- 1 teaspoon baking powder
- 1/2 cup coconut milk
- 2 tablespoons coconut sugar
- A pinch of sea salt
- 1 egg
- 2 tablespoons melted butter
- 2 ounces fresh blueberries

Directions

In a mixing bowl, thoroughly combine all the ingredients.

Drop a spoonful of batter onto the greased Air Fryer pan. Secure the air-frying lid.

Cook in the preheated Air Fryer at 360 degrees F for 10 minutes, flipping them halfway through the cooking time.

Repeat with the remaining batter and serve warm. Enjoy!

Per serving: Calories: 195; Fat: 8g; Carbs: 25.4g; Protein: 4.9g; Sugars: 6.9g; Fiber: 1g

581. Chocolate and Peanut Butter Fudge [PC]

(Ready in about 35 minutes | Servings 6)

Ingredients

- 1 cup all-purpose flour
- 1 teaspoon baking powder
- 1 cup granulated sugar
- 1/2 cup peanut butter
- 2 eggs, beaten
- 1/2 cup cocoa powder
- A pinch of grated nutmeg
- 1/4 teaspoon ground cardamom
- 1/4 teaspoon ground cinnamon
- 1/2 cup chocolate chips

Directions

Thoroughly combine all the ingredients in a mixing bowl. Pour the mixture into a lightly greased baking pan.

Place a metal trivet and 1 cup of water in the inner pot. Lower the baking pan onto the metal trivet.

Secure the pressure-cooking lid. Pressure cook for 20 minutes at High pressure. Once cooking is complete, use a natural pressure release for 10 minutes; carefully remove the lid.

Enjoy!

Per serving: Calories: 378; Fat: 11g; Carbs: 61.1g; Protein: 12g; Sugars: 31.1g; Fiber: 4.7g

582. Classic Cinnamon Rolls [AF]

(Ready in about 15 minutes | Servings 4)

Ingredients

9 ounces refrigerated crescent rolls
1 tablespoon coconut oil
4 tablespoons caster sugar
1 teaspoon ground cinnamon

Directions

Separate the dough into rectangles. Mix the remaining ingredients until well combined.

Spread each rectangle with the cinnamon mixture; roll them up tightly.

Place the rolls in the Air Fryer cooking basket. Secure the air-frying lid.

Bake the rolls at 300 degrees F for about 5 minutes; turn them over and bake for a further 5 minutes.

Bon appétit!

Per serving: Calories: 356; Fat: 20.5g; Carbs: 39.4g; Protein: 2.8g; Sugars: 24.2g; Fiber: 1.1g

583. The Best Dulce de Leche Ever [PC]

(Ready in about 35 minutes | Servings 2)

Ingredients

1 (14-ounce) can sweetened condensed milk

Directions

Add a metal trivet and steamer basket to the inner pot. Place the can of milk in the steamer basket.

Add in water until the can is covered.

Secure the pressure-cooking lid. Pressure cook for 20 minutes at High pressure. Once cooking is complete, use a natural pressure release for 10 minutes; carefully remove the lid.

Don't open the can until it is completely cooled.

Enjoy!

Per serving: Calories: 360; Fat: 8.5g; Carbs: 66.1g; Protein: 7.1g; Sugars: 57g; Fiber: 0.8g

584. Chocolate Mug Cake [AF]

(Ready in about 25 minutes | Servings 1)

Ingredients

2 tablespoons all-purpose flour
2 tablespoons almond flour
2 tablespoons cocoa powder, unsweetened
2 tablespoons agave nectar
1/4 teaspoon baking powder
1 teaspoon pure vanilla extract
A pinch of kosher salt
A pinch of grated nutmeg
2 tablespoons coconut oil, at room temperature
2 tablespoons full-fat milk

Directions

Thoroughly combine all the ingredients; mix until well combined.

Spoon the mixture into a mug and place it in the Air Fryer cooking basket. Secure the air-frying lid.

Air fry the mug cake at 350 degrees F for approximately 20 minutes. Bon appétit!

Per serving: Calories: 476; Fat: 39g; Carbs: 28.5g; Protein: 8.8g; Sugars: 7g; Fiber: 6.2g

585. Caramel Chocolate Cake [PC]

(Ready in about 30 minutes | Servings 10)

Ingredients

1 cup cake flour
1/2 cup coconut milk
1/4 cup cocoa powder
A pinch of sea salt
A pinch of grated nutmeg
4 tablespoons butter, softened
1/4 cup brown sugar
1 teaspoon pure vanilla extract
1/2 cup chocolate chips
1/2 cup caramel bits
2 cups chocolate frosting

Directions

Add 1 cup of water and a metal trivet to the inner pot of your Instant Pot Duo Crisp. Spritz a baking pan with a nonstick cooking spray.

In a mixing bowl, thoroughly combine the flour, milk, cocoa powder, salt, nutmeg, butter, brown sugar, and vanilla extract.

Scrape the batter into the prepared pan. Lower the baking pan onto the trivet.

Secure the pressure-cooking lid. Pressure cook for 20 minutes at High pressure. Once cooking is complete, use a natural pressure release for 5 minutes; carefully remove the lid.

Transfer the cake to a cooling rack; then, frost the cake and place it in your refrigerator until ready to serve.

Bon appétit!

Per serving: Calories: 422; Fat: 23.3g; Carbs: 49.4g; Protein: 3.6g; Sugars: 28.2g; Fiber: 3.5g

DESSERTS

586. Apricots with Mascarpone Cheese and Coconut [AF]

(Ready in about 20 minutes | Servings 4)

Ingredients

8 apricots, halved and pitted
1 tablespoon coconut oil, melted
2 tablespoons honey
1 teaspoon ground cinnamon
2 ounces mascarpone cheese
1 tablespoon coconut flakes

Directions

Toss the apricots with the coconut oil, honey, and cinnamon.

Place the apricots in a lightly oiled Air Fryer cooking basket. Secure the air-frying lid.

Cook the apricots at 340 degrees F for 16 minutes. Top the fried apricots with mascarpone cheese and coconut flakes.

Bon appétit!

Per serving: Calories: 176; Fat: 6.8g; Carbs: 28.3g; Protein: 2.8g; Sugars: 26g; Fiber: 1.8g

587. Gooey Pinch Me Cake [PC]

(Ready in about 40 minutes | Servings 9)

Ingredients

2 (12-ounce) packages refrigerated biscuit dough
1/2 cup brown sugar
1/2 teaspoon ground cloves
1/2 teaspoon ground cardamom
1 teaspoon ground cinnamon
1 teaspoon vanilla
1/2 cup pistachios, chopped
1 stick butter, melted
1/2 cup honey

Directions

Add 1 cup of water and a metal trivet to the inner pot of your Instant Pot Duo Crisp. Brush a Bundt pan with a nonstick cooking spray and set aside.

Cut the biscuits into quarters. Thoroughly combine the brown sugar, spices, and pistachios.

In another bowl, whisk the butter and honey. Dip the biscuits in the melted butter mixture and roll them in the spice/sugar mixture.

Arrange the rolls in the prepared Bundt pan. Cover the pan with a piece of aluminum foil; allow it to rise overnight at room temperature.

On an actual day, lower the pan onto the trivet. Secure the pressure-cooking lid.

Pressure cook for 25 minutes at High pressure. Once cooking is complete, use a natural pressure release for 10 minutes; carefully remove the lid.

Bon appétit!

Per serving: Calories: 476; Fat: 21.7g; Carbs: 66.4g; Protein: 6.7g; Sugars: 34.1g; Fiber: 3g

588. Banana Rum Galettes [AF]

(Ready in about 25 minutes | Servings 4)

Ingredients

3/4 cup all-purpose flour
3/4 cup water
1 tablespoon rum
4 tablespoons butter
1 banana, mashed
1 tablespoon caster sugar
1/4 teaspoon salt
1/4 teaspoon grated nutmeg

Directions

In a mixing bowl, thoroughly combine all the ingredients.

Drop a spoonful of batter onto the greased Air Fryer pan. Secure the air-frying lid.

Cook your galettes at 360 degrees F for 10 minutes, flipping them halfway through the cooking time.

Repeat with the remaining batter and serve warm. Enjoy!

Per serving: Calories: 235; Fat: 11.7g; Carbs: 26.7g; Protein: 3g; Sugars: 5.6g; Fiber: 1.4g

589. Ginger Crumb Cake with Berries [PC]

(Ready in about 25 minutes | Servings 5)

Ingredients

1 pound mixed berries
1/4 cup butter, melted
1 teaspoon crystallized ginger
1/2 cup granulated sugar
2 large eggs, whisked
1 teaspoon vanilla extract
1/3 cup milk
3/4 cup oats
1/2 teaspoon ground cinnamon
A pinch of sea salt

Directions

Place the berries on the bottom of the inner pot. Sprinkle the berries with butter, ginger, and sugar.

In a mixing bowl, thoroughly combine the remaining ingredients to make the streusel topping. Place the streusel topping on top of the berry layer.

Secure the pressure-cooking lid.

Pressure cook for 10 minutes at High pressure. Once cooking is complete, use a natural pressure release for 10 minutes; carefully remove the lid. Bon appétit!

Per serving: Calories: 283; Fat: 13.5g; Carbs: 33.6g; Protein: 7.7g; Sugars: 15.3g; Fiber: 4.4g

590. Traditional Unnakai Malabar [AF]

(Ready in about 15 minutes | Servings 1)

Ingredients

1 plantain, peeled
1/4 cup coconut flakes
1/4 teaspoon cinnamon powder
1/4 teaspoon cardamom powder
1 tablespoon ghee
2 tablespoons brown sugar

Directions

Toss the plantain with the remaining ingredients.

Secure the air-frying lid.

Bake the prepared plantain in the preheated Air Fryer at 390 degrees F approximately 13 minutes, flipping it halfway through the cooking time.

Bon appétit!

Per serving: Calories: 545; Fat: 35g; Carbs: 54.4g; Protein: 6.1g; Sugars: 36g; Fiber: 3.1g

591. Apple Walnut Crisp Cake [PC]

(Ready in about 20 minutes | Servings 4)

Ingredients

1 pound apples, peeled and sliced	1/2 teaspoon ground cinnamon
1 tablespoon lemon juice	1 cup rolled oats
2 tablespoons brown sugar	1 teaspoon vanilla extract
1/2 teaspoon ground cardamom	1/4 cup walnuts, chopped
	1/4 cup coconut oil

Directions

Arrange the apples on the bottom of the inner pot. Sprinkle the apples with lemon juice, brown sugar, cardamom, and cinnamon.

In a mixing bowl, thoroughly combine the rolled oats, vanilla, walnuts, and coconut oil. Drop the mixture by the spoonful on top of the apples.

Secure the pressure-cooking lid. Pressure cook for 8 minutes at High pressure. Once cooking is complete, use a natural pressure release for 10 minutes; carefully remove the lid.

Bon appétit!

Per serving: Calories: 382; Fat: 19.8g; Carbs: 47.3g; Protein: 7.7g; Sugars: 16.1g; Fiber: 7.4g

592. Fluffy Apple Crumble Cake [AF]

(Ready in about 20 minutes | Servings 3)

Ingredients

1/3 cup all-purpose flour	2 eggs, beaten
1/4 cup coconut flour	1/2 teaspoon pure vanilla extract
1/2 teaspoon baking powder	1/4 cup full-fat milk
1/2 teaspoon ground cinnamon	2 small apples, peeled, cored, and grated
3 tablespoons brown sugar	
A pinch of kosher salt	

Directions

Mix all the ingredients to make the batter. Pour the batter into the inner pot.

Secure the air-frying lid.

Bake your cake at 350 degrees F for about 13 minutes or until it is golden brown around the edges.

Bon appétit!

Per serving: Calories: 215; Fat: 5.5g; Carbs: 34.7g; Protein: 6.2g; Sugars: 19.9g; Fiber: 3.6g

593. Raspberry Peanut Butter Cake [PC]

(Ready in about 35 minutes | Servings 9)

Ingredients

1 cup vanilla cookies, crushed	1 cup caster sugar
1/2 cup peanut butter	1 cup heavy whipped cream
1/4 cup demerara sugar	4 tablespoons all-purpose flour
2 eggs	1 lemon, zested and juiced

Directions

Mix the crushed cookies, maple syrup, and peanut butter. Press the crust mixture into the prepared ramekins.

Thoroughly combine the remaining ingredients. Pour this mixture into ramekins and cover them with a piece of foil.

Place a metal trivet and 1 cup of water in the inner pot. Lower the ramekins onto the trivet.

Secure the pressure-cooking lid. Pressure cook for 25 minutes at High pressure. Once cooking is complete, use a natural pressure release for 10 minutes; carefully remove the lid.

Bon appétit!

Per serving: Calories: 133; Fat: 0.2g; Carbs: 34.3g; Protein: 1.5g; Sugars: 19.6g; Fiber: 1.4g

594. Old-Fashioned Almond Cupcakes [AF]

(Ready in about 20 minutes | Servings 6)

Ingredients

3/4 cup self-raising flour	1 cup granulated sugar
1/4 cup cocoa powder	1/2 cup almond milk
2 eggs, beaten	2 ounces almonds, slivered
1 stick butter, at room temperature	

Directions

Mix all the ingredients in a bowl. Scrape the batter into silicone baking molds; place them in the Air Fryer basket.

Secure the air-frying lid.

Bake your cupcakes at 330 degrees F for about 15 minutes or until a tester comes out dry and clean.

Allow the cupcakes to cool before unmolding and serving. Bon appétit!

Per serving: Calories: 373; Fat: 24.5g; Carbs: 33.6g; Protein: 7.7g; Sugars: 18.1g; Fiber: 2.8g

595. Baked Apples with Honey and Raisins [PC]

(Ready in about 10 minutes | Servings 4)

Ingredients

6 large apples, cored (leave the bottom 1/2 inch of the apples intact)
1/4 cup raisins
1/4 cup walnuts, chopped
1 teaspoon ground cinnamon
2 tablespoons honey
2 tablespoons butter

Directions

Add a metal rack and 1 cup of water to the inner pot. Prepare your apples.

Mix the remaining ingredients to make a stuffing. Stuff your apples with the prepared mixture and place them on the rack.

Secure the pressure-cooking lid. Pressure cook for 3 minutes at High pressure. Once cooking is complete, use a quick pressure release; carefully remove the lid.

Serve warm apples and enjoy!

Per serving: Calories: 260; Fat: 9.6g; Carbs: 47.4g; Protein: 1.7g; Sugars: 34.9g; Fiber: 8.7g

596. Better-Than-Box-Mix Brownies [AF]

(Ready in about 25 minutes | Servings 6)

Ingredients

1/2 cup butter, melted
1/2 cup granulated sugar
2 eggs, whisked
3/4 cup self-raising flour
1/4 cup cocoa powder
1 teaspoon vanilla extract
1/2 cup chocolate chips

Directions

In a mixing bowl, beat the melted butter and sugar until fluffy. Next, fold in the eggs and beat again until well combined.

After that, add in the remaining ingredients. Mix until everything is well incorporated.

Now, spritz the sides and bottom of a baking pan with a nonstick cooking spray. Scrape the batter into the pan.

Secure the air-frying lid.

Bake your brownie at 340 degrees F in the preheated Air Fryer for approximately 20 minutes. Enjoy!

Per serving: Calories: 304; Fat: 20.9g; Carbs: 26.1g; Protein: 4.8g; Sugars: 10.4g; Fiber: 2.4g

597. Apple Pie and Ginger Curd [PC]

(Ready in about 20 minutes | Servings 8)

Ingredients

2 pounds apples, peeled, cored, and chopped
1 cup water
1 cup sugar
1 tablespoon fresh lemon juice
1 teaspoon ground cinnamon
1/2 teaspoon grated nutmeg
1 teaspoon ground ginger
1/8 teaspoon ground cloves

Directions

Place all the ingredients in the inner pot of your Instant Pot Duo Crisp. Secure the pressure-cooking lid.

Pressure cook for 4 minutes at High pressure. Once cooking is complete, use a natural pressure release for 15 minutes; carefully remove the lid.

Bon appétit!

Per serving: Calories: 110; Fat: 0.3g; Carbs: 28.7g; Protein: 0.4g; Sugars: 24g; Fiber: 3g

598. Dutch Baby Pancake [PC+AF]

(Ready in about 25 minutes | Servings 4)

Ingredients

1 pear, peeled, cored and sliced
1 tablespoon lemon juice
1 tablespoon coconut oil
1/2 cup all-purpose flour
1/2 teaspoon baking powder
2 tablespoons brown sugar
1/2 teaspoon cinnamon
2 eggs, whisked
1/2 cup milk
1/2 teaspoon vanilla extract

Directions

Drizzle the pear slices with the lemon juice and melted coconut oil; arrange the pear slices in the inner pot. Pour in 1 cup of water.

Secure the pressure-cooking lid. Pressure cook for 8 minutes at High pressure. Once cooking is complete, use a natural pressure release for 10 minutes; carefully remove the lid.

Mix the remaining ingredients to make the batter. Pour the batter over the pears.

Secure the air-frying lid.

Air fry your pancake at 350 degrees F for about 13 minutes or until it is golden brown around the edges.

Bon appétit!

Per serving: Calories: 183; Fat: 6.6g; Carbs: 24.6g; Protein: 5.7g; Sugars: 10.1g; Fiber: 2.1g

599. Lebanese Moghli Pudding [PC]

(Ready in about 10 minutes | Servings 5)

Ingredients

1 ½ cups basmati rice
1 cup water
1 cup canned coconut milk
1/2 cup brown sugar
1 star anise
1 cinnamon stick
1/2 cup dried apricots, sliced

Directions

Place all the ingredients in the inner pot of your Instant Pot Duo Crisp.

Pressure cook for 4 minutes at High pressure. Once cooking is complete, use a quick pressure release; carefully remove the lid.

Bon appétit!

Per serving: Calories: 305; Fat: 3.3g; Carbs: 63.3g; Protein: 6.4g; Sugars: 19.6g; Fiber: 2.9g

600. Classic Apple and Cranberry Cookies [PC+AF]

(Ready in about 20 minutes | Servings 4)

Ingredients

1/2 cup all-purpose flour
1/2 cup oats, ground
1/2 teaspoon baking powder
1 apple, peeled and grated
1/4 cup dried cranberries
2 tablespoons butter
1/2 teaspoon ground cinnamon
1/2 cup full-fat milk
1 egg, whisked

Directions

Add a metal trivet and 1 cup of water to the Instant Pot.

Mix the ingredients and divide the batter between mason jars. Top your mason jars with tin foil.

Secure the pressure-cooking lid. Pressure cook for 5 minutes at High pressure. Once cooking is complete, use a quick pressure release; carefully remove the lid.

Secure the air-frying lid and select the "Bake" function.

Remove the foil and bake your cookies at 360 degrees F for 5 minutes more.

Enjoy!

Per serving: Calories: 247; Fat: 9g; Carbs: 34g; Protein: 7.7g; Sugars: 8.2g; Fiber: 3.8g

Made in the USA
Middletown, DE
08 November 2021